Rodale's Sensational Desserts

by Joan Bingham and Dolores Riccio

Rodale Press, Emmaus, Pa.

Library of Congress Cataloging in Publication Data

Bingham, Joan.
    Rodale's sensational desserts.
    Includes index
    1. Desserts.   I. Riccio, Dolores, 1931-
II. Title.   III. Title: Sensational desserts.
TX773.B5   1985   641.8′6   85-2523
ISBN 0-87857-542-1   hardcover
ISBN 0-87857-585-5   paperback

2   4   6   8   10   9   7   5   3   1   hardcover
2   4   6   8   10   9   7   5   3   1   paperback

Rodale's Sensational Desserts

To Don and Rick with love

Authors' Note

Although this book is the work of two people, it is written in the first person singular for the sake of style and clarity.

Contents

Acknowledgments

We owe many "thank you's" to many people who helped make this book a reality.

First, to Charles Gerras, our good friend and favorite editor, for his advice and direction.

To Camille Bucci for her amazing attention to detail and her cheerful willingness to help with any problems.

To Anita Hirsch, JoAnn Brader, Natalie Updegrove, and Karen Haas of the Rodale Test Kitchen, who supervised the testing and made helpful suggestions.

To Kay Lichthardt, Laura Reifsnyder, Barbara Fritz, Elinor Wilson, and Kathryn Sommons, the talented food stylists who dreamed up and constructed lovely settings in which to photograph our recipes.

To Carl Doney, Mitch Mandel, Alison Miksch, Angelo Caggiano, John P. Hamel, Christie Tito, and Sally Ullman, who spent hour upon hour taking photographs from just the right angles to produce spectacular pictures.

To Anita G. Patterson and Lynn Foulk for the beautiful book design and Jean Gardner for her detailed illustrations.

And also to Rick Riccio; Don Bingham; Lucy and Charlie Anderson; Sally, Gary, Jason, and Heather Batchelder; Stephanie, Doug, Peter, and Wendy Gorman; Ardeth and Jim Bolin; Phyllis and Allan Watts; and Ron and Marty Roof who taste-tested and critically evaluated our recipes, we give our warmest appreciation.

Introduction

Wonderful, luscious, magnificent desserts. I love them! But I also love my family and friends, and I want to make everything I cook for them as wholesome as possible without sacrificing flavor. Toward that end, I've created hundreds of dessert recipes and adapted hundreds more over the years. With each new dish I am convinced once more that food value and delicious taste are two sides of the same coin.

Some of the ingredients you'll find in this book differ from those in most dessert cookbooks. My dessert recipes feature fresh and dried fruits, whole grains, honey, and sweet butter. I use no sugar or salt, and very little white flour. You won't find chocolate in any of my recipes either; I use low-fat carob instead. I've found that desserts made with these superior ingredients taste at least as delicious as those made with the conventional ingredients.

FLOURS

The flour I use in most of my dessert recipes is whole wheat pastry flour. This flour, milled from soft wheat, is a nutritious choice for cakes, cookies, and pastries. For breads, I use regular whole wheat flour. Because whole wheat flour yields a heavier product than white flour, I sometimes use half of this flour and half unbleached white flour when lightness is especially desirable. While unbleached white flour is not as rich in nutrients, it makes such a difference in the texture of some desserts that I think it's worth using on occasion. Of course, if you prefer, you can use all whole wheat flour or whole wheat pastry flour in place of the unbleached white flour when it is called for in the recipes.

Soy flour, which has a high protein and high fat content, can be added to whole wheat flour to produce slightly lighter baked goods than you get using whole wheat flour alone. But soy flour does tend to burn easily and has a pronounced flavor. When I use it, I lower the oven temperature by 25 degrees, and I never replace more than one-quarter of the flour with soy flour.

When recipes in this book call for whole wheat or unbleached white flour, the flour should be sifted once before measuring for cakes and cookies. For breads, rolls, and pastry, just stir with a fork or whisk in the canister to make sure the flour hasn't packed down, since that would give you an inaccurate measure. Some recipes specify sifting the flour three times with other ingredients to insure careful blending and to promote lighter texture.

For recipes calling for cornmeal, I use water-ground corn-meal because it retains the germ.

Oat flour is a tasty addition to some recipes. There's no need to purchase it, however, since you can make your own.

Oat Flour

1¼ cups uncooked quick oats

In a food processor or blender, process oats until powdery. Use in place of flour where called for.

Yields about 1 cup

EGGS

I always use large eggs, and all the recipes in this book call for them. That equates to 2 ounces per egg or ¼ cup, 24 ounces per dozen eggs.

I buy locally produced eggs. They're always fresher than eggs that are imported from another part of the country. You can store eggs refrigerated in the cartons in which you buy them for up to four weeks. But be aware that the quality goes down as storage time goes up.

It's frustrating to get a dozen eggs home from the store and find that one or more of them is cracked. Tempting as it may be to use the cracked ones, don't do it. Eggs that aren't protected by the shells are very susceptible to harmful bacteria. Should you inadvertently crack a few eggs yourself, use them immediately, or separate them, putting the whites in a covered container and the unbroken yolks in a jar of cold water where they'll stay fresh, refrigerated, for about four days.

If you have a half dozen egg whites in a jar, and you need to remove two for a recipe, figure on 2 tablespoons for each egg white called for. Egg whites can be frozen in a plastic container for up to a year. They may be defrosted during that time and refrozen after you've removed what you need.

Few things are so disheartening to a cook as breaking several eggs into a bowl and discovering that the last one is bad or even doubtful, thus spoiling the entire batch. Therefore, always make it a practice to break each egg into a cup before adding it to other ingredients.

Adding eggs yolks to a hot liquid isn't as tricky as you might suppose. Just add a small amount of the hot liquid to the beaten yolks while whisking constantly. Continue to add more of the hot liquid in the same manner until you've added about a third of it to the yolks, then pour the egg mixture directly into the remainder of the hot liquid while whisking.

Many people prefer to cook a mixture containing delicate egg yolks in the top of a double boiler set over simmering water. This method may take a bit longer than cooking them over direct heat, but it's more likely to result in a smooth mixture. However, with careful stirring, there's no reason that many mixtures containing eggs can't be cooked successfully over low, direct heat. If the worst happens (and it happens sometimes, even when using a double boiler) and the sauce or pudding curdles, you can often redeem it by beating it smooth with a blender or food processor, or with a fast whisking.

In making desserts, you'll be required to separate eggs often. This is easier when the eggs are cold. I usually return the yolks to the refrigerator unless I'm going to use them immediately since they're such a good medium for the growth of bacteria.

Egg yolks do break sometimes during the separating process, and even the tiniest bit of egg yolk will ruin egg whites for beating due to the oil in the yolk. If you do get a speck of yolk in the white, don't try to remove it with your finger, which has natural skin oil on it. Instead, fish it out with the edge of the empty egg shell, which will cut through the resistant white and pick up the speck.

Egg whites beat up to the largest volume when they're at room temperature. The classic way to beat them is in a copper bowl because copper provides the acid leavener that promotes fluffy beaten whites. In lieu of that, you can use a regular mixing bowl and add cream of tartar. For less than three egg whites, use a narrow bowl such as the small bowl of an electric mixer so the whites will be in full contact with the beaters and not spread out underneath them. If you're using an electric mixer, beat the whites at low speed until they're

foamy. Then add cream of tartar, and increase the speed to high. Cream of tartar is acid potassium tartrate, a powder refined from the process of fermenting grapes to make wine. Since it has an acid character, it acts as a stabilizer (just as the copper bowl does), and keeps whites from getting watery after they're beaten.

When egg whites are beaten for a meringue, they should form stiff peaks. However, for a soufflé, beat them only until the peaks are formed but fall over. In either case, don't beat them until they're dry.

Beaten egg whites are often folded into other ingredients. This simple process can be crucial to the success of a recipe. If they're stirred in rather than folded, the whites will deflate, letting out all the air you've beaten in, and, just like a leaky balloon, your dessert will shrink. Start the folding process by stirring one-quarter of the beaten whites into the mixture. This will lighten it. Then spoon the remaining whites on top and fold them in by making a cut down the center with a spatula. Pull the spatula over against the sides and bottom of the bowl, turning the mixture over

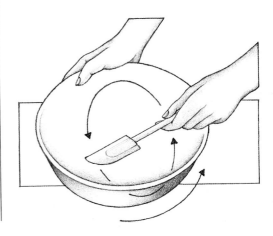

as you do. Continue to do this until all the whites are folded in and no streaks remain. Folding shouldn't take more than a minute or two.

To make failproof meringue toppings for pies or puddings, spread the meringue over a warm filling. This will keep the meringue from "weeping" or oozing condensation. Spread the meringue so that it covers the entire filling. It should seal the edges of the crust or dish and be at least 1 inch thick at the middle. Otherwise, it will shrink into a thin, rubbery layer, and not be the luxurious topping it should be.

DAIRY PRODUCTS

Cream, milk, buttermilk, sour cream, and yogurt are all used to give body and texture to desserts. Good fresh whipped cream, fat and calories notwithstanding, is still a great favorite as a dessert topping.

A few years ago when ultrapasteurization was developed by the dairy industry, I was pleased with the prospect of purchasing ultrapasteurized heavy cream to have on hand for use as a topping, knowing it would keep far longer than the standard pasteurized cream. What a disappointment! It took forever to whip the cream, and I never did achieve the beautiful high mounds I wanted. I've given up using this cream with little going for it but a long shelf life.

While egg whites should be at room temperature when beaten, the formula for beating cream is just the opposite. For the best results, the cream, the bowl, and the beaters all should be thoroughly chilled. The cream should be beaten until soft peaks form when you gently lift the beaters out of it. I like whipped cream without any flavoring or sweetening, but my family prefers it with a touch of honey and a bit of vanilla or almond flavoring, depending on what it's to be used for.

Whipped cream need not, as is commonly thought, be whipped at the last minute (although, admittedly, this is preferable). If you whip it ahead of time, put the whipped cream in a fine mesh strainer over a bowl, cover, and store in the refrigerator. Any liquid that separates out will then drain into the bowl instead of pooling at the bottom of the cream. Kept this way, cream can be whipped several hours in advance of use.

Occasionally, on a hot muggy day, cream just won't whip into a fluffy mound. Placing the bowl of cream into a larger bowl of ice usually solves the problem. If this doesn't work, whip in a few drops of lemon juice, a drop at a time.

A tempting variation of whipped cream is chantilly cream, a flavored whipped cream usually piped through a pastry bag to add a fancy touch. It's a delicious decoration for many desserts.

Nonfat dry milk is an ingredient I use often. It gives body to many frostings and candies that would ordinarily be provided by powdered sugar, which I don't use. I always buy nonfat dry milk that's marked U.S. Extra Grade to insure getting a high-quality product. Noninstant milk powder has a little more nutritional value than the instant, but it takes longer to dissolve. In fact, in some recipes it won't dissolve at all, so I always use the instant for desserts.

SHORTENING

By definition, shortening is a solid fat that comes either from an animal or a vegetable source. The denser the shortening, the more shortening power it has. However, the term "shortening" has been broadened so that in general usage it now often applies to oils that are used in baking as well.

Unsalted butter is my first choice in shortening. I love the marvelous taste and texture it imparts, but butter is expensive and high in fats; also there are recipes in which it just won't work, so I sometimes substitute vegetable oil. With spices, raisins, carob, or other dominant flavors, vegetable oil is often acceptable. Can you use butter and oil interchangeably? Not really. They produce a different texture, so, unless you have specific dietary restrictions, it's best to use oil when oil is called for and butter when butter is listed as the shortening. I never use any solid shortening except butter. It should be kept in mind, however, that whipped butter is unsatisfactory for baking. It's full of air and thus impossible to measure correctly.

Greasing pans may seem like an insignificant part of cooking, but it's important because the flavor of the grease lingers on the surface of whatever is baked in the pan. Without exception, I grease pans for baking with butter. But you don't need much. The paper in which butter is wrapped generally has sufficient residue on it to grease a pan.

When you purchase butter, look for the words "Made from Sweet Cream" on the package. (Some butter is made from sour cream, and it's decidedly inferior.) U.S. Grade AA and U.S. 93 Score are the best butter grades. Solid pounds of butter are a few cents cheaper than the pounds that are divided into quarters, but I use the divided quarters—they're so much easier for cooking since the wrappers are marked by tablespoons.

If you opt to use the solid pounds, you can measure the amount of butter using the water displacement method. To get ⅓ cup of butter, fill a 1-cup measure with ⅔ cup water. Then add butter until the water fills the cup. Pour off the water, and you'll have ⅓ cup of butter remaining. You can measure any amount of solid shortening this way.

When I use oil, safflower, sunflower, or corn oil are my choices since their mild flavors don't overpower other ingredients. Oil should be stored in a cool, dark place.

THICKENERS

Eggs, cornstarch, tapioca, flour, arrowroot, and gelatin are used to thicken dessert sauces and puddings. The most delicate sauces and puddings—those with a custard base—use eggs or egg yolks. Cornstarch and tapioca are frequently the thickening agents in fruit sauces and fillings. Flour can also be used, but the recipe must be cooked longer to rid it of the raw flour flavor. In addition, flour makes an opaque sauce, whereas with cornstarch or tapioca a sauce becomes translucent, showing the attractive color of a fruit to advantage. Arrowroot can be used to thicken a sauce that isn't going to be reheated since reheating breaks it down.

Gelatin is a temperature-sensitive ingredient that becomes firm when it chills. It is used in desserts which are to be molded.

LEAVENING

Leavening agents are used in desserts such as cakes, breads, and some cookies to give them a light texture. Baking soda works only when used with sour ingredients such as sour cream or sour milk. Baking powder is often the choice for cakes or cookies and is sometimes used in conjuction with baking soda.

Yeast is the preferred leavener for breads, unless they're quick breads. You'll notice that the recipes in this book call for powdered rather than cake yeast. This is simply because powdered yeast is more readily available in the supermarkets. For more information on yeast, see page 154.

Eggs and beaten egg whites are the leavening agents of choice for certain desserts such as Italian Sponge Cake (page 10). They produce a particularly light texture.

Eggs and yeast are natural leaveners. While baking powder and baking soda are artificial leaveners, they're important in creating many desserts and are used only in small amounts.

SWEETENERS

One of the questions I'm frequently asked is, "How do you make desserts without using sugar?" The truth is, I don't miss sugar at all. There are several alternatives that aren't merely just as good—they're better.

Honey is the sweetener most often used as a replacement for sugar, and it's a fine choice. I won't tell you honey is a great nutritional food—it isn't, but it has two advantages over sugar. First, because it is sweeter than sugar, you don't need to use as much of it. Second, honey does contain some nutrients in small quantities—iron, copper, and phosphorus, among others.

I always use what is labeled "pure honey" in cooking, because honey that isn't labeled "pure" may contain from 1 to 19 percent corn syrup or sugar.

Some honeys have a stronger flavor than others. Buckwheat honey, for example, has a pronounced taste that would overpower most of the ingredients used in desserts. On the other hand, clover honey, wildflower honey, and orange blossom honey are mild and unobtrusive. They make wonderful sweeteners, even in the most delicate desserts.

Raw honey, which is less expensive than processed honey, is available in many supermarkets and most natural foods stores. I don't recommend raw honey for use in desserts because it has a strong flavor that varies from batch to batch, depending on the source. It's also deep in color, which will darken desserts that should be delicate and pale, such as custard. I'd rather spend an extra few pennies for a lighter, more consistent honey.

Recipes that call for a small amount of sugar, such as recipes for breads and muffins, can be converted to honey by merely using less honey than the sugar called for, about half to three-quarters as much. But in converting a recipe that uses a large amount of sugar, such as a cake, you'll also need to decrease the amount of liquid called for in the recipe to compensate for the moisture the honey adds. Reduce liquid by ¼ cup for every cup of honey used, unless you're also converting from white flour to whole wheat flour in which case no reduction of liquid is necessary. Whole wheat absorbs moisture more readily than white flour does.

Cakes, cookies, and breads made with honey will have a denser texture than those made with white sugar. I prefer this texture, just as I prefer the texture of whole grain bread to the air-puffed, mass-produced white bread that used to be the popular choice among Americans but has fallen from grace during the past few years.

Another plus for honey is its preservative powers. You'll find that baked goods made with this sweetener don't dry out nearly so fast as those made with sugar.

Honey is indisputably sticky stuff, and that makes it difficult to measure in the conventional way. However, if you lightly oil a cup or spoon before using it to measure honey, the honey will slip off the oiled surface. If you're going to measure butter or oil anyway, do that first and your measuring utensil will be ready for honey. Or you can rinse a glass measure in very cold water to achieve the same result.

Although honey should be kept at room temperature (it may crystallize in the refrigerator), even at room temperature it's slow to pour. When I'm going to cook with honey, I set the bottle in a pan of warm water. This thins it out to a pourable consistency without actually heating it.

Some recipes in this book call for boiling honey. Be sure you do this in a very large pan since honey expands to many times its volume when boiled. Should it boil over on your range, you'll find it extremely difficult to clean up.

Pure maple syrup, which is the boiled sap of sugar maple trees, is a delightful sweetener for some desserts. It should be used in recipes where its flavor will enhance and not overpower the other ingredients. Grade A, the most expensive, is light in both color and flavor. I prefer Grade B when I want a stronger maple taste. This darker, more flavorful syrup isn't as easy to come by, but some natural foods stores do carry it. Not as sweet as honey, maple syrup can be substituted for sugar in equal measure.

Molasses is rich in iron and contains other nutrients as well. I use it sparingly in recipes where a strong flavor is needed. I've found that 1 or 2 tablespoons of molasses combined with a much larger amount of honey in a dessert will produce the taste of brown sugar.

An interesting alternative sweetener, date sugar, is available in natural foods stores. Since it doesn't dissolve well and costs the world, I limit its use mostly to dessert toppings. It's a great replacement for brown sugar on a streusel topping.

Fruits and fruit juices also provide an abundant source of natural sweetness.

CAROB

When I first decided to eliminate chocolate from my pantry, there was an uproar from my family. However, they soon learned that I could make truly delicious desserts featuring carob, known also as St. John's bread or locust bean. In some recipes the carob taste truly resembles chocolate; in others, the natural carob flavor is welcome on its own terms.

Why do I bother? Because carob is a more healthful food than chocolate. It doesn't contain caffeine as chocolate does. Since carob is naturally sweet, there's no need to add the large amount of sweetener necessary to make chocolate palatable. In fact, carob is a dieter's delight because it is low in calories and contains only 2 percent fat compared to chocolate's 52 percent.

Carob is sold in several forms. Powdered carob is found on the shelves of most natural foods stores, and carob chips are now available in many supermarkets, as well as in natural foods stores. My favorite form of carob is milk carob chips, which are the closest in flavor to chocolate. So if you're a chocoholic who has been forbidden this treat, try the milk chips. Any recipe in this book that calls for carob chips can be made either with the milk carob chips or the regular chips. Although the milk carob chips aren't as readily obtainable, they're worth the effort it might take to locate them.

To melt carob chips, place them with some butter in the top of a double boiler set over hot water. If you don't include butter, the chips just get soft and burn instead of melting.

Powdered carob can be made into a syrup (see below) that facilitates its use in recipes. This syrup will keep for months stored, covered, in the refrigerator. But be sure to stir it well before each use since it tends to lump in the middle.

Basic Carob Syrup

1 cup sifted powdered carob
2 cups water

In a medium-size saucepan, mix carob into water. Bring to a boil over low heat, and boil until smooth, stirring constantly.

Cool. Store, covered tightly, in refrigerator. Stir well before each use.

Yields about 2 cups

FRUITS

You'll notice that many of the recipes in this book contain fruit. That's because fruit can bring such wonderful qualities to desserts. It's a natural sweetener, allowing you to cut down on the amount of honey used or to rely entirely on the fruit itself for sweetness. Also, most fruits provide the kind of fiber that's so lacking in American diets. The following chart gives the fiber content of some fruits commonly used in desserts.

Fiber in Fruit

VARIETY	PERCENT OF FIBER
Apples (peeled)	0.50
Apples (unpeeled)	0.77
Bananas	0.50
Cherries	0.97
Peaches	0.64
Pears (unpeeled)	1.40
Plums	0.61
Raisins	0.67
Rhubarb	0.70

SOURCE: *Composition of Foods: Fruits and Fruit Juices; Raw, Processed, Prepared,* United States Department of Agriculture, revised 1982.

Fresh fruit is bursting with goodness, but some fruits are quite perishable and should be refrigerated soon after purchase. Berries, grapes, cherries, pineapples, and citrus fruits don't ripen any further after picking, so there's no point in leaving them at room temperature. Inspect the fruit you purchase for any signs of soft spots or blemishes.

Fresh pineapple is lovely, but it can't be used in recipes that include gelatin, as many of the desserts in this book do; an enzyme in fresh pineapple interferes with the jelling of gelatin. I use unsweetened canned pineapple in gelatin recipes.

I use commercial unsweetened flaked coconut in most of the recipes calling for coconut. But fresh coconut is tastier if you have it at hand and have the time to prepare it. A coconut has three eyes, one of which is soft. This is the one you puncture to drain out the coconut milk. After this is done, place the coconut in a 400°F oven for 20 to 25 minutes. Break open the coconut shell, and with a small paring knife, peel off the brown inner skin and grate the coconut meat. If you prefer, you can shred coconut in a food processor.

Dried fruits are wonderful! Raisins, prunes, and dried apricots, apples, or peaches all have a long shelf life when kept in a cool dry place. And because they're dehydrated the vitamin content is intensified. One caution concerning currants: don't confuse dried currants with fresh currants. If a recipe calls for currants, it means the fresh red, green, black, or white berries that make exquisite jams and jellies. Dried currants are entirely different, coming not from berries but from tiny seedless grapes.

Unsulfured dried fruit is commonly available in the markets today. Although this type of dried fruit is desirable, it tends to be drier than its counterpart that's preserved with sulfur. Therefore, I often plump dried fruit before using it by covering it with boiling water and letting it stand for 15 to 20 minutes; then

I drain the fruit thoroughly before adding it to the recipe.

Another way of plumping dried fruit is to place it in a shallow ovenproof bowl, cover it with water, and put it in a slow (200°F) oven for 10 to 15 minutes. I've never found this necessary, but if the fruit you purchase is excessively dry, perhaps you'll want to try this method.

To cut up dried fruit use kitchen shears dipped in hot water (or use a food processor). If the shears get sticky, just dip them in the water again and continue cutting. When planning to use cut pieces of dried fruit in a batter, shake them in a bag with just enough flour to keep them separate so they won't clump.

Citrus fruits impart marvelous, tart flavors to desserts. Lemons and limes stored whole in a jar filled with water and kept in the refrigerator will yield quite a bit more juice. If time doesn't allow use of this method, cover each lemon or lime with hot water and let it stand for about 15 minutes before squeezing it. These procedures coax about twice as much juice from the fruit.

Save the rinds of citrus fruits and store them in the refrigerator or freeze them to make grated rinds. In this way you eliminate the need to ruin a whole fruit just to obtain a little grated rind. When you grate the rinds be sure you get only the top skin and none of the white pith underneath. This white substance will give your delicate desserts a bitter flavor.

Recipes often require special preparation of fruit, such as peeling, pitting, or soaking in acidulated water. Thin-skinned fruits, like peaches, are often difficult to peel without mutilating them. The best way I've found to skin them, leaving the meat of the fruit intact, is to cover the fruit with boiling water; let it stand for one minute; then easily peel off the skin with a knife. If this is done right, nothing but the skin will come off.

But when you peel oranges or other thick-skinned fruits, you want to remove not only the rind but the pith as well. Peel citrus fruits from the stem end in large pieces.

There are cherry pitters on the market, but I find that pesky job can be done just as efficiently with the point of a knife inserted at the stem end, twisted down under the pit, and pulled upward.

Some recipes call for putting fruit, such as apple slices, in acidulated water — water to which lemon juice or vinegar has been added in a ratio of 1 tablespoon lemon juice to 1 quart water. This prevents browning of foods that oxidize when exposed to air. Unless otherwise specified, in this book acidulated water is made with lemon juice, not vinegar.

Fresh fruit, presented attractively in a bowl, alone or with cheese, is a simple, yet magnificent dessert. I sometimes prefer to poach fruit in a syrup of 1 part honey to 16 parts water until the fruit is just tender. Soft fruits, such as cherries or plums, poach in about 5 minutes. Hard fruits, such as pears, take 30 minutes or longer.

GELATIN

The base for many desserts, gelatin is light, low in calories, and easy to work with. I never use the artificially flavored, presweetened gelatins, but add my own flavorings to plain gelatin which contains no sweetener at all. (See the chapter on Ice Cream Parlor Frozen and Chilled Desserts.)

NUTS

Another nutritious dessert ingredient I use lavishly in cooking, nuts come in a wide assortment and so provide a great variety of tastes and textures, depending on how they're prepared. I never buy chopped or ground nuts, which are more expensive and not as fresh.

Nuts are simple to grind in either a food processor or blender. I much prefer a food processor for this, however. With a blender you must stop and scrape down the sides many times to get an even grind. A food processor takes care of the job in a few seconds with no stopping and scraping, and a processor will also chop nuts, if you use an on/off motion.

When preparing ground almonds for certain recipes, you may want to blanch and toast them before you grind them. To do this, first drop the shelled nuts into a saucepan of boiling water. Remove the pan from the heat and allow to stand for four minutes. Drain the nuts, and slide the skins off with your fingers. Dry them well, spread them on a baking sheet and bake in a 350°F oven for six to ten minutes, or until lightly browned. Don't overbrown or the nuts will taste burnt.

I often use walnuts in recipes that usually are made with pecans. Walnuts are much less expensive, and they're also slightly sweeter. If you wish to make this exchange in any of the recipes in this book, feel free to do so.

FLAVORINGS

Even the good flavor of fruit often can be enhanced by the addition of an extract or spice. For the most part, the flavorings I use are entirely natural. Vanilla beans are delightful—they impart a delicious vanilla taste that can't be duplicated with an extract. But the vanilla extract is much less expensive and easier to use, so it's often my choice, depending on the dessert I'm making and how important a role the vanilla flavor will play. However, for a fine

Dessert Flavorings

NAME	FLAVOR AND FORM	USES
Allspice	Tastes like a combination of cinnamon, cloves, and nutmeg—usually ground	Cakes, pies, puddings
Almond	Flavor is strong and similar to nut—extract	Candies, breads, cakes, cookies, pies, puddings
Anise	Licorice flavor—seeds or extract	Candies, coffee cakes, cookies, rolls
Cardamom	Strong, spicy taste—seeds or ground	Coffee cakes, rolls
Cinnamon	Fairly mild, spicy flavor—ground or stick	Breads, cakes, coffee cakes, cookies, pies, preserves, puddings
Cloves	Pungent flavor—ground	Cakes, cookies, pies, preserves
Ginger	Spicy, warm flavor—ground or stick	Cakes, cookies, gingerbreads, puddings, preserves
Lemon	Tart—extract	Cakes, cookies, frostings, pies, puddings
Mace	Similar to nutmeg but milder taste—ground	Cakes, preserves
Nutmeg	Pungent, spicy flavor—ground	Coffee cakes, custards, puddings
Orange	Citrus—extract	Cakes, cookies, frostings, pies, puddings
Vanilla	Extract, bean	Breads, most desserts

NOTE: Since some of the flavoring cooks off, desserts which require no cooking need less flavoring. Freezing also weakens flavoring, so you should allow for this in a recipe you plan to freeze.

vanilla pudding or ice cream, there's nothing as wonderful as the taste of the bean itself. Vanilla beans, when used whole, can be washed, dried, and saved to be used again in another pudding or sauce. I like to add a vanilla bean and a cinnamon stick to the liquid in which I poach pears or peaches, and I often save both to use again.

CANDY AND SWEET SNACKS

I make candy and sweet snacks using honey, date sugar, and ground coconut as sweetners. This *is* limiting. It takes high temperatures to get really hard candy, and honey *does* burn much more readily and at lower temperatures than sugar.

Over the years, I've found a variety of tasty candies that can be made without using higher temperatures. (Although with careful watching and diligent stirring, you can make harder candy with honey.) But whether it's soft ball or hard crack stage—whether you're using honey or another sweetener to make cooked candy—a candy thermometer is a must. The temperature is just too critical a factor to trust to the old, cold-water method.

In addition to a candy thermometer, to cook candy you'll need a very deep pan that will hold four to five times the volume you plan to use. Honey expands greatly as it boils. This pan also should have a heavy bottom so it won't burn the delicate honey. And you'll need a long-handled, wooden spoon for stirring. No other special equipment is necessary.

Many traditional candies, such as fudges, penuches, and fondants that rely on sugar to crystallize for proper texture, are difficult to make and usually turn out poorly when made with honey. I avoid them. But my Easy Peanut Butter Fudge recipe (page 235), for example, is different because it gets its texture from the peanut butter, not the honey.

There are many candies and treats which can be made successfully with honey or maple syrup. They rely on butter, cream, or other ingredients for their textures.

DECORATING

You'll find instructions in the various chapters on how to use a pastry bag and decorating kit to turn desserts into visual masterpieces for special occasions. When you don't want to go to this extra work, you can resort to simple decorations. Bear in mind, they should be compatible in taste, texture, and color with the dessert you're decorating.

Nuts, whole, chopped, or ground, can be attractively used to dress up cakes, pies, or cookies. Coconut, either ground into Coconut Sugar or just flaked, adds an extra note of flavor, as well as being an eye-pleasing addition to myriad desserts, from frozen ice cream balls to crepe toppings. I often use Coconut Sugar as a "shake on" to replace powdered sugar.

Coconut Sugar

1¼ cups unsweetened flaked coconut

In a food processor or blender, process coconut until texture is fine, about 1 to 2 minutes. Use to dust cakes and candies.

Yields about 1 cup

You may choose to embellish lemon or lime pie with thin slices of fresh lemon or lime. For fancy citrus slices, score a lemon, orange, or lime with a zester, then slice fruit thinly, cut slices in halves, and twist them slightly. The rind of an orange or lemon can be grated and used as a decoration as well as an ingredient.

Pieces of dried fruit can be used to decorate puddings or to create faces on a child's cake or on gingerbread people. Cinnamon, nutmeg, or powdered carob add contrast when sprinkled on light-colored puddings, white frostings, or whipped cream.

Candy is another attractive decoration. The use of carob leaves (see below) makes any cake look like a professional job.

Carob Leaves

These decorative leaves are fun to make. Use them as a border for a cake, or gather them at the center. You might even want to decorate individual servings of pudding with carob leaves.

1 cup milk carob chips
2 tablespoons butter
  about 12 plant leaves approximately 1 to 1½ inches long (washed and dried)

In the top of a double boiler set over hot water, melt together carob chips and butter. Coat backs of leaves with mixture. Allow to set, and then carefully peel off and discard leaves.

Makes about 12 leaves

A FEW TIPS FOR EASE AND EFFICIENCY

One of the basics for a smooth operation in any type of cooking is to assemble all ingredients and equipment before you start. In dessert making this is especially important since timing is often critical. You don't want to be rooting around in the cabinet, looking for an ingredient, while you should be doing something crucial such as folding in egg whites.

Cooking is much easier if you do all the paring, chopping, grating, grinding, and any other preparation in advance of the actual blending of ingredients. This is the way master chefs do it, in order to concentrate more on perfection of method.

Few ovens are entirely trustworthy. Invest a couple of dollars in an oven thermometer to make sure that the temperature you set is the temperature you get. Dessert making often requires precise temperatures that would never be demanded for a roast or a casserole.

Make it a rule not to test baked goods too early. Many a cake or bread has fallen because of the cook's anxiety to prod it. An oven with a glass door is extremely helpful to impatient cooks. But seeing isn't everything; use your sense of smell, too. A cake or bread will emit a heavenly fragrance when it's just ready to be tested, and your nose will tell you, too, if the bottom is sticking a bit.

Sometimes baked goods will overbrown on the top before they're cooked through, especially in a temperamental oven. If this happens, lay a piece of foil right on top of the dessert, *without* tucking it around the baking pan in any way.

As a general rule, when you want baked goods to brown fast on the top (as you do with muffins), you place them in the upper third of the oven, and when you want the underside to be crusty (as you do with pizza) you use the very bottom shelf. That's why cakes go in the middle—you want them to cook very evenly throughout.

It's tricky to use more than one oven shelf at a time. Pans reflect extra heat onto what's beneath them; therefore they must be staggered so that one pan will not be directly above another.

SUBSTITUTING INGREDIENTS

There are times when you may want to, or have to, substitute one ingredient for another. For example, all of us who cook a greal deal have had the experience of being ready to make a certain recipe only to discover, while assembling the ingredients, that there's one we're out of. Then sometimes a recipe may call for a small amount of an ingredient which you don't expect to use again, so you just don't want to buy it.

Simple Substitutions

INGREDIENT	SUBSTITUTION
1 cup skim milk	1 cup reconstituted nonfat dry milk
1 cup sour milk	1 tablespoon lemon juice in 1 cup whole milk (allow to stand for 10 minutes)
1 cup buttermilk	1 tablespoon lemon juice in 1 cup whole milk (allow to stand for 10 minutes), or 1 cup yogurt
1 cup heavy cream (except for whipping)	¾ cup milk and ⅓ cup melted butter
1 cup sifted cake flour	½ cup unbleached white flour and ½ cup whole wheat pastry flour, less 2 tablespoons
1 tablespoon flour (for thickening)	2 teaspoons cornstarch
1 tablespoon baking powder	¼ teaspoon baking soda and ½ teaspoon cream of tartar
1 whole egg	¼ cup egg whites
1 square unsweetened chocolate	3 tablespoons powdered carob and 1 tablespoon melted butter
1 cup sugar	½ to ¾ cup honey
confectioner's sugar (for decoration)	coconut sugar

Or you may be converting a recipe to more healthful ingredients, cutting back on fats or eliminating chocolate or sugar.

EQUIVALENTS

Shopping for ingredients for a specific recipe can be confusing. You know you need ¾ cup honey, for example, but honey is sold by the pound. The following information should alleviate some of the confusion.

FREEZING DESSERTS

Cookies, cakes, pies, and breads are all good candidates for freezing. But they should be thoroughly cooled before they're wrapped for this type of storage.

Cookies can be frozen either before or after baking, but I've found that freezing the dough is more desirable. Cookies baked before freezing tend to dry out more quickly when they're defrosted. The logs of dough for refrigerator cookies are my first choice for freezing. They fit

Equivalent Amounts For Some Common Ingredients

INGREDIENT	EQUIVALENT AMOUNT	INGREDIENT	EQUIVALENT AMOUNT
1 pound whole wheat flour	about 3¾ cups, sifted	1 pound unshelled almonds	⅔ cup, shelled
1 pound unbleached white flour	about 4 cups, sifted	1 pound shelled walnuts	4 cups
1 stick butter	½ cup	1 pound unshelled walnuts	1½ cups, shelled
1 cup heavy cream	2½ cups whipped cream	1 pound shelled pecans	4 cups
1 pound honey	1⅓ cups	1 pound unshelled pecans	1¼ cups, shelled
juice of 1 large lemon	¼ cup juice	1 pound raisins	3¼ cups
rind of 1 large lemon	1 tablespoon grated rind	1 large apple	1¼ cups, sliced
juice of 1 large lime	2 tablespoons juice	1 pound apples	3 cups, sliced
juice of 1 large orange	¾ cup juice	1 large banana	½ cup, mashed
rind of 1 large orange	2 tablespoons grated rind	1 slice soft bread	½ cup bread crumbs
1 pound shelled almonds	3 cups		

neatly and compactly into the freezer. When I want to bake a batch, it's easy to slice off the desired amount of dough, let it defrost, then slice it into cookies and pop them into the oven.

If you choose to bake cookies before freezing them, place a piece of wax paper between each baked cookie, then wrap the batch tightly before putting it into the freezer. Delicate cookies may need more protection. I usually put the wrapped packages into rigid plastic containers to insure the edges of the cookies against breakage.

Cookie dough will keep about five months in the freezer and may be defrosted in the refrigerator or at room temperature. Baked cookies freeze well for about three months. To thaw baked cookies of the crisp type, defrost them in a single layer at room temperature. Moist, chewy cookies such as hermits should be thawed in the refrigerator, wrapped.

If crisp cookies have lost their snap and appeal after being frozen, preheat your oven to about 300°F, lay the cookies on a baking sheet, and heat them for about two minutes.

Cakes freeze well, except for a few types, and they're quick to defrost. But it's best to freeze them sans frostings and fillings. Most frostings don't fare well during the freezing process, and they make the cake soggy. But if you know you're not going to have time to frost a cake after it has been frozen and want to take it from freezer to table, use a frosting with a butter base.

A frosted cake will keep well in the freezer for about two months while an unfrosted one should stay fresh for four months.

To defrost a cake, first unwrap it. Then cover it lightly. A covered cake dish provides the ideal atmosphere. If you don't have one, lightly cover the cake with plastic wrap, leaving air space on the sides. Allow about one hour for defrosting before you plan to frost, fill, and serve a cake.

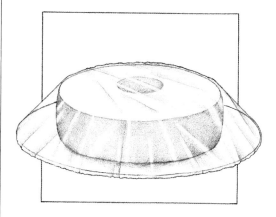

I've found that spice cake is one type of cake that loses its quality when frozen. The flavor turns bitter, leaving an aftertaste. While many cooks claim this doesn't occur if cloves are left out, I've not been pleased with the taste of any spice cake I've frozen.

Pies can be made completely and frozen, or you can freeze empty piecrusts to be filled later. Both can be frozen either baked or oven-ready. Crusts that are short, meaning they contain a large quantity of butter, retain their flakiness better than those that use less shortening.

I like to have several frozen, unfilled pie shells on hand to use if I am in a hurry. For bottom crusts or one-crust pies, I roll out the dough and line foil pans with it. Then I freeze the shells, unwrapped. After they're frozen, I wrap them individually and then stack them, wrapping the whole stack together. If I want top crusts, I roll them out and freeze them separated by pieces of wax paper. Then I wrap the frozen stack.

If you prefer, you can freeze the pie-crust dough in a ball, and roll it out after it's defrosted. This eliminates breakage that may occur with a frozen pie shell, but the dough must be rolled when it's thoroughly defrosted, yet still very cold. It's also harder to handle than a dough that hasn't been frozen.

Before you fill a pie that's to be frozen unbaked, brush the inside of the bottom crust with a little melted butter. This will keep the crust from becoming soggy. If there's a top crust, brush it with melted butter when it's in place.

Some fillings freeze better than others. Fruit fillings are especially suited to freezing, but you must double the amount of thickener (such as tapioca, cornstarch, or flour) called for in a recipe if you're going to freeze the pie unbaked. Fruit pies will keep well for up to six months. An uncooked, frozen pie should be baked, unthawed, in a hot oven, about 425°F, for the first 20 minutes. The temperature should then be reduced to 350°F and baking continued until the filling is bubbly and the crust is golden brown, about 45 minutes more.

Cream-filled or custard pies don't do well when home-frozen—the filling separates. Those that you see in the markets have been frozen in much colder, more sophisticated freezers than any that are available for home use. A chiffon pie can be frozen if you fold ½ cup to 1 cup of whipped cream into the filling before you put it into the baked shell, but I think the quality suffers a little. Allow chiffon pie to defrost at room temperature before serving.

To serve a precooked, frozen pie hot, take it right from the freezer to a preheated 400°F oven, and bake until the filling is bubbly. This usually takes from 25 to 45 minutes, depending on the filling.

Breads, both quick breads and yeast breads, freeze well and thaw rapidly. If they're sliced before freezing, you can gently separate the slices, thereby accelerating the thawing process. For my taste, frozen breads do lose that wonderful, just-baked flavor, so I freeze them only when I know I'm not going to get the chance to bake.

Puddings as a general rule don't freeze well because they're delicate and often have a custard base. Cobblers and steamed fruit puddings are an exception. They'll still be tasty after being in the freezer for as long as a year. Thawed at room temperature for about eight hours and then heated in a steamer, these puddings will have a delightful freshness.

TO WRAP IT UP

There are many types and brands of food wraps. Each has its own special jobs.

Plastic wrap is a latter-day wonder that is perfect for covering cakes, pies, cookies, puddings, or any other food for short-term storage—either in or out of the refrigerator. A heavy-duty plastic wrap can even be used for short-term freezer storage.

Wax paper may be considered old-fashioned by some, but this inexpensive wrap still has many kitchen uses. While it won't cling like plastic wrap will, it's wonderful for separating pie shells, cookies, and crepes for freezing. It's also useful for lining baking sheets that are to be used for drop candies or other sticky goodies you're not going to bake.

Foil is available in many weights and serves a variety of purposes. The lightweight foil is a good wrap for short-term storage of baked goods, either in a refrigerator or freezer or at room temperature. The heavyweight foil is unexcelled for long-term freezer storage.

Plastic food bags are great for storing cookies, cupcakes, candies, or other small treats. And they're wonderful for foods (such as ice cream bars or cupcakes) that you want to keep separated but stored together in a freezer.

The best of these bags come with ziplock openings that enable you to seal them airtight.

The following pages contain a selection of my favorite dessert recipes along with instructions and tips on making and serving them. Some of these desserts, while scrumptious and wholesome, are also very rich so I reserve them for true occasions or those days when I think my family needs a special treat. For everyday dining, I favor my lighter desserts—a simple pudding, a refreshing sorbet, or a piece of succulent fruit. Whatever your personal requirements might be, I feel confident that the wide variety of desserts presented here will provide you with opportunities to make the perfect choices.

CHAPTER

Winning Cakes and Cupcakes

Most cakes and cupcakes are easy to make. They can be prepared well ahead of serving time. And they're delicious. So when company is coming, I often say, "Let them eat cake!"

The cakes in this book come under two general classifications: butter cakes (the larger group) and sponge cakes. I've included many of my favorite recipes for butter cakes. This category embraces cakes that contain oil as well as those made with butter. Sponge cakes (also known as foam cakes) contain no shortening. Fruit cakes, pound cakes, and most layer cakes fall into the first group, and they're baked in many forms including cupcakes, sheet cakes, and loaves. Sponge cakes are usually baked in a tube pan although they can also be baked in layers or sheets.

Coconut Dream Cake   Page 6

SELECTING PANS

If you don't have the size pan called for in a recipe, you can use an alternate size, but you'll have to alter the baking time. A pan that's smaller than the specified size produces a thicker cake and, therefore, requires a bit more baking than a larger one. For instance, if your recipe calls for 9-inch round pans and you're using 8-inch round pans, add about ten minutes to the baking time. Of course, the reverse is true, too. If a recipe calls for 8-inch pans and you're using 9-inch pans, you'll have to reduce the baking time by about ten minutes.

Two 9 × 9 × 2-inch square pans can be used interchangeably with three 8 × 1½-inch round pans. The baking time, of course, will be longer for the square pans than for the round ones. Two 8-inch square pans are equivalent to one 13 × 9 × 2-inch pan or two

9-inch round pans. A cake baked in the 13-inch pan will need the longest baking time, followed by the 8-inch square pans and then the 9-inch round pans—in decreasing order. A 9 × 5 × 3-inch loaf pan and a 9-inch square pan are good substitutes for each other. The cake in the loaf pan requires the longer baking time.

I have a good supply of cake pans in all sizes. If you're going to make cakes frequently, I suggest you invest in a number of pans. The following is a list of pans I recommend for cake baking:

3 8-inch round layer cake pans
3 9-inch round layer cake pans
1 8-inch square pan
1 9-inch square pan
1 Bundt pan
1 9-inch tube pan
1 9-inch springform pan
2 9 × 5 × 3-inch loaf pans
1 jelly-roll pan
1 or 2 13 × 9 × 2-inch pans

Sponge cakes are traditionally baked in tube pans so that the heat can penetrate the batter from the middle as well as from the edges, thus promoting even rising. But they also rise well when baked in layer cake or jelly-roll pans because these pans are thin enough to allow the bottom and top of the cake to cook evenly through to the middle.

In general, butter cakes are baked in pans that are well coated with butter. Sometimes these butter-coated pans are dusted lightly with flour to produce a beautifully delicate golden crust. If I'm making a carob cake, I often vary the coating by dusting the pans with powdered carob.

Sponge cakes are baked in ungreased pans since the fragile batter must cling to the pan's surface as it rises. Sometimes, however, the bottom of the pan is buttered and lined with parchment paper to facilitate removal of the cake.

INGREDIENTS

Cake baking is a more exact science than most other forms of cooking. Measure ingredients accurately. Flavoring is the one area in which you'll find it's safe to experiment. Taste a speck of the batter. If it seems too bland, add more flavoring. Baking decreases the strength of most flavorings.

It helps to understand the role each ingredient plays in cake baking. Unsalted butter or oil make the cake rich and tender. Eggs, which in a butter cake are added after the butter is creamed, are binders. They also add protein and flavor and increase the volume of the cake, acting either with other leaveners or independently. To produce the lightest possible cake, egg whites are often beaten and then folded into other ingredients.

Honey not only sweetens cake, it also increases its tenderness, moisture, and shelf life. (To prevent a sliced cake from drying out quickly, place a cut lemon next to the cut edges of the cake before covering it with plastic wrap or storing it in a covered cake dish.)

The chief ingredient of cakes, with the exception of some sponge cakes, is flour. I sometimes use half whole wheat pastry flour and half unbleached white flour when lightness is especially important. Regular whole wheat flour contains more gluten and makes a heavier cake. The addition of unbleached white flour provides lightness without taking too much away from the nutritional properties.

Leaveners are responsible for the volume of a cake. They form the tiny air bubbles that cause a cake to rise. In butter cakes, baking powder and baking soda are the main leavening agents. They're often assisted by eggs or beaten egg whites.

Liquids in the form of milk, buttermilk, water, or fruit juice expand the gluten and starch in the flour. Then, of course, the flavoring from fruits, juices, or extracts is added. When a cake is made with butter, flavoring isn't as critical because butter adds its own delightful taste.

STEP BY STEP

Assembling ingredients, turning on the oven, and preparing pans are the first three steps in cake making. An even heat is essential, so it's always necessary to preheat the oven in which you're going to bake a cake.

For a butter cake, you first cream the shortening to give the cake a fine texture. This is usually done with an electric beater, but there are cooks who prefer the old-fashioned wooden spoon. After the butter is fluffy, the eggs or egg yolks and honey are beaten in. You can't overbeat at this point, since you're just adding air that will increase the cake's volume.

Flour and liquid are added next — sometimes alternately. Beating is kept to a minimum so the gluten won't be toughened. The ingredients should be mixed just enough to blend them thoroughly. Then the flavoring is mixed in.

If the eggs have been separated, the beaten whites are folded quickly and thoroughly into the batter (see page xiii). Folding in beaten egg whites as a final step instead of adding whole eggs to the batter will lighten the cake, but if you fail to fold in all of the beaten whites, leaving pieces of them in the batter, your cake will have a coarse texture.

FILLING THE PANS

Don't overfill cake pans or the batter may rise over the top, spilling onto your oven. Two-thirds full is a good rule of thumb. Should you get some batter on the pan's edge, wipe it off before putting the pan into the oven or it will burn and smoke.

Thick cake batters tend to rise more in the middle than on the edges while baking. This is a particular problem with layer cakes — the layers don't sit well on top of each other if they're not even. To prevent this irregularity, take a spatula and spread the batter so that it's a bit higher on the edges than in the center. It will level off as it bakes.

BAKING

For cake baking, oven shelves should be placed as close to the center of the oven as possible. If you have four shelf positions, use the second from the bottom.

When baking more than one layer at a time, careful placement of pans is important for even baking. The pans should never touch the walls of the oven or each other. If you're baking more than two layers, you'll need two oven shelves. Hot air must be able to circulate freely for cakes to bake evenly. Stagger the pans so that they're not directly above each other. Put two pans toward, but not touching, the back of the oven, and the others toward, but not touching, the oven door. In spite of staggering the pans, you may notice that one side of a cake layer is browning or rising before the other side. To correct this, very gently turn the pan around.

The baking times I give are approximate since many conditions influence the length of time needed to bake a cake. Oven temperatures aren't always accurate. Altitude also is a factor, as well as the number of layers being baked in the oven at one time.

You can test the doneness of a cake by inserting a cake tester or food pick into the center. If it comes out clean, the cake is finished baking. A butter cake will shrink slightly from the sides of a pan when it's done. Should it be completely separated from the pan, remove it from the oven immediately. The cake will be overdone and dry but probably still edible. The touch test is one of the best criteria, especially for sponge cakes. Gently press on the center of the cake. If the imprint remains, the cake is underbaked, but if the surface springs back, the cake is ready to be removed from the oven.

COOLING

A butter cake should cool slightly in the pan on a wire rack or it will break apart. But if you allow it to cool thoroughly in the pan the cake will continue to cook from the steam generated between the pan and the cake. Therefore, it's important, after 10 minutes, to turn the cake out onto a wire rack to cool completely.

A sponge cake should cool completely in the pan, inverted and slightly elevated so that the cake "hangs" above the surface of the counter top, before removing it from the pan to a wire rack.

Wire racks permit the air to circulate around all the cake's surfaces and thus prevent further cooking.

WHAT CAUSES FAILURES?

You can select the best recipe, use the best ingredients, and make your best effort and still end up with a cake that's less successful than you'd hoped for. The types of failures and the reasons for them are numerous.

If a butter cake falls, is crumbly, or seems leaden, you may have used too much shortening or may have overdone it with the honey. Either of these can make the cake heavy and inhibit the rise.

A cake that's underbaked or baked in too slow an oven will be soggy and unable to sustain its height.

Dry butter cakes often result from using more flour or leavening than is needed or too little shortening. And, of course, baking a cake at an excessively high temperature will dry it out, too.

You may find that a butter cake doesn't have the tender texture you expected. This happens when the butter hasn't been creamed long enough or the beaten egg whites haven't been folded in well. If you've skimped on the flour, the texture will be adversely affected, too.

Have you ever baked what was to be a big, airy cake and had it turn out an undersized, compact failure? This sometimes happens when a cook is hurrying and doesn't allow time for ingredients to reach room temperature.

A layer cake that's split on the top is usually a bit on the dry side, indicating that it contains too much flour or was baked at too high a temperature. When this occurs the outer surface bakes faster than the inside and splits from the expanding inner batter.

The problems with sponge cake are different but just as vexing. Beating eggs well is especially important for a high-quality sponge cake since there's often no other leavening. A coarse or grainy cake can be the result of underbeating. But overbeating will reduce the air you're trying to beat in, and the cake will be heavy and may fall.

If you use a pan that's too large for the amount of batter, heat won't circulate freely on the top of the cake during baking, and the cake will be heavy and lacking in volume. If the oven's too hot, the sponge cake will have a rubbery texture instead of being light and delicate.

Many cakes in this chapter are rich and filling. I save these for special occasions and serve only small portions. Others, made with fewer egg yolks and less butter, are good, wholesome everyday fare. I enjoy many of these cakes without frostings. But if you want topping on your cakes, you'll find many from which to choose in the chapter titled Triumphant Toppings, Fillings, and Sweet Spreads.

CAKES

Coconut Dream Cake

This truly spectacular sponge cake is a wonderful choice for special occasions.

  ½ cup butter
  9 eggs, separated
  ¾ cup honey
1½ teaspoons vanilla extract
  ¾ cup sifted whole wheat pastry
     flour
  ¾ cup sifted unbleached white flour
  1 tablespoon baking powder
1½ teaspoons baking soda
  1 cup unsweetened flaked coconut
  1 cup Creamy Cake Filling
     (page 273)
  2 cups Coconut Cream Frosting
     (page 267)
     toasted unsweetened flaked
     coconut (optional)

Preheat oven to 350°F. Butter and flour 3 9-inch layer cake pans.

In a small saucepan, melt butter. Set aside to cool.

In a large bowl, beat egg yolks, honey, and vanilla for 5 minutes.

Sift together whole wheat pastry flour, unbleached white flour, baking powder, and baking soda into a medium-size bowl. Stir into egg yolk mixture. Beat in butter.

In a large bowl, beat egg whites until stiff peaks form. Fold into batter. Then fold in coconut. Turn into prepared pans, and bake on middle shelf of oven for 25 to 30 minutes, or until cake springs back when pressed in the center.

Cool in pans for 15 minutes.

Turn out onto wire racks. Cool well before frosting.

Spread Creamy Cake Filling between layers, and frost with Coconut Cream Frosting. Decorate with flaked coconut, if desired.

8 to 10 servings

Carob-Prune Cake

  1 cup pitted prunes
  ½ cup boiling water
1¼ cups sifted whole wheat pastry
     flour
1¼ cups unbleached white flour
  1 tablespoon baking powder
  1 teaspoon baking soda
2½ tablespoons sifted powdered
     carob
1½ teaspoons ground allspice
  ⅔ cup vegetable oil
  ¾ cup honey
  2 eggs
  1 cup buttermilk
1½ teaspoons vanilla extract

Place prunes in a small bowl, cover with boiling water, and set aside to plump for 15 to 20 minutes.

Preheat oven to 350°F. Butter and flour (or sprinkle with carob) a 9 × 9 × 2-inch pan.

Sift together whole wheat pastry flour, unbleached white flour, baking powder, baking soda, carob, and allspice into a medium-size bowl.

In a large bowl, beat together oil, honey, eggs, buttermilk, and vanilla.

Drain any excess liquid from

prunes, and then chop in a food processor (using on/off motion) or blender.

Add dry ingredients to wet ingredients gradually, mixing with electric mixer. Add prunes, and mix until blended. Turn into prepared pan, and bake for 25 minutes, or until top springs back when lightly pressed in the center.

Serve with Carob Whip (page 266).

10 to 12 servings

Carob-Strawberry Torte

    8 egg whites, at room temperature
    ¼ teaspoon cream of tartar
    ½ cup honey
1½ teaspoons vanilla extract
    4 cups Carob Whip (page 266)
1½ cups sliced fresh strawberries
       whole fresh strawberries

Preheat oven to 250°F. Butter and flour 2 large baking sheets. With a 7-inch saucepan cover, trace 2 circles on each baking sheet.

In a large bowl, beat together egg whites and cream of tartar until foamy. Gradually beat in honey and vanilla, and continue beating until whites are stiff but not dry. Divide between circles on prepared baking sheets, spreading evenly to edges of circles. Bake on middle shelf of oven until lightly browned, 45 to 50 minutes. (After about 25 minutes, reverse baking sheets.)

Remove from oven, and cool on baking sheets.

To assemble, place 1 meringue on a serving plate, spread with 1 cup Carob Whip, and top with ½ cup sliced

Lady Baltimore Cake   Page 9

strawberries. Repeat until top layer is in place. Spread remaining Carob Whip on top, and decorate with whole strawberries. Store in refrigerator.

Cut with serrated knife.

8 to 10 servings

VARIATIONS

Carob-Orange Torte: Substitute 1½ cups chopped unsweetened mandarin oranges for the sliced strawberries and ½ cup mandarin orange sections for the whole strawberries.

Carob-Apricot Torte: Substitute 1½ cups chopped apricots for the sliced strawberries and apricot halves for the whole strawberries.

Carrot Cake Roll

A light, delicate cake roll with orange flecks throughout and a creamy raisin filling.

CAKE

⅓ cup whole wheat flour
⅓ cup unbleached white flour
2 tablespoons cornstarch
1 teaspoon baking powder
½ teaspoon ground cinnamon
3 eggs, separated
½ cup honey
1 teaspoon grated lemon rind
½ teaspoon vanilla extract
1 cup grated carrots, loosely packed
¼ teaspoon cream of tartar
2 tablespoons Coconut Sugar
    (page xxii)

FILLING

1 cup cream cheese, softened
2 tablespoons honey
½ teaspoon vanilla extract
½ cup chopped raisins
    Coconut Sugar, for sprinkling

Preheat oven to 350°F. Butter a jelly-roll pan, and line it with wax paper.

To make the cake: Sift together whole wheat four, unbleached white flour, cornstarch, baking powder, and cinnamon into a small bowl.

In a medium-size bowl, beat egg yolks until light and thick. Beat in honey, lemon rind, and vanilla. Stir in dry ingredients until just blended. Stir in carrots.

In another medium-size bowl, beat egg whites until foamy throughout. Sprinkle with cream of tartar and beat until stiff peaks form. Stir about one-quarter of the egg whites into batter to lighten it, then fold in the rest. Spoon batter into prepared pan, spreading it right to edges. Bake for 12 to 15 minutes, or until golden brown on top and dry inside when tested with a cake tester or food pick.

Sprinkle a tea towel with Coconut Sugar. Loosen edges of cake with a sharp knife, and turn it out onto towel. Gently peel off wax paper. Roll cake up lengthwise in towel, and let stand for 1 minute. Unroll, and let stand for 3 minutes. Then roll up again, and let stand until cool.

To make the filling: In a medium-size bowl, beat cream cheese until fluffy. Beat in honey, vanilla, and raisins.

Unroll cake. Remove towel. Spread filling right to edges of cake. Reroll cake, and place gently, seam-side down,

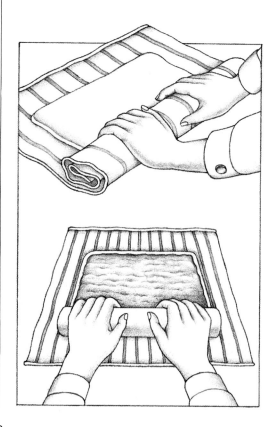

on tray or other server. Sprinkle with Coconut Sugar. If filling does not show well at ends, trim about ½ inch off each end with a serrated knife.

12 to 14 servings

Lady Baltimore Cake

¼ cup raisins
1⅓ cups sifted whole wheat pastry flour
1⅓ cups sifted unbleached white flour
4 teaspoons baking powder
¾ cup honey
⅔ cup vegetable oil
1 cup milk
1 teaspoon vanilla extract
5 egg whites
4 cups Seven-Minute Frosting (page 268)
½ cup chopped walnuts
¼ cup chopped dried figs

Preheat oven to 350°F. Butter and flour bottoms and sides of 2 8-inch layer cake pans.

Place raisins in a small bowl, cover with boiling water, and set aside to plump for 15 to 20 minutes.

Sift together whole wheat pastry flour, unbleached white flour, and baking powder 3 times. Place into a large bowl. Mix in honey, oil, milk, and vanilla. Beat with an electric mixer for 2 minutes.

In a large bowl, beat egg whites, and then fold into batter. Turn into prepared pans, and bake for 25 to 30 minutes, or until a cake tester or food pick inserted into the center comes out clean.

Cool in pans for 10 minutes. Remove to wire racks to cool completely.

Spoon 1 cup Seven-Minute Frosting into a medium-size bowl, and add walnuts, drained raisins, and figs. Spread between cake layers. Frost top and sides with remaining frosting (or, if desired, use less frosting and frost only top).

10 to 12 servings

Currant-Walnut Bar Cake

¾ cup whole wheat pastry flour
¾ cup unbleached white flour
1 teaspoon baking powder
1 teaspoon ground ginger
1 cup dried currants
1 cup coarsely chopped walnuts
3 eggs
½ cup buttermilk
¾ cup honey

Preheat oven to 350°F. Butter a 13 × 9 × 2-inch pan.

Sift together whole wheat pastry flour, unbleached white flour, baking powder, and ginger into a medium-size bowl. In another medium-size bowl, toss currants and nuts with ¼ cup of the flour mixture.

In a large bowl, beat together eggs, buttermilk, and honey. Add flour mixture and stir just to mix. Stir in currants and nuts. Turn into prepared pan, and bake for 30 to 35 minutes, or until top springs back when lightly pressed in center.

Cool in pan on wire rack. Cut into bars, and serve with Orange Custard Sauce (page 270).

Makes about 2 dozen

Italian Sponge Cake
(Pane di Spugna)

This useful cake can be the basis of many desserts, using different toppings, or it can be split and filled with pastry cream or fruit filling. I use it to make my favorite Fourth of July cake (page 185).

¾ cup sifted whole wheat pastry
    flour
¾ cup sifted unbleached white flour
10 eggs, separated
¼ teaspoon cream of tartar
2 tablespoons water
1 cup honey
2 teaspoons almond extract
1 teaspoon grated lemon rind

Preheat oven to 350°F. Line an ungreased 13 × 9 × 2-inch pan with a sheet of parchment or wax paper cut to fit the bottom.

In a medium-size bowl, sift together whole wheat pastry flour and unbleached white flour.

In the large bowl of an electric mixer, beat egg whites until foamy. Sprinkle with cream of tartar, and continue to beat until stiff peaks form.

In the small bowl of an electric mixer (it is not necessary to clean beaters), combine egg yolks with water. Beat until very light. Gradually add honey, and continue to beat until mixture nearly fills bowl. Remove from mixer. Stir in almond extract and lemon rind. Use a whisk or spatula to fold flour mixture into egg yolk mixture. Use the same whisk to fold egg-flour mixture into egg whites until no white

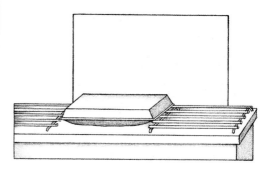

streaks show. Spoon batter into prepared pan. Bake for 35 to 45 minutes, or until cake is golden brown and springs back when lightly touched at the center with a finger.

Invert cake in pan, using 2 wire racks to hold up ends of pan. When completely cool, remove cake from pan and strip off paper.

12 to 16 servings

Ladyfingers

3 eggs, separated
¼ cup honey
½ teaspoon vanilla extract
½ cup sifted whole wheat pastry flour
½ cup sifted unbleached white flour
1 tablespoon cornstarch
⅛ teaspoon cream of tartar

Preheat oven to 350°F. Line 2 baking sheets with parchment paper.

In a large bowl, beat egg yolks until golden. Add honey and beat for 10 minutes, or until very thick. Add vanilla.

Sift together whole wheat pastry flour, unbleached white flour, and cornstarch into a medium-size bowl. Mix with fork to blend well. Fold flour mixture into egg yolk mixture, a little at a time.

In another medium-size bowl, beat together egg whites and cream of tartar until stiff peaks form. Fold into batter. Transfer to pastry bag with about a ¾-inch opening. Squeeze onto prepared baking sheets in 3-inch lengths, 1 inch apart (or spoon onto parchment in 1 by 3-inch lengths). Bake on middle shelf of oven for 10 to 12 minutes, or until lightly browned.

Remove carefully with a spatula, and cool on wire racks.

Makes 1½ to 2 dozen

Old-Fashioned Pound Cake

Pound cake freezes well and serves as a useful basic recipe for many beautiful desserts. It is equally good served plain, especially at tea time.

    ¾ cup whole wheat pastry flour
    ¾ cup unbleached white flour
    2 teaspoons baking powder
    ¼ teaspoon baking soda
    ¼ teaspoon ground mace (ground
        nutmeg may be substituted)
    ⅔ cup butter, softened
    ¾ cup honey
    3 eggs
    1 teaspoon vanilla extract

Preheat oven to 350°F. Butter an 8½ × 4½ × 3-inch loaf pan, and line bottom with ungreased parchment paper. (Wax paper may be substituted.)

In a medium-size bowl, sift together whole wheat pastry flour, unbleached white flour, baking powder, baking soda, and mace.

In the large bowl of an electric mixer, beat butter until fluffy. Add honey in a slow stream, then eggs, 1 at a time, and vanilla. Do not rush this stage, but beat thoroughly after each addition.

Add flour mixture in 4 additions, beating just enough to blend each time. Spoon batter into prepared pan, and bake on middle shelf of oven for 45 to 50 minutes. If cake browns before it's done, lay a sheet of aluminum foil loosely over the top as it bakes. Do not test until cake has risen and split; the split should not appear moist. A cake tester or food pick inserted into the center should come out clean and dry.

Cool cake in pan on a wire rack until it can be handled. Remove from pan, and cool completely. Do not remove parchment paper until cake is sliced.

8 to 10 servings

VARIATIONS

Raisin Pound Cake: Mix ½ cup raisins with 2 tablespoons flour from recipe. Fold into batter just before spooning batter into pan.

Raisin Nut Pound Cake: Mix ½ cup raisins and ½ cup chopped walnuts with 2 tablespoons flour from recipe. Fold into batter just before spooning batter into pan.

Lemon Pound Cake: Substitute 1 teaspoon grated lemon rind for vanilla. Fold into batter just before spooning batter into pan.

Carob-Cranberry Layer Cake

- 1½ cups whole wheat pastry flour
- 1 cup unbleached white flour
- ½ cup sifted powdered carob
- 2½ teaspoons baking powder
- 2 teaspoons baking soda
- 1½ teaspoons ground cinnamon
- 1 cup milk
- 2 teaspoons vanilla extract
- 2 cups finely chopped cranberries
- 2 teaspoons grated orange rind
- ¾ cup butter, softened
- 1 cup honey
- 3 eggs
    - Cranberry Frosting and Filling (page 267)

Preheat oven to 350°F. Butter 2 9-inch layer cake pans, and line them with rounds of buttered wax paper.

In a medium-size bowl, sift together whole wheat pastry flour, unbleached white flour, carob, baking powder, baking soda, and cinnamon 3 times.

Combine milk and vanilla in a small bowl. Combine cranberries and orange rind in another small bowl.

In a large bowl, cream butter until fluffy. Beat in honey and then eggs, 1 at a time. Add flour mixture alternately with milk, beginning and ending with flour. Fold in cranberry mixture. Divide batter evenly between prepared pans. Bake on middle shelf of oven for 35 to 40 minutes, or until cake springs back when lightly pressed in the center and a cake tester or food pick inserted into the center comes out clean and dry.

Cool layers on wire racks for 5 minutes, turn out of pans, strip off wax paper, and turn right side up to finish cooling.

When cold, spread each layer with Cranberry Frosting and Filling. On a serving dish, place 1 layer on top of the other, frosting sides up. Keep cool. Refrigerate leftovers.

10 servings

Mandarin Tangerine Steamed Cake

CAKE
- ½ cup whole wheat flour
- ½ cup unbleached white flour
- ½ cup whole wheat cracker crumbs (dry whole grain bread crumbs may be substituted)
- 2 teaspoons baking powder
- ½ cup butter, softened
- ⅓ cup honey
- 2 eggs
- 1 tablespoon grated orange rind
- 3 tablespoons orange juice
- ¼ cup chopped dried papaya (dried apricots may be substituted)
- ¼ cup chopped dried figs (dates may be substituted)

SAUCE
- 1¼ cups orange juice
- 1 egg
- 1 tablespoon cornstarch
- 2 tablespoons butter
- ¼ cup honey
- 1 cup peeled, seeded tangerine sections
- 1 teaspoon rum extract

To make the cake: Butter a 1-pound coffee can generously. Select a large pot that will hold the coffee can upright. Place a trivet or rack on the bottom of the pot.

In a medium-size bowl, mix together whole wheat flour, unbleached white flour, cracker crumbs, and baking powder.

In a large bowl, cream butter. Beat in honey, then eggs and grated orange rind. Stir flour mixture into butter mixture. Blend in orange juice. Fold in dried fruit. Spoon batter into prepared can. Cover can loosely with a square of foil secured with a rubber band. Allow top of foil to form a dome. (See illustration on page 157.) Stand can on trivet or rack in pot, and add enough water to come three-quarters up sides of can, but not enough to make can float. Bring water to a boil, reduce heat, cover, and steam for 2 hours.

Remove can from pot, and stand it on a rack. When cool enough to handle, remove cake by loosening sides with a long thin knife. Stand cake on a serving plate, and serve warm with sauce poured over and around it.

To make the sauce: Combine orange juice, egg, and cornstarch in a medium-size bowl, and beat until blended. Pour mixture into a saucepan, and cook over medium-low heat, whisking constantly, until it simmers. Stir in butter and honey. Cook 1 minute longer, while whisking. If necessary, sieve sauce. (It will seem thick, but the tangerines will thin it.) Stir in tangerines and rum extract.

6 to 8 servings

Lemon *Gateau*

8 eggs, separated
1¼ cups sifted whole wheat pastry
    flour
1 cup unbleached white flour
1 tablespoon baking powder
¾ cup honey
½ cup vegetable oil
½ cup lemon juice
½ teaspoon finely grated lemon rind
1½ teaspoons lemon extract, divided
½ teaspoon cream of tartar
2 cups heavy cream
¼ cup honey
    fresh raspberries or strawberries
    (optional)

Preheat oven to 325°F. Butter and flour a 10-inch tube pan.

Beat egg yolks slightly. Allow egg whites to come to room temperature.

In a large bowl, sift together whole wheat pastry flour, unbleached white flour, and baking powder. Make a well in the middle, and add ¾ cup honey, oil, egg yolks, lemon juice, lemon rind, and 1 teaspoon lemon extract. Beat with a spoon until blended.

In another large bowl, beat together egg whites and cream of tartar until stiff peaks form. Fold into batter, and then pour into prepared pan. Bake on middle shelf of oven for 50 to 60 minutes, or until top springs back when lightly pressed in the center with fingers.

Cool in pan for 10 minutes, then turn out onto a wire rack, and allow to cool thoroughly.

In a medium-size bowl, beat together heavy cream, ¼ cup honey, and ½ teaspoon lemon extract. Frost top and sides of cooled cake. Refrigerate.

Just before serving, decorate with berries.

10 to 12 servings

Raspberry-Peach Layers

2 cups heavy cream, divided
¼ cup butter
½ cup whole wheat pastry flour
½ cup unbleached white flour
¾ teaspoon baking soda
1 teaspoon baking powder
6 egg yolks
2 eggs
⅓ cup honey
1½ teaspoons vanilla extract
2 tablespoons honey
2 cups fresh raspberries
3 large peaches, peeled, pitted, and
    chunked

Preheat oven to 350°F. Butter and flour 2 9-inch layer cake pans.

In a small saucepan, heat together ¼ cup cream and butter until butter has melted. Set aside to cool slightly.

Sift together whole wheat pastry flour, unbleached white flour, baking soda, and baking powder 3 times.

In a large bowl, beat egg yolks, eggs, and ⅓ cup honey for 10 minutes. Beat in vanilla. Fold in flour and cream-butter mixtures. Turn into prepared pans, and bake on middle shelf of oven for about 15 minutes, or until tops spring back when pressed lightly with fingertips.

Cool for 10 minutes in pans, and then turn out onto wire racks to cool completely.

In a medium-size bowl, beat 1¾ cups cream and 2 tablespoons honey until soft peaks form. When ready to serve, spread half of the whipped cream on 1 cake layer. Top with half of the raspberries and half of the peaches. Place the other layer on top, spread with remaining whipped cream, and decorate with remaining fruit. Serve immediately.

8 to 10 servings

Raspberry Chestnut Torte

This delectable cake contains no flour at all. Its velvety texture is reminiscent of cheesecake, but its flavor is more delicate.

1 cup cooked, peeled chestnuts
4 eggs, separated
½ cup honey
½ teaspoon orange extract
3 tablespoons Basic Carob Syrup, (page xviii)
⅛ teaspoon cream of tartar
1 package (10-ounces) unsweetened frozen raspberries, thawed and drained with juice reserved
2 teaspoons cornstarch
1 teaspoon honey

Preheat oven to 350°F. Butter a 9-inch layer cake pan, and line bottom with buttered parchment paper.

In a food processor, grind chestnuts to a fine texture. Add egg yolks, ½ cup honey, and orange extract. Process until well blended and creamy, stopping machine to scrape sides and bottom at least twice. Blend in Basic Carob Syrup. Transfer mixture to a large bowl.

In a medium-size bowl, beat egg whites until foamy. Sprinkle with cream of tartar. Continue beating until stiff peaks form.

Stir about one-quarter of the egg whites into chestnut mixture to lighten it. Carefully fold in the rest of the egg whites. Spoon mixture into prepared pan, and bake on middle shelf of oven for 30 to 35 minutes, or until a cake tester comes out dry when inserted into the center and top of cake is lightly browned.

Place pan on a wire rack, and let cake cool completely in pan. It will shrink slightly and become more compact.

Pour reserved raspberry juice into a medium-size saucepan. Stir in cornstarch until there are no lumps. Cook over medium heat, stirring constantly, until mixture bubbles and thickens. Add raspberries and 1 teaspoon honey to pan and cook ½ minute longer, or just until glaze bubbles again. Refrigerate sauce to cool completely.

Invert cake onto a plate, and remove parchment paper. Turn cake upright on a serving plate. Spread raspberry glaze over cake, and let it drip down sides. Keep in a cool place until ready to serve.

12 servings

Mango Gold Cake

1 cup whole wheat pastry flour
1 cup plus 2 tablespoons
   unbleached white flour
2½ teaspoons baking powder
¼ teaspoon ground allspice
¼ teaspoon ground cloves
½ cup butter, softened
¾ cup honey
5 egg yolks
½ cup milk
½ cup yogurt
1 teaspoon vanilla extract
1 mango, peeled and diced (about
   2 cups loosely packed)
   Vanilla Cream (page 273)
1 tablespoon date sugar (optional)

Preheat oven to 325°F. Butter 2
9-inch layer cake pans, and line bottoms with wax paper.

Sift together whole wheat pastry
flour, unbleached white flour, baking
powder, and spices 3 times.

In a large bowl, cream butter until
fluffy. Beat in honey and then egg yolks.
Add about one-third of the flour, blending well. Beat in milk. Add another
third of the flour, then yogurt, and
vanilla. Add remaining flour. Blend well
after each addition. Divide batter
between the 2 prepared pans. Sprinkle
mango over top, and press down just
to surface of batter. Bake layers on
middle shelf of oven for 40 to 45 minutes or until golden brown and beginning to shrink away from sides of pan.
Layers will be moist.

Cool for 5 minutes, then carefully
remove from pans, peel off wax paper,
and turn right-side up. Spread Vanilla
Cream between layers. Sprinkle date
sugar on top, if desired.

10 servings

Orange Surprise Cake

1 cup sifted whole wheat pastry flour
1 cup unbleached white flour
2 teaspoons baking powder
1 cup honey
½ cup butter
2 eggs, separated
¼ cup orange juice
1 large orange, peeled, seeded, and
   chopped
   Orange Frosting (page 267)
½ orange, peeled, seeded, and
   sectioned

Preheat oven to 350°F. Butter an
8 × 8 × 2-inch pan.

Sift together whole wheat pastry
flour, unbleached white flour, and baking powder 3 times.

In a large bowl, beat together honey
and butter until fluffy. Beat in egg
yolks and orange juice. Add flour mixture, a little at a time, mixing well.
Fold in chopped oranges.

In a small bowl, beat egg whites
until stiff peaks form. Fold into batter.
Bake in prepared pan on middle shelf
of oven for 35 to 45 minutes, or until a
cake tester or food pick inserted into
the center comes out clean.

Cool completely, and frost with
Orange Frosting. Decorate with
orange sections.

9 to 12 servings

Pineapple Sunshine Carrot Cake

1 cup whole wheat pastry flour
1 cup unbleached white flour
2 teaspoons baking powder
2 teaspoons baking soda
1 teaspoon ground nutmeg
1 teaspoon ground cinnamon
½ cup honey
½ cup maple syrup
4 eggs, separated
1 cup vegetable oil
1 teaspoon vanilla extract
2 cups finely shredded carrots
1 can (8 ounces) unsweetened
   crushed pineapple, drained
1 cup unsweetened flaked coconut

Preheat oven to 350°F. Butter a 13 × 9 × 2-inch pan.

In a medium-size bowl, sift together whole wheat pastry flour, unbleached white flour, baking powder, baking soda, nutmeg, and cinnamon.

In a large bowl, beat together honey, maple syrup, and egg yolks. Beat in oil and vanilla. Sift flour mixture into liquid ingredients, beating well.

In another medium-size bowl, beat egg whites until stiff peaks form, and then fold into batter.

Fold in carrots, pineapple, and coconut. Turn into prepared pan, and bake on middle shelf of oven for 50 to 60 minutes, or until a cake tester or food pick inserted into the center comes out clean.

Cool in pan for 10 minutes. Then turn out onto a wire rack.

12 to 16 servings

CUPCAKES

Pumpkin Cupcakes

1½ cups whole wheat pastry flour
1 teaspoon baking soda
½ teaspoon ground cinnamon
¼ teaspoon ground allspice
¼ teaspoon ground cloves
¼ teaspoon ground ginger
¼ teaspoon ground nutmeg
½ cup chopped dried papaya (golden
   raisins may be substituted)
½ cup vegetable oil
2 eggs, at room temperature
¾ cup honey, slightly warmed
1 cup thick pumpkin puree
   Basic White Frosting (page 268)

Preheat oven to 350°F. Line a 12-cup muffin tin with paper liners.

Sift together flour, baking soda, and spices into a large bowl. Stir in papaya.

In a medium-size bowl, beat oil with eggs until light and well blended. Beat in honey and then pumpkin. Pour into flour mixture, and stir until blended. Spoon batter into prepared muffin tin, filling each cup about two-thirds full, and bake on middle shelf of oven for 30 minutes, or until a cake tester or food pick inserted into the center of a cake comes out clean and dry.

As soon as they can be handled, remove cupcakes to a wire rack to cool. Frost with Basic White Frosting.

Makes 1 dozen

17

Boston Cream Cupcakes

1 cup sifted whole wheat pastry flour
¾ cup sifted unbleached white flour
2 teaspoons baking powder
2 eggs, separated
½ cup butter, softened
½ cup honey
¾ cup milk
1 teaspoon vanilla extract
  Lemon Cream (page 273)
  Carob Fudge Glaze (page 266)

Preheat oven to 375°F. Line a 12-cup muffin tin with paper liners, or butter and flour the tin.

In a medium-size bowl, sift together whole wheat pastry flour, unbleached white flour and baking powder.

In the small bowl of an electric mixer, beat egg whites until stiff peaks form. Remove bowl and cover with a plate. It is not necessary to wash beaters.

In the large bowl of an electric mixer, cream butter until fluffy. Beat in honey, then egg yolks.

Pour milk into a small bowl and stir in vanilla.

Add dry ingredients alternately with milk to creamed mixture in 3 to 4 portions, beginning and ending with dry ingredients and mixing only enough to blend thoroughly each time. Remove from mixer. Stir in about one-quarter of the beaten egg whites to lighten. Fold in the rest of the egg whites. Immediately spoon batter into prepared muffin tin, filling each cup about two-thirds full. Bake on middle shelf of oven for 20 minutes, or until cupcakes are risen, golden and dry in the center when tested with a cake tester or food pick. Place tin on a wire rack. When it can be handled, remove cupcakes, and allow to cool completely on wire racks.

Place wire racks over a sheet of wax paper. If paper liners were used, remove them from cupcakes, and cut each cupcake in half horizontally at the middle. Spread Lemon Cream on bottom halves; put tops back on. Spread Carob Fudge Glaze on tops, and let it drip down sides. Chill cupcakes until served. These cupcakes are not finger food, so serve with forks.

Makes 1 dozen

VARIATION

Orange Butterflies: Substitute 1 teaspoon finely grated orange rind for vanilla extract. Instead of ¾ cup milk, use ½ cup milk and ¼ cup orange juice.

When cupcakes are baked and cooled, do not remove paper liners. Slice off tops of cupcakes above liners. Spread bottoms with Orange Filling (page

272) or whipped cream. Cut each cupcake top into 2 "wings." Fix the wings at a slant in the filling of each cupcake.

Ginger Cupcakes

These old-fashioned cakes have the two characteristics so often found in early American recipes: They are easy to mix up, and the recipe makes a generous amount.

    ¾ cup molasses
    ½ cup honey
    1½ cups boiling water
    1 teaspoon baking soda
    ½ cup butter, cut into thin slices
    3 cups plus 2 tablespoons whole
        wheat flour
    1 tablespoon ground ginger
    1 tablespoon baking powder
    1 cup uncooked quick oats
    1 egg

Stand molasses and honey jars in a pan of hot water to warm and thin them a bit before measuring. Combine measured molasses and honey in a medium-size bowl. Stir in boiling water, then baking soda. Blend in butter. Allow mixture to cool to warm, stirring occasionally. The butter will melt during this time.

Preheat oven to 350°F. Generously butter 3 6-cup muffin tins, or line with paper liners.

Sift flour, ginger, and baking powder into a large bowl. Stir in oats.

Beat egg into molasses mixture. Pour liquid ingredients all at once into dry ingredients, and stir just to blend well. Spoon batter into prepared muffin tins, filling each cup about

two-thirds full, and bake on middle shelf of oven for 25 minutes, or until a cake tester or food pick inserted into the center of a cake comes out clean and dry.

Let cupcakes cool in muffin tins on wire racks for 5 minutes. Then remove and cool completely on the racks.

Homemade applesauce makes a nice accompaniment to these cupcakes.

Makes 1½ dozen

Chipper Cupcakes

    1½ cups whole wheat pastry flour
    ¾ teaspoon baking soda
    ¼ teaspoon cream of tartar
    ¼ cup butter, softened
    ¾ cup honey
    1 egg
    1½ teaspoons vanilla extract
    ¼ teaspoon almond extract
    ¾ cup sour cream
    1 cup milk carob chips

Preheat oven to 350°F. Line 3 6-cup muffin tins with paper liners.

Sift together flour, baking soda, and cream of tartar 3 times.

In a large bowl, cream butter until fluffy. Beat in honey, egg, vanilla, and almond extract in that order. Add dry ingredients alternately with sour cream, beginning and ending with flour mixture. Fold in chips. Spoon batter into prepared muffin tins, filling each cup about three-quarters full. Bake for 20 to 25 minutes, or until they are golden and spring back when lightly pressed with fingertips.

Remove from pan, and cool on wire racks. No frosting is necessary.

Makes 1½ dozen

Cup Cheesecakes

For company, I like to make these with two different toppings and arrange them on a three-tiered cookie plate.

CUPCAKES
1 cup crumbs from Good Old Butter
    Cookies (page 48)
¼ cup butter, melted
12 ounces cream cheese, softened
⅓ cup honey
1 egg
1 teaspoon vanilla extract
TOPPING
½ cup Apricot Jam (page 276)
2 cups diced peeled peaches
       or
Blueberry Flummery (page 104)
       or
German Red Fruit Pudding
    (page 107)

Preheat oven to 350°F. Line a 12-cup muffin tin with paper liners.

To make the cupcakes: In a small bowl, mix cookie crumbs with butter. Press a rounded teaspoon of mixture on bottom of each paper liner.

Whip cream cheese in a medium-size bowl. Beat in honey, then egg, and vanilla until fluffy and well blended. Divide the cheese mixture evenly between the paper liners, and bake on middle shelf of oven for 12 minutes. Turn off oven but do not open door. Leave cheesecakes in oven 12 minutes longer and then remove.

Cool cheesecakes in muffin tin on a wire rack.

To make the topping: Melt jam in a small saucepan. Mix in peaches. The Blueberry Flummery and German Red Fruit Pudding are ready to use. Divide desired topping among cheesecakes, and chill in refrigerator until serving time.

If desired, prepare half portions of any two toppings so that you can have half of one flavor and half of another.

Makes 1 dozen

Peach Cupcakes

¾ cup sifted whole wheat pastry flour
¾ cup sifted unbleached white flour
1 teaspoon baking powder
6 eggs, separated
⅔ cup honey
1 teaspoon vanilla extract
1 cup Peach Preserves (page 276)
¼ teaspoon cream of tartar

Preheat oven to 350°F. Line 2 12-cup muffin tins with paper liners.

Sift together whole wheat pastry flour, unbleached white flour, and baking powder into a medium-size bowl.

In a small bowl, beat egg yolks. Add to flour mixture along with honey, vanilla, and Peach Preserves. Beat until mixed.

In a large bowl, beat egg whites and cream of tartar until stiff peaks form. Fold in flour mixture, half at a time. Spoon batter into prepared muffin tins, filling each cup almost to the top, and bake on middle shelf of oven for about 20 minutes, or until cupcakes spring back when pressed in the center.

Remove from oven, and cool completely before removing from tins.

Makes 2 dozen

Carrot Cake Roll   Page 8

Spongy Cupcakes with Raisins

1 cup raisins
2 cups whole wheat pastry flour
2 teaspoons baking powder
1 teaspoon baking soda
½ cup butter
½ cup honey
3 eggs
⅓ cup milk
1 teaspoon vanilla extract

Preheat oven to 350° F. Butter 3 6-cup muffin tins.

Dust raisins with ¼ cup flour.

Sift together 1¾ cups flour, baking powder, and baking soda 3 times.

In a large bowl, beat together butter and honey. Beat in eggs. Add flour mixture and milk alternately. Mix in vanilla, and fold in raisins. Spoon batter into prepared muffin tins, filling each cup about two-thirds full, and bake on middle shelf of oven for about 20 minutes, or until a cake tester or food pick inserted into the center of a cake comes out clean.

Remove from tins, and cool on wire racks.

Makes 1½ dozen

Moist Carob Cupcakes

¼ cup butter, softened
¼ cup vegetable oil
1¼ cups honey
2 eggs
1½ teaspoons vanilla extract
2 cups sifted whole wheat pastry
   flour
1 teaspoon baking powder
1 teaspoon baking soda
6 tablespoons sifted powdered
   carob
¾ cup milk
   Carob Whip (page 266)

Preheat oven to 350°F. Butter 2 12-cup muffin tins.

In a large bowl, beat together butter, oil, and honey. Beat in eggs and vanilla.

Sift together flour, baking powder, baking soda, and carob 3 times. Add to batter, alternating with milk and blending well between additions, beginning and ending with flour mixture. Pour into prepared muffin tins, filling each cup about half full, and bake on middle shelf of oven for about 20 minutes, or until a cake tester or food pick inserted into the center of a cake comes out clean.

Remove from tins, and cool on wire racks. Frost with Carob Whip.

Makes 2 dozen

Orange-Filled Cupcakes

2½ cups sifted whole wheat pastry
   flour
1 tablespoon baking powder
2 teaspoons baking soda
½ cup butter, softened
½ cup honey
3 eggs
¼ cup milk
⅓ cup orange juice
1 cup Orange Filling (page 272)

Preheat oven to 325°F. Line 3 6-cup muffin tins with paper liners.

Sift together flour, baking powder, and baking soda into a medium-size bowl. Stir with fork to blend.

In a large bowl, beat together butter and honey. Beat in eggs, then milk, and orange juice. Mix in flour mixture, and then beat to blend well. Spoon batter into prepared muffin tins, filling each cup about one-third full. Make slight indentations in centers, and fill each with 1 heaping teaspoon Orange Filling. (It will overflow a bit.) Spoon batter on top of filling. (Tins should be almost full.) Bake on middle shelf of oven for 20 to 25 minutes, or until golden.

Remove to wire rack to cool.

Makes 1½ dozen

CHAPTER

Naturally
Smart Cookies

Nothing I cook brings back so many heartwarming memories as cookies. My mother baked them every week (as so many mothers did), and I could scarcely wait for them to cool enough to bite into. I've followed my mother's practice of engaging in a weekly cookie baking session, but the cookies I make, while just as delicious, are more wholesome than those my mother made.

Whole grain flours provide an interesting range of textures and flavors that blend well with the other cookie ingredients. Whole wheat flour produces a firm, usually thick cookie, although the amount of liquid used in a recipe also affects thickness. Whole wheat pastry flour is my selection for a thin or delicate cookie.

You don't have to invest in special equipment to make cookies. Most of what's required is already standard in the average kitchen. You will need two baking sheets, sometimes called cookie sheets. If you don't own baking sheets, avoid pans with high sides as replacements. The sides will reflect the heat, and the result will be overbrowned cookies that may be difficult to remove from the pans. Instead, turn the pans over, and use the bottoms as baking sheets.

A roll of parchment paper is helpful. I bake thin or delicate cookies on greased parchment paper placed on the baking sheet. I can then remove the paper from the pan and allow the cookies to cool slightly before sliding them gently onto cooling racks. The paper can be used again for another batch.

One baking sheet at a time in the oven is a good rule to follow. But if you

27

have a large batch of cookies to bake, you may have neither the time nor the patience for this. When you do use two baking sheets, arrange your oven racks in the two center positions. Place one baking sheet on the top rack as far to one side of the oven as it will go without coming nearer than 1 inch from the oven's side. Place the other sheet on the rack below on the opposite side of the oven. When half the cooking time has elapsed, switch the positions of the baking sheets. Alternating baking sheets in this way will give you fairly evenly baked cookies. Whether you're using one baking sheet or two, it's important that they don't touch the oven's sides and that the cookies themselves are placed on the sheets so that they're at least 2 inches from the oven walls. Otherwise, the cookies nearest the walls will be in danger of overbrowning.

Cookies made with honey or maple syrup stay deceptively soft until they're cool. Therefore, you can't rely on touch to estimate degree of doneness. Watch for the edges to brown slightly. If this doesn't happen after the cookies have been in the oven the specified amount of time, lift a cookie to see whether the bottom is lightly browned—a signal that the cookies are done.

When you remove a baking sheet from the oven, don't put more dough on it until it has cooled thoroughly. To save time, alternate two baking sheets. While one is in the oven, arrange the dough for the next batch on a second one. Then, as you take one batch out of the oven, you can pop in the second baking sheet, take the cookies off the first one (putting them on a rack to cool), clean off the warm baking sheet, allow it to cool, and arrange another

batch of dough on it. This mini-assembly line can continue until all the cookies are baked.

Cool cookies on wire racks in a single layer. Never stack them until they're completely cooled—they'll stick together and break when you try to pull them apart.

You don't want to bake cookies too far ahead of the time you'll be serving them, but you can still make the cookie dough well in advance and either refrigerate it for up to two weeks or freeze it. The dough will keep for several months in the freezer.

Most cookie dough handles better if it has been refrigerated for an hour or two before baking. It should never be left at room temperature.

BAR COOKIES

The first cookies I ever made were bar cookies—the traditional brownies—and I've been a devotee of this type of cookie ever since. They're so tasty and so reliable, you almost can't go wrong. Just mix the batter, smooth it in a buttered pan (bar cookie dough is soft and spreadable), and bake it. If you're making a particularly thin, delicate bar, lightly flour the pan after you've buttered it.

Always use the size pan called for in a recipe when you're making bar cookies. A smaller pan will produce a cake rather than a cookie, and a larger pan will spread the dough out too thin, causing the bars to be dry. After the dough has been baked, it can be cut into bars, squares, or fingers. Allow the bars to cool for 5 minutes, then score them (cut just through the top crust); cool completely before you finish cutting, and remove them from the pan.

Bar cookies are a good choice for picnics because they travel well. I take them right in the pan in which they were baked.

DROP COOKIES

Small children love to help in the kitchen, and there's no better task to start them with than drop cookies. They're the easiest of all cookies to make.

Drop cookies are made of a soft, light dough that slides off a spoon. Small dabs of meringue flecked with tiny pieces of dried fruit or cradling delicious jams are the elite of drop cookies.

If you're preparing drop cookies that include nuts or dried fruits in the food processor, you can drop the nuts or fruits, whole, down the feed tube into the batter. The steel blade will chop them to an appropriate size. Or if you prefer, chop the nuts first, then fold them into the prepared cookie batter.

Drop cookies are traditionally small—usually about a teaspoon of dough is used to produce a 1- or 2-inch cookie. But I also make giant cookies this way, increasing the baking time a bit. It doesn't matter what size cookie you choose to make, but it is important that all the cookies baked on one baking sheet be the same size. If they're not uniform, the small ones will burn before the big ones are done.

Spacing is important, too. Drop the dough on the baking sheet, leaving enough room between each spoonful so that the cookies can spread as they bake without running together.

PRESSED COOKIES

Cooks who will tackle almost any recipe are sometimes intimidated by pressed cookies. There's really no need to be. The trick is getting the dough to the right consistency. It must be soft enough that you can push it through a cookie press or pastry bag, yet firm enough that the cookies will hold their shapes. They're a bit more work than many other types of cookies may be. I don't consider them everyday cookies, but for special occasions, they're well worth the effort.

Most doughs used for pressed cookies are rich. Although they may seem expensive to make, they're more satisfying and filling than other types of cookies, so they go further.

MOLDED COOKIES

Pieces of dough hand-shaped to form balls, crescents, criss-crosses, or other shapes that are flattened or baked as is, are known as molded cookies. These cookies are simple to make, but the hand-shaping does take a little time.

When dough is difficult to shape, chilling will make it more malleable. If the dough doesn't hold the shape you mold it to, you need to add more flour; but if it cracks when you form or flatten it, more liquid is needed.

When I flatten molded cookies, I usually use the bottom of a glass, but the tines of a fork or your fingers, slightly dampened, will work as well. Ball cookies are rolled between the palms of the hands. Crescent-shaped cookies are enhanced by rolling them in Coconut Sugar (page xxii) after they've been baked and are still warm.

REFRIGERATOR COOKIES

I like these cookies. They're easy to make, and the end product is quite delicate. The dough, which is stiffer than that used for drop cookies and softer than that used for rolled cookies, is made ahead of time, then rolled into logs, wrapped with plastic wrap or wax paper, and stored in the refrigerator for a period ranging from several hours to two weeks. (It can also be kept in the freezer for up to three months.) To make perfectly cylindrical rolls, you can pack dough into small cans from which you've removed both ends.

I use frozen cookie dough when I want particularly dainty cookies — it can be sliced thinner than dough that's right out of the refrigerator. The slices should be about ⅛ inch thick. For even slices, always use a sharp knife. You can give the cookies a tasty, decorative border by rolling the logs in ground nuts, coconut, or finely chopped dried fruit before refrigerating them.

ROLLED COOKIES

Rolled cookies take more time and effort than any other type of cookie, but they're also the most versatile. They can be cut into all kinds of shapes, stuffed with imaginative fillings, or made into pinwheels.

Cutting cookie dough into animal shapes dates back to pre-Christian times when animal cookies were part of the ritual accompanying the winter solstice. Eventually cookie cutters were invented by some enterprising person to speed up the shaping process, and now cookie cutters are made in many shapes other than the original animal forms. You may find that rolled cookies made with honey are softer than those made with sugar, and so the shapes may not be quite as well defined and the texture not as crisp.

Using too much flour during the rolling process is to be avoided since it toughens the cookies. If the dough is too soft to roll out, don't add more flour; instead, lengthen the chilling time. And you won't need to flour the rolling pin before you roll this cookie dough if you use a rolling pin cover or roll the dough between pieces of wax paper. On a hot sticky day, the dough may become too soft before you've had time to roll all of it. To prevent this problem, roll the dough in small portions, leaving what you're not working with in the refrigerator until you're ready to use it.

Rolled cookie dough sometimes sticks to the cookie cutters. Dipping them briefly in warm water, in coconut sugar, or in flour before cutting each cookie will prevent this difficulty.

Filled cookies are just two rolled cookies filled with jams or preserves, nut fillings, dried fruits, or whatever your imagination suggests — and they are scrumptious. But the looks and often the flavor are ruined if they leak while they're baking. To eliminate this common problem, don't overfill the dough. Leave plenty of room around the edges and seal each cookie well by pressing the edges together with the tines of a floured fork. Then cut a vent in the top so that steam can escape.

STORAGE TIPS

Different kinds of cookies should be stored in their own containers. If you mix them, each will take on the characteristics of the others—for example, crisp cookies will lose their crispness and soft cookies their moisture. Flavors will also mingle. The spicy flavor of gingersnaps will permeate the delicate taste of the almond wafers with which they're stored.

A piece of bread placed in a container of soft cookies will help keep them fresh and moist. The bread should be replaced every two days.

Any cookies you intend to keep longer than a week will fare better stored in the refrigerator or freezer. Cookies freeze nicely in large containers with wax paper between layers and will keep this way for three months. They defrost rapidly when you're ready to serve them.

THE TRAVELING COOKIE

Cookies make marvelous, thoughtful gifts. I often send them at holiday time to people who are too busy to make their own homemade treats. I wrap each one individually in a small piece of plastic wrap or foil. Since bar cookies travel well, I use them often as gifts. Because they are the most substantial cookies, they go at the bottom of a tin container. I continue to pack the goodies in the order of their durability with the most delicate on top. Meringues go in last. As I pack the tin, I fill the empty space with popcorn. Then I put the tin into a cardboard box, filling in all around it with popcorn. Since I've used this method of packing, the cookies have always arrived intact—even when they have to go through the hustle of holiday mails.

SERVING SUGGESTIONS

When you arrange a cookie assortment, consider textures and flavors, making sure they're different yet go well together. Don't serve all drop cookies, all bar cookies, or all refrigerator cookies if you're offering a selection. Add sweet snacks such as stuffed dates to the plate for variety. I always like to have one brightly colored goody to brighten the plate.

There are many occasions when cookies are just right and many ways to serve them. They're wonderful in lunch boxes. As desserts, cookies can be topped with ice cream and a carob or fruit sauce. At other times, cookies are a welcome treat served with pudding or fresh fruit. They go well with a glass of milk at bedtime or make a satisfying snack to tide over a hungry soul until dinner. And they're standard picnic fare.

In these days of busy, hurried living, home-baked cookies say you care enough to take the time for those you love. But the secret of the cookies in this book is that they don't take too much time, and most of them are really easy to make.

BAR COOKIES

Fig Squares

These chewy squares keep well and are excellent lunch-box treats.

 3 eggs
 ½ cup honey, at room temperature
 1 teaspoon vanilla extract
 ½ cup whole wheat flour
 ½ cup unbleached white flour
 1 teaspoon baking powder
 2 cups chopped dried figs

Preheat oven to 325°F. Butter a 13 × 9 × 2-inch pan.

In a medium-size bowl, beat eggs until they are light and thick. Beat in honey and then vanilla. Stir in whole wheat flour, unbleached white flour, and baking powder until well blended. Fold figs into batter. Spread batter evenly in prepared pan, and bake on middle shelf of oven for 25 minutes, or until a cake tester or food pick inserted into the center comes out clean.

Cool in pan on a wire rack before cutting.

Makes 1 dozen

Golden Honey Hermits

You will find these a popular lunch-box or after-school treat.

 3 cups sifted whole wheat flour
 1 teaspoon baking soda
 1 teaspoon ground cinnamon
 1 teaspoon ground cloves
 ¾ cup butter, softened
 ¾ cup honey
 ¼ cup molasses
 3 eggs
 1¼ cups golden raisins
 ½ cup chopped walnuts

Preheat oven to 350°F. Butter a 15½ × 11-inch jelly-roll pan with a ½-inch rim.

Sift together into a medium-size bowl flour, baking soda, and spices.

In a large bowl, cream butter. Beat in honey, molasses, and then eggs. Stir in flour mixture until well blended. Fold in raisins and nuts. Spread batter in prepared pan, and bake on middle shelf of oven for 20 minutes, or until a cake tester or food pick inserted into the center comes out dry.

Cool in pan on a wire rack. When cool, make 7 even cuts on the long side and 3 cuts on the opposite side.

Makes 32

Lemon Coconut Bars

 1 cup plus 3 tablespoons whole
   wheat pastry flour
 1½ teaspoons baking powder
 ½ cup butter, softened
 ¼ cup honey
 1½ cups unsweetened flaked coconut
 3 eggs
 ½ cup honey
 ⅓ cup lemon juice

¼ teaspoon grated lemon rind
¼ cup Coconut Sugar (page xxii)

Preheat oven to 350°F. Butter a 9 × 9 × 2-inch pan.

Into a small bowl, sift together flour and baking powder.

In a medium-size bowl, cream butter until fluffy. Beat in ¼ cup honey. Stir in flour mixture and coconut. Press into prepared pan, and bake on middle shelf of oven for 18 minutes, or until lightly browned.

In another medium-size bowl, beat eggs until light and thick. Beat in ½ cup honey. Stir in lemon juice and lemon rind. Pour over baked pastry, and bake an additional 25 minutes.

Cool in pan on a wire rack. Sprinkle with Coconut Sugar.

Makes 9 to 12

Benne Wafers   Page 35

Peanut Butter Carob Bars

  5 tablespoons butter, softened
  ½ cup honey
  2 eggs
  1 tablespoon vanilla extract
  ¼ cup Basic Carob Syrup
    (page xviii)
  1 cup sifted whole wheat pastry
    flour
  ¾ cup peanut butter
  ¾ cup unsweetened flaked coconut
1½ tablespoons butter
  ⅓ cup milk carob chips

Preheat oven to 350°F. Butter a 7 × 11 × 2-inch pan.

In a large bowl, beat together softened butter and honey. Beat in eggs. Mix in vanilla and Carob Syrup. Beat in flour until well blended. Pour into prepared pan, and bake on middle shelf of oven for 25 minutes.

Cool in pan on a wire rack. Spread with peanut butter and sprinkle with coconut.

In a small bowl set over hot, but not boiling water, stir together 1½ tablespoons butter and carob chips. Drizzle over coconut-peanut butter topping.

Makes 15 to 20

Raspberry Meringue Squares

Mixing up the batter for these goodies only takes a few minutes. There is no need even to use an electric mixer. The assembly is more complicated, but the result is well worth the effort.

¾ cup whole wheat flour
¾ cup unbleached white flour
1½ teaspoons baking powder
½ teaspoon ground cinnamon
½ cup honey
3 eggs, separated
½ cup butter, melted and cooled
½ teaspoon vanilla extract
1 cup chopped pecans
½ cup uncooked quick oats
1 cup Raspberry Jam (page 273)
¼ teaspoon cream of tartar
2 teaspoons honey

Preheat oven to 350°F. Butter a 7 × 11 × 2-inch pan.

In a medium-size bowl, sift together whole wheat flour, unbleached white flour, baking powder, and cinnamon.

Warm ½ cup honey by standing open jar in a pan of hot water. Do not use direct heat as this will make honey too warm to mix with egg yolks.

In a large bowl, beat egg yolks and warmed honey together until light and well blended. Beat in butter and vanilla.

In another medium-size bowl, mix together pecans and oats.

This part is tricky, so follow directions carefully. Measure ½ cup pecan mixture, and stir into batter. Then measure ½ cup batter and stir into pecan mixture. Use your fingers to blend batter into pecans. You now should have 2 mixtures: a cake-type batter with some pecans mixed through it and a pecan-oat crumb mixture with a little batter blended into it. Spoon cake-type batter into prepared pan and smooth with a spatula.

Whip jam with a spoon to make it more spreadable, and dribble across batter. Smooth with a spatula to within ½ inch of edges of pan, but do not stir into batter. Crumble pecan-oat mixture across top as evenly as possible. Bake on middle shelf of oven for 18 to 20 minutes, or until golden and dry inside when tested with a cake tester or food pick.

While squares are baking, beat egg whites in a medium-size bowl until foamy. Sprinkle with cream of tartar and continue beating until stiff peaks form. Gradually beat in 2 teaspoons honey. Cover bowl with a plate.

Remove pan from oven and spread meringue on top, right to edges of pan. Keep top smooth as peaks will over-brown. Return pan to top shelf of oven, and bake for about 8 minutes, or until meringue is golden brown.

Makes 16

Strawberry Cheesecake Bars

½ cup cold butter
½ cup date sugar
1 cup whole wheat pastry flour
8 ounces cream cheese
⅓ cup honey
1 egg
1 cup chopped fresh strawberries

Preheat oven to 350°F.

In a food processor or with a pastry blender, combine butter, date sugar, and flour until mixture resembles coarse crumbs. Reserve ¾ cup mixture, and press remainder of crumbs into an 8 × 8 × 2-inch pan. Bake on middle shelf of oven for 10 minutes.

In a large bowl, beat cream cheese until fluffy. Beat in honey and egg. Fold in strawberries, and spread mixture on top of crust in pan. Sprinkle with reserved crumb mixture, and bake on middle shelf of oven for 20 minutes.

Cool before cutting into 2-inch squares.

Makes 16

DROP COOKIES

Benne Wafers

This crunchy sesame seed cookie from the South is a perfect choice to accompany iced lemon tea or milk.

½ cup sesame seeds
¼ cup butter, softened
½ cup honey
1 egg
½ teaspoon vanilla extract
1 cup minus 2 tablespoons whole
  wheat flour
1 teaspoon baking powder

Preheat oven to 350°F. Line 2 baking sheets with foil.

In a heavy skillet, toast sesame seeds, while stirring, over low heat until they are just golden (not brown).

In a large bowl, cream butter until fluffy. Beat in honey, then egg, and vanilla. Mix in flour and baking powder. Stir in sesame seeds. Drop by teaspoon-

fuls onto foil 2 inches apart. Bake for 10 minutes, or until edges are golden.

Remove foil with cookies on it. Reline pan with more foil to bake second batch. Allow baked cookies to cool on foil until firm. Then remove, and cool thoroughly on wire racks.

Makes about 2½ dozen

Coconut-Carob Drops

1 cup whole wheat flour
1 teaspoon baking powder
¼ teaspoon ground cinnamon
½ cup butter, softened
½ cup honey
1 egg
1 teaspoon vanilla extract
1 cup uncooked quick oats
1 cup unsweetened flaked coconut
1 cup milk carob chips

Preheat oven to 350°F. Lightly butter 2 baking sheets.

In a medium-size bowl, mix together flour, baking powder, and cinnamon.

In a large bowl, beat together butter, honey, egg, and vanilla. Mix in flour, then oats, coconut, and carob chips. Drop by heaping tablespoonfuls onto prepared baking sheets, flattening with back of spoon. Allow about 1½ inches between cookies. Bake each batch on middle shelf of oven for 10 to 12 minutes, or until edges are browned.

Remove to wire racks. Cookies will firm up as they cool.

Makes about 2½ dozen

Colossal Molasses Cookies

2¾ cups whole wheat flour
1 cup uncooked quick oats
½ cup nonfat dry milk
1 teaspoon baking soda
¾ cup vegetable oil
½ cup dark molasses
½ cup honey
2 eggs
2 teaspoons vanilla extract
1 cup walnut halves
1 cup Monukkah raisins (an extra-large raisin available in health food stores; regular raisins may be substituted)

Preheat oven to 350°F. Butter a baking sheet.

In a large bowl, combine flour, oats, dry milk, and baking soda; stir to blend well.

In medium-size bowl, combine oil, molasses, honey, eggs, and vanilla. Beat well. Pour liquid ingredients into dry ingredients, and stir to blend. Mix in walnuts and raisins. Pour quarter-cupfuls of batter onto prepared baking sheet. (There will be room for 5 or 6.) Flatten slightly with your hand, and bake for 12 to 15 minutes, or until lightly browned on top. Check undersides so that they do not overbrown. Repeat the same procedure until batter is finished.

Cool on wire racks.

Makes about 1½ dozen 4½-inch cookies

Priscilla's Oatmeal-Peanut Butter Cookies

These no-flour cookies are moist and chewy, unlike other kinds of oatmeal cookies. The small amount of molasses combined with honey gives a "brown sugar" taste.

½ cup butter, softened
½ cup peanut butter, at room temperature
¾ cup honey
2 teaspoons vanilla extract
2 teaspoons molasses
2 eggs
1 teaspoon baking soda
2½ cups uncooked quick oats

Preheat oven to 325°F. Butter 2 baking sheets.

In a large bowl, cream butter and peanut butter together by hand, or with an electric mixer, until well blended. Creaming can also be done in a food processor. Mix in honey, vanilla, and molasses. Beat in eggs, 1 at a time. If using a food processor, remove mixture to a large bowl at this point. Stir in baking soda and then oats.

Drop by rounded teaspoonfuls onto prepared baking sheets 3 inches apart. Bake each batch on top shelf of oven for 12 minutes, or until lightly browned.

Cool cookies on baking sheets until removed easily, about 3 minutes. Complete cooling on wire racks.

Makes about 3½ dozen

Double Cashew Crunchies

These crunchy frosted cookies pack a real protein punch.

¾ cup uncooked quick oats
½ cup butter, softened
½ cup honey
1 tablespoon molasses
1 egg
1 teaspoon vanilla extract
½ cup whole wheat pastry flour
¼ cup soy flour
½ teaspoon baking soda
1 cup broken cashews
　Cashew Frosting (page 266)

Preheat oven to 350°F. Butter 2 baking sheets.

In a blender or food processor, process oats to the consistency of coarse flour.

Cream butter in a large bowl. Beat in honey, molasses, egg, and vanilla, in that order. Mix in oat flour, whole wheat pastry flour, soy flour, and baking soda. Fold in nuts. Drop by heaping teaspoonfuls onto prepared baking sheets, 2 inches apart. Bake cookies for 10 to 12 minutes, or until lightly browned on top. Check undersides to avoid overbrowning.

Cool on wire racks over sheets of wax paper. When cool, frost with warm Cashew Frosting. Store in a cool place in single layers.

Makes about 2½ dozen

Pumpkin Treats

1 cup dried currants
½ cup butter, softened
½ cup honey
¼ cup date sugar (optional)
2 eggs
1½ cups pumpkin puree
2 teaspoons vanilla extract
2½ cups sifted whole wheat pastry
　flour
2 teaspoons baking powder
1 teaspoon baking soda
2½ teaspoons ground cinnamon
1½ teaspoons ground ginger
1 cup chopped walnuts

Preheat oven to 350°F. Butter 2 baking sheets.

Place currants in a small bowl, cover with boiling water, and set aside to plump for 15 to 20 minutes.

In a large bowl, beat together butter and honey. Beat in date sugar, eggs, pumpkin, and vanilla.

In a medium-size bowl, sift together flour, baking powder, baking soda, cinnamon and ginger. Add to liquid ingredients, mixing well. Fold in drained currants and walnuts. Drop by heaping tablespoonfuls onto prepared baking sheets, and bake on middle shelf of oven for 15 to 20 minutes, or until lightly browned.

Cool on wire racks.

Makes about 3 dozen

Oatties

This is one of my favorite cookies—good old-fashioned oatmeal with many variation possibilities.

½ cup butter, softened
1 cup honey
1 egg
1 teaspoon vanilla extract
1½ cups whole wheat flour
½ teaspoon baking powder
½ teaspoon baking soda
½ teaspoon ground cinnamon
¼ teaspoon ground cloves
2 cups uncooked quick oats
½ cup raisins
½ cup chopped walnuts

Preheat oven to 350°F. Butter 2 baking sheets.

Cream butter in a large bowl. Beat in honey, then egg, and vanilla. Stir in flour, baking powder, baking soda, and spices until mixture is well blended. Fold in oats, then raisins and walnuts. Drop by heaping teaspoonfuls, 2 inches apart, on prepared baking sheets. Bake on middle shelf of oven for 10 to 12 minutes, or until edges are golden.

Cool on wire racks.

Makes 3 to 4 dozen

VARIATIONS
Persimmon Oatties: Substitute 1 cup chopped dried persimmons for raisins and walnuts.
Toll House Oatties: Substitute ¾ cup milk carob chips for raisins and ½ cup chopped pecans for walnuts.
Raisin Chip Oatties: Substitute ¾ cup milk carob chips for walnuts.

Meringue Kisses

This light, elegant cookie is deceptively easy to make.

4 egg whites, at room temperature
¼ teaspoon cream of tartar
2 tablespoons honey
1 teaspoon almond extract

Preheat oven to 375°F. Butter and flour 2 baking sheets.

In a large bowl, beat egg whites and cream of tartar until foamy. Beat in honey and almond extract until egg whites form stiff peaks. Drop by tablespoonfuls onto prepared baking sheets. Place 1 baking sheet on middle shelf of oven, and turn oven off immediately. Leave cookies in oven for 1 hour.

Remove to wire racks.

Preheat oven to 375°F again. Bake remaining cookies in the same manner.

Makes about 4 dozen

Pignolis

1 cup Almond Paste (page 277)
½ cup honey
½ teaspoon almond extract (optional)
4 egg whites
⅛ teaspoon cream of tartar
⅔ cup whole wheat pastry flour
about ½ cup pine nuts

Preheat oven to 300°F. Line a baking sheet with parchment paper.

Place Almond Paste in a small bowl, and break up into small pieces. Blend in honey to make a smooth paste. If you like a pronounced almond flavor, as I do, add almond extract. (This part can be done in a food processor.)

In a medium-size bowl, beat egg whites until foamy throughout. Sprinkle cream of tartar on top, and continue beating until stiff peaks form. Stir almond paste mixture into egg whites with a wooden spoon. This is not a "fold in" process; it's all right to stir mixture gently. Stir slowly until completely blended. Fold in flour. Drop batter by heaping teaspoonfuls, 1 inch apart, onto prepared baking sheet. Sprinkle tops with pine nuts. (I use a demitasse spoon, and this is just about the right amount for each cookie.) Press pine nuts slightly so that they hold to batter. One baking sheet will take about half the batter. Bake on middle shelf of oven for 25 minutes, or until lightly browned at edges.

Scrape cookies off parchment paper with a sharp spatula, and cool on wire racks. Turn parchment paper over, and prepare second batch. Bake the same way.

Makes 26

PRESSED COOKIES

Almond Spirals

    1 cup butter, softened
    ½ cup honey
    1 egg
    1 teaspoon almond extract
    2¼ cups whole wheat pastry flour
    ¾ cup ground almonds

In a large bowl, cream butter until soft and fluffy. Beat in honey, then egg,

and almond extract. Stir in flour and almonds until well blended. Chill dough until firm.

Preheat oven to 375°F. Fit a cookie press with spiral disk. Turn dough into press, and pipe cookies onto ungreased baking sheets, lifting press as soon as dough appears on sheet. Bake for 7 minutes, or until edges are delicately browned. Do not overbrown.

Cool on wire racks.

Makes about 5 dozen

Lemon Spritz

Pressed cookies are more likely to stay where you place them while baking if you chill the baking sheets first.

    1 cup butter, softened
    ⅓ cup honey
    3 egg yolks
    1 teaspoon lemon extract
    1⅓ cups whole wheat pastry flour
    1¼ cups unbleached white flour

In a large bowl, cream butter until light and fluffy. Beat in honey and then egg yolks and lemon extract. Stir in whole wheat pastry flour and unbleached white flour until well blended. Chill dough for at least 1 hour.

Preheat oven to 400°F. Fit a cookie press with a flower or star-shaped tube. Turn dough into press, and pipe cookies onto ungreased baking sheets, lifting press as soon as dough appears on sheet. Bake for 7 minutes, or until edges and bottom are delicately browned.

Cool on wire racks.

Makes about 6 dozen

Anise Stars

This is a pressed cookie, but if you don't have a cookie press (or cookie gun, as it is sometimes called), the dough, when chilled, can be rolled and cut with a star cookie cutter. Stars made with a cookie cutter are larger than those made with a press; therefore, the recipe will make fewer cookies when the dough is rolled.

     1 cup butter, softened
    ⅓ cup honey
     3 egg yolks
     1 teaspoon anise extract
    1⅓ cups whole wheat pastry flour
    1¼ cups unbleached white flour
     1 cup Anise Icing (page 268),
        optional
        date sugar, for sprinkling
        (optional)

In a large bowl, cream butter until light and fluffy. Beat in honey, then egg yolks, and anise extract. Stir in whole wheat pastry flour and unbleached white flour until well blended. Chill dough for at least 1 hour.

Preheat oven to 400°F. Fit a cookie press with large star tube. Turn dough into press, and pipe cookies onto ungreased baking sheets, lifting press as soon as dough appears on sheet. Bake for 7 minutes, or until edges and bottom are delicately browned.

Cool on wire racks. If necessary to reuse baking sheets, they should be cooled first.

To make a fancier cookie for festive occasions, frost tops with Anise Icing, and sprinkle with date sugar.

Makes about 6 dozen

Carob Pistachio Fingers

     1 cup butter, softened
    ⅓ cup honey
     3 egg yolks
    1½ teaspoons vanilla extract
    1⅓ cups whole wheat pastry flour
    1¼ cups unbleached white flour
     3 tablespoons sifted powdered
        carob
    ½ cup milk carob chips
     1 tablespoon butter
    ⅔ cup chopped pistachios

In a large bowl, cream softened butter until light and fluffy. Beat in honey, then egg yolks, and vanilla. Stir in whole wheat pastry flour, unbleached white flour, and carob until well blended. Chill dough for at least 1 hour.

Preheat oven to 375°F. Fit a cookie press with large plain tube. Turn dough into press, and pipe cookies onto ungreased baking sheets, making each about 2½ inches long. Bake for 7 minutes, or until edges and bottom are delicately browned. Do not overbrown.

Cool on wire racks. If necessary to reuse baking sheets, they should be cooled first.

Place carob chips and 1 tablespoon butter in top of a small double boiler. Set over simmering water, and stir until melted and well blended. Dip end of each cookie into melted carob; then press pistachios into carob while it is still soft. Cool on wire racks until firm.

Makes about 4 dozen

MOLDED COOKIES
Almond Crescents

1 cup butter, softened
½ cup honey
1½ teaspoons almond extract
1 cup whole wheat pastry flour
1 cup unbleached white flour
1 cup ground almonds

In a large bowl, beat butter until fluffy. Beat in honey and almond extract.

Sift together whole wheat pastry flour and unbleached white flour into a medium-size bowl. Stir in almonds. Mix thoroughly into butter mixture. Chill until firm, about 1 hour.

Preheat oven to 300°F.

Divide dough into pieces, and roll them into logs about ½ inch thick. Cut into 2½-inch lengths. Taper ends with fingers, and bend into half-moon shapes. Place about ½ inch apart on ungreased baking sheets, and bake on middle shelf of oven for 20 to 25 minutes, or until lightly browned.

Cool on wire racks.

Makes about 4 dozen

Priscilla's Oatmeal-Peanut Butter Cookies   Page 36
Strawberry Almond Cookies   Page 44
Spicy Prune Chews   Page 43

Chinese Dessert Cookies

Try them with Ginger-Melon Ice Cream (page 122) as the perfect conclusion to a Chinese dinner.

  1 cup butter, softened
  ½ cup honey
  1 egg
  1 teaspoon almond extract
  1 cup whole wheat pastry flour
  1 cup unbleached white flour
  1 teaspoon baking powder
    about 40 blanched whole almonds

In a large bowl, beat butter until fluffy. Beat in honey and then egg and almond extract. Sift in whole wheat pastry flour, unbleached white flour, and baking powder, blending well. Chill dough until firm enough to shape, about 1 hour.

Preheat oven to 350°F. Butter 2 baking sheets.

With hands, roll cookie dough into 1-inch balls. Place on baking sheets 2 inches apart. Flatten slightly, and press an almond into center of each. Bake in batches for 12 to 15 minutes, or until browned at edges. Check undersides; do not overbrown.

Cool on wire racks.

Makes about 40

Orange-Ginger Cookies

  2 cups brown rice flour
  2½ teaspoons ground ginger
  1 teaspoon baking powder
  1 teaspoon baking soda
  ½ teaspoon ground cinnamon
  ½ cup butter, softened
  ⅓ cup honey
  2 tablespoons molasses
  1 egg
  1 tablespoon grated orange rind

Preheat oven to 350°F.

In a medium-size bowl, sift together flour, ginger, baking powder, baking soda, and cinnamon.

Cream butter in a large bowl. Beat in honey and molasses, then egg, and orange rind. Blend in flour mixture.

Form rounded tablespoonfuls of dough into balls by rolling between palms of your hands. (If dough is a bit too soft, chill for 5 minutes in freezer.) Place balls 2 inches apart on ungreased baking sheets. Bake for 10 minutes, or until golden on top. Centers will be soft.

Remove from baking sheets, and cool on wire racks.

Makes 2 dozen

Peach Prints

  ¾ cup butter, softened
  ½ cup honey
  2 egg yolks
  2 teaspoons vanilla extract
  1½ cups brown rice flour (whole wheat pastry flour may be substituted)
  1½ cups whole wheat pastry flour
  ¼ cup Peach Preserves (page 276)

In a large bowl, beat together butter and honey. Beat in egg yolks and vanilla. Mix in rice flour and whole wheat pastry flour. Roll dough into a ball, wrap with plastic wrap, and chill until firm, about 2 hours.

Preheat oven to 325°F.

Divide dough into 24 pieces, and roll each piece into a ball between palms of your hands. Press balls flat with heel of hand onto ungreased baking sheets. Make an indentation in the middle of each cookie with a finger. Fill indentations with Peach Preserves. Bake in 2 batches on middle shelf of oven for 15 to 18 minutes.

Allow to cool on baking sheets.

Makes 2 dozen

Snappy Cookies

⅔ cup butter, softened
⅔ cup honey
2 tablespoons molasses
2 eggs
2½ cups whole wheat pastry flour
1 tablespoon ground ginger
2 teaspoons ground allspice
1 teaspoon baking soda

Preheat oven to 350°F.

In a large bowl, beat together butter and honey. Beat in molasses and eggs.

In a medium-size bowl, sift together flour, ginger, allspice, and baking soda, stirring with a fork to blend. Mix into butter mixture. Form dough into 1-inch balls by breaking off pieces and rolling between palms of your hands. Place on ungreased baking sheets 3 inches apart. Bake on middle shelf of oven for 8 minutes, or until browned.

Cool on wire racks.

Makes about 3 dozen

Spicy Prune Chews

2 cups whole wheat flour
1 tablespoon ground cinnamon
1 teaspoon ground nutmeg
1 teaspoon baking powder
½ teaspoon baking soda
1 cup ground walnuts
3 eggs
¾ cup honey
12 ounces pitted dried prunes,
   finely chopped

In a medium-size bowl, sift together flour, cinnamon, nutmeg, baking powder, and baking soda. Mix in nuts.

In a large bowl, beat together eggs and honey. Stir prunes into egg-honey mixture, separating prune bits with edge of spoon. Mix in dry ingredients. Wrap dough with plastic wrap, and chill until firm, about 2 hours.

Preheat oven to 375°F. Butter 2 baking sheets.

With floured hands, roll dough into 1½-inch balls, and place 1 inch apart on prepared baking sheets. Bake on middle shelf of oven for 10 minutes.

Cool on wire racks.

Makes about 4 dozen

Strawberry Almond Cookies

¾ cup butter, softened
½ cup honey
2 eggs, separated
1 teaspoon vanilla extract
2 cups whole wheat flour
1 cup ground almonds
½ cup Strawberry Jam (page 273)

In a large bowl, beat together butter and honey. Add egg yolks and vanilla, and beat until fluffy.

Sift in flour, blending well. Form dough into a ball, wrap with plastic wrap, and chill until firm, about 1 hour.

Preheat oven to 350°F. Butter 2 baking sheets.

Divide dough into 24 pieces. Flour palms of hands, and roll each piece into a ball.

In a small bowl, gently beat egg whites until just foamy. Roll each ball in egg whites and then in nuts. Place balls 2 inches apart on prepared baking sheets. With a floured finger, make an indentation in each cookie, pressing almost to bottom, but not breaking through. Fill each cookie with jam, and bake on middle shelf of oven for 20 to 25 minutes.

Cool on wire racks.

Makes 2 dozen

REFRIGERATOR COOKIES

Braga Cornflowers

This crisp Portuguese cookie is ideal to serve with tea, especially mint tea.

¼ cup butter, softened
¼ cup honey

2 teaspoons grated lemon rind
1 teaspoon vanilla
½ cup whole wheat flour
½ cup unbleached white flour
1 teaspoon baking powder

In a medium-size bowl, cream butter. Beat in honey, lemon rind, and vanilla. Blend in whole wheat flour, unbleached white flour, and baking powder. Spoon dough onto a sheet of wax paper, and chill until it can be molded.

Form dough into a log about 7 inches long. Pat into a square rather than a round shape. Chill until quite firm.

Preheat oven to 350°F.

Slice dough into ⅛-inch slices. Place ½ inch apart on ungreased baking sheets, and bake for 10 minutes, or until golden on bottom. Tops will be pale.

Cool on wire racks.

Makes 3 dozen

Designer Cookies

1¼ cups whole wheat pastry flour
1¼ cups unbleached white flour
1 teaspoon baking powder
1½ cups butter, softened
¾ cup honey
2 eggs
2 teaspoons vanilla extract, divided
3 tablespoons Basic Carob Syrup (page xviii)

Line an 8½ × 4½ × 2½-inch loaf pan with wax paper.

Sift together whole wheat pastry flour, unbleached white flour, and baking powder into a medium-size bowl.

In a large bowl, beat butter until fluffy. Beat in honey, eggs, and 1 teaspoon vanilla. Add flour mixture, and blend well. With floured hands, divide dough in half. Leave 1 half in large bowl, and place the other half in a separate bowl. To 1 half, add 1 teaspoon vanilla, mixing in thoroughly. To the other half, add carob syrup, mixing thoroughly.

Pat light dough on bottom of prepared pan. Pat carob dough on top. Cover, and refrigerate until firm, at least 4 hours.

Preheat oven to 350°F. Butter 2 baking sheets.

Remove dough from pan, cut crosswise with a sharp knife into ¼-inch-thick slices, and place on prepared baking sheets. Bake on middle shelf of oven for about 12 minutes, or until lightly browned.

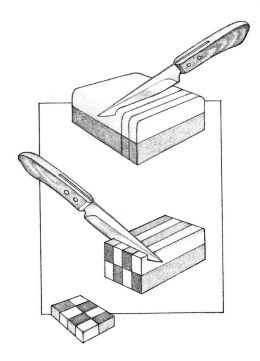

To make a checkerboard pattern, press together 4 ¼-inch slices, reversing every other one, and then cut crosswise. Each slice will then have an 8-square checkerboard pattern. Bake for 8 minutes, or until lightly browned.

Cool on wire racks.

Makes about 2 dozen slices or 5 dozen checkerboards

Old-Fashioned Refrigerator Date Cookies

1¼ cups whole wheat flour
¾ cup oat flour (page xii)
1 teaspoon baking soda
½ cup butter, softened
½ cup honey
1 egg
½ teaspoon vanilla extract
½ cup finely chopped dates
½ cup ground almonds or walnuts

Sift together whole wheat flour, oat flour, and baking soda in a medium-size bowl.

In a large bowl, beat together butter and honey. Beat in egg and vanilla. Gradually blend in flour mixture. Fold in dates and almonds or walnuts. Divide dough in half, shape into 2 logs, and refrigerate until firm, about 3 hours.

Preheat oven to 350°F. Butter 2 baking sheets.

Slice logs into rounds about ¼ inch thick. Place 1 inch apart on prepared baking sheets, and bake on middle shelf of oven for 8 to 10 minutes, or until browned.

Cool on wire racks.

Makes about 2½ dozen

Raspberry Pinwheels   Page 49
Peach Prints   Page 42
Brambles   Page 46
Meringue Kisses   Page 38

ROLLED COOKIES

Basic Honey Cookies

½ cup butter, softened
½ cup honey
1 egg
½ teaspoon vanilla extract
2 tablespoons lemon juice
2 cups whole wheat pastry flour
1 egg white, slightly beaten

Butter 2 baking sheets.
In a large bowl, beat together butter and honey. Beat in egg, vanilla, and lemon juice. Sift flour into liquid ingredients, stirring to blend. Form into a ball, wrap with plastic wrap, and chill in refrigerator for 1 hour.

Preheat oven to 350°F.
On a lightly floured surface, roll out dough to a ¼-inch thickness. With a cookie cutter or the top of a glass, cut dough into 2- to 2½-inch rounds. Brush with egg white. Place on prepared sheets, and bake on middle shelf of oven for about 10 minutes, or until lightly browned.

Makes about 2 dozen

Brambles

Here is a pastry cookie that is especially pleasing as a variation when you are preparing a selection of cookies.

¾ cup raisins
1 egg
1 tablespoon lemon juice
½ teaspoon grated lemon rind
   pastry for 2 Basic Flaky Piecrusts
   (page 57)
   cinnamon, for sprinkling

Grind or very finely chop raisins. (A food processor can be used to advantage for this job.) Place raisins into a medium-size bowl.
Break egg into a small bowl, and beat slightly. Beat in lemon juice. Reserve 2 tablespoons of egg mixture, and beat the rest into raisins, adding grated lemon rind. Mixture should be very well blended. Spoon into a small saucepan, and cook over low heat, stirring constantly, until mixture thickens. Set aside to cool.
Preheat oven to 400°F. Butter a baking sheet.
On a lightly floured surface, roll out pastry to a ⅛-inch thickness. Cut into rounds with a cookie cutter or the

top of a glass (about 2½ inches across) dipped into flour.

Place a teaspoonful of filling on half the rounds. Cover with the other half of the rounds. Seal edges of cookies with tines of a fork, and place on prepared baking sheet.

Reroll scraps of pastry, and make as many cookies as possible the same way. Brush with reserved egg mixture. With the point of a paring knife, cut a very small *v* in the top of each. Sprinkle with cinnamon. Bake for about 20 minutes, or until browned.

Cool on wire racks.

Makes about 16

VARIATION
Prune Brambles: Substitute Prune Filling (page 272) for raisin mixture.

Cookie Leaves

1¾ cups whole wheat pastry flour
1 teaspoon baking powder
1 teaspoon baking soda
½ cup butter, softened
⅓ cup honey
1 egg
1 teaspoon anise extract or
   1½ teaspoons vanilla extract
1½ cups Vanilla Icing (page 268),
   divided
   natural green food coloring

Sift together flour, baking powder, and baking soda into a medium-size bowl.

In a large bowl, beat butter until fluffy. Beat in honey and egg. Stir in anise or vanilla extract. Add dry ingredients, mixing in well. Form into a ball, wrap with plastic wrap, and chill until firm, at least 3 hours.

Preheat oven to 350°F.

On a lightly floured surface, roll out dough to a ⅛-inch thickness. The dough will be soft. Cut with a leaf-shaped cookie cutter, or cut a leaf from a piece of cardboard, and trace around it on dough with a knife. Place leaves on ungreased baking sheets, and bake on middle shelf of oven for about 7 minutes, or until golden.

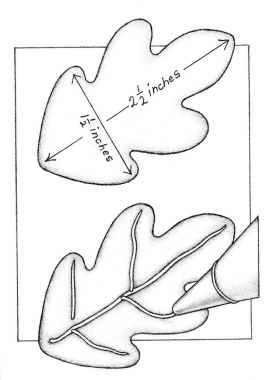

Cool on wire racks.

To 1 cup Vanilla Icing, add enough green food coloring to make a light green color. Frost cooled cookies. To remaining ½ cup frosting, add enough green food coloring to make a dark green color. Place dark green icing into a pastry bag with a writing tip, and make dark green veins on leaves.

Makes 3 to 4 dozen

Good Old Butter Cookies

1 cup butter, softened
¾ cup honey
1 egg
2 tablespoons unsweetened frozen
    orange juice concentrate
1½ teaspoons vanilla extract
2¾ cups whole wheat pastry flour
1 teaspoon baking powder

In a large bowl, beat together butter and honey. Beat in egg, orange juice concentrate, and vanilla. Mix in flour and baking powder, blending well. Form into a ball, wrap with plastic wrap, and chill for about 2 hours, or until firm enough to roll.

Preheat oven to 400°F.

Divide dough in half. Roll out 1 half on a lightly floured surface to a ⅛-inch thickness. Work quickly; the dough tends to soften. Cut with the top of a glass or a cookie cutter into 2½-inch rounds, and place on ungreased baking sheets. Repeat procedure with the other half. Bake on middle shelf of oven for 8 to 10 minutes, or until lightly browned.

Cool on wire racks.

Makes about 3 dozen

Italian Honey Cluster Cookies

"Finger-lickin' good" certainly describes these sticky but delicious nibbles.

1 cup whole wheat flour
1 cup unbleached white flour
3 eggs, beaten
1 teaspoon vanilla extract
½ teaspoon almond extract
    vegetable oil, for deep frying
¾ cup honey
    cinnamon, for sprinkling
    Coconut Sugar (page xxii), for
    sprinkling

Stir whole wheat flour and unbleached white flour together in a medium-size bowl. Make a well in the center. Pour in eggs and vanilla and almond extracts, and mix into a stiff dough; or mix in a food processor. Dough should be stiff enough to roll out on a lightly floured surface without sticking. If it seems a bit too soft, add a little more flour. Divide dough in half. Roll out half the dough into a 12 by 8-inch rectangle. Trim off uneven edges. Cut into strips ½ inch in width. Roll each strip into a straw shape. Cut the straw-shaped strips into ¼-inch pieces. (There should be a hollow center.) Repeat with the rest of the dough and the trimmings.

Heat oil in a large heavy saucepan to 400°F. Fill a large slotted spoon with the little rolls, and place in hot fat. Fry for about 2 minutes, turning occasionally, until just golden brown, and drain on paper towels. While one batch is frying, fill another slotted spoon with more rolls.

Heat honey in a small skillet until it just begins to bubble, and simmer for 5 minutes.

Lay wire racks on top of each other with wires running in opposite directions so that cookies won't fall through, and place racks on a sheet of wax paper. Using the 2 slotted spoons, pick up some of the fried rolls and turn them over in the honey. Let them drain for 1 minute before laying them on crossed wire racks. Sprinkle with cinnamon, and let stand for 30 minutes.

Cut a round of wax paper to fit a dinner plate. Using the 2 slotted spoons, mound cookies on plate in pyramid. Sprinkle pyramid with Coconut Sugar.

Makes an 8-inch pyramid

Raspberry Pinwheels

½ cup butter, softened
⅓ cup honey
1 egg
1 teaspoon vanilla extract
2 cups whole wheat pastry flour
½ teaspoon baking powder
½ cup Raspberry Jam (page 273)
½ cup ground walnuts

In a large bowl, beat together butter and honey. Beat in egg and vanilla.

Sift together flour and baking powder into a medium-size bowl. Stir with a fork to blend. Mix flour into butter mixture just until well blended. Cover with plastic wrap, and refrigerate until firm, about 1 hour.

Roll dough between 2 pieces of wax paper (the bottom one lightly floured), to an 11×11-inch square. Remove top piece of wax paper.

Spoon jam into a small bowl, and whisk to make it spreadable. Spread on top of dough, leaving a ½-inch margin at front and back but extending it all the way to both sides. Sprinkle nuts over jam. Using wax paper as a guide, roll dough up, jelly-roll fashion, from front to back. Wrap with the wax paper and freeze.

Preheat oven to 350°F. Butter a baking sheet (even if it has a non-stick surface). Cut frozen dough into rounds ¼ inch in thickness. Bake on prepared baking sheet on top shelf of oven for about 15 minutes, or until lightly browned.

Makes about 2½ dozen

CHAPTER
3

Elegant Pies and Tarts

I love good pastry, the kind that's tender, yet not crumbly — the kind that melts in the mouth. I'm surprised that so many fine cooks are hesitant about making basic flaky pastry. It's not that difficult once you learn the classic techniques and get some practice.

The ingredients of good pastry couldn't be simpler — just flour, butter, and water with a little lemon juice — but it's the method of mixing and handling them that produces the magic of a light, delicate piecrust.

It's important to know the chemistry involved if you want to understand the rules of making pastry. Bits of butter are incorporated into flour in order to lighten it, and water is added to make it hold together. When the piecrust is baked at a high temperature, the butter melts and the water steams away. This leaves empty spaces between layers of flour (now flavored with the rich taste of butter), giving the crust that sought-after flakiness that characterizes a fine piecrust.

The ingredients are kept cold so that the butter will not melt into the flour before it is baked. If melting occurs before baking, those delightful flakes will not form in the pastry. Therefore, pastry cooks use cold butter and ice water; in hot weather, it's not going too far to chill the flour also. Many cooks use a marble slab to roll out piecrust, because marble is always a little cooler than room temperature, and it's wonderfully smooth as well. I use a piece of marble that once topped a small bureau for rolling out pastry. Now it has a permanent place on my kitchen counter top, where it is useful for

Fresh Papaya and Kiwi Tart   Page 64

kneading bread too. I also favor a marble rolling pin, although any good hardwood rolling pin will do.

Flour for piecrusts need not be sifted, but it should be stirred with a fork before measuring in case it has packed down in the canister.

The butter is "cut into" the flour using two knives or a pastry blender, so that it will remain in minute pieces and not melt into the flour. Some cooks rub the butter in with their fingers, but this is not advisable because the warmth of the hands may cause some of the butter to melt no matter how fast and sure the cook works. The size of the butter bits needn't be uniform but should vary between the size of a grain of rice and the size of a small pea.

Adding just the right amount of water is critical. Unfortunately, the amount given in recipes can never be quite specific, because it varies with the density of the flour, the kind of flour (whole wheat flour absorbs more than white flour), and the humidity of the air. Therefore, recipes usually instruct you to use your judgment. This can be very frustrating for a novice cook. Following the principle that water can always be added but cannot be removed, use it very frugally—add just a tablespoon at a time, sprinkling it over whatever part of the flour mixture seems driest, and then toss very lightly with two forks. Toward the end of the blending, you may want to add just a teaspoon or a few drops at a time. All this doesn't take as long to do as it takes to explain it.

A little lemon juice added to the ice water increases flakiness and enhances flavor. I especially like this addition, since I don't use salt in pastry, and lemon seems to bring out the naturally nutty flavor of the whole grain.

You'll know when you have added just the right amount of water because the mixture will form a dough when pressed against the side of the bowl, but it won't feel sticky, like paste. If too dry, the edges of the crust will crumble while you're rolling it out. If too wet, the crust will stick to the surfaces it touches. Either way, too dry or too wet, the piecrust will be tougher than it should be when baked.

Work as quickly as possible, and handle the pastry gently to avoid developing the gluten in the flour. Gluten, which is present in all wheat flours (see the chapter on Easy-Does-It Breads, Muffins, and Coffee Cakes) makes the dough elastic, hard to handle, and tough. If you find that your pastry resists being rolled out easily, it may be gluten that's the cause. Let the pastry rest in the refrigerator for 20 minutes or so to relax the gluten; then try again. Some cooks always chill pastry briefly before rolling anyway because it makes the dough easier to handle. But if you chill it for a long time, it may become too cold and stiff to roll out. In that case, just let it rest for a few minutes at room temperature before rolling.

Pastry for piecrust should be rolled out from the center so that the edges won't be too thin. When you have rolled out the pastry, it should be ⅛ inch thick at the center and slightly thicker at the edges, so they won't tear. After placing the pastry in the plate, trim the edges so that there's about a 1-inch overhang. I like to use a scissors, but a sharp paring knife will do. On a one-crust pie, fold the overhang under to build up the rim, then flute or press with the tines of a fork. On a two-crust pie, leave a 2-inch overhang on the top, and fold the top edge over the bottom edge. Flute or press with a fork to seal.

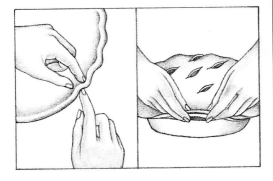

A two-crust pie needs a vent to allow steam to escape. Otherwise, the top crust would be lifted by the steam. Don't go overboard on this, however, or the contents will not cook well. Just cut two or three *v*'s in the top crust, each about 2 inches long.

To glaze the top crust of a two-crust pie, brush with ice water (you'll have some left over from mixing), cream, or beaten egg before putting the pie into the oven.

Pastry is baked at a high temperature, 425°F, so that the melting of butter and steaming of water will happen quickly, thereby promoting extra flakiness. If the filling of the pie needs long cooking, reduce the heat after 15 minutes to accommodate the filling. You will already have given the crust the good fast start it needs.

Glass or enamel pie plates may reduce standard cooking time by a few minutes. Nonshiny metal pans produce the brownest bottom crust.

The bottom crust of a filled pie must be protected from a moist filling so that it will not become soggy. For a custard-based pie, there are two effective methods. The first is to prebake the crust for five to seven minutes before adding the filling. The second is to brush the inside of the crust with egg white, beaten just until it's foamy, and let this coating dry for a few minutes before adding the filling and baking the pie.

For fruit pies, the fruit is tossed with a thickener, such as cornstarch, tapioca, or flour, before being added to the pie shell. As the fruit exudes its juice during cooking, it's absorbed by the thickener, which keeps it from penetrating the shell completely. (Remember that fruit shrinks as it cooks, so heap up the filling of a fruit pie.)

My pastry is made of whole wheat flour, which has different properties from white flour. Whole wheat flour is more flavorful but less fine in texture than white flour. Because white flour is processed to remove the bran and the germ, leaving only the tender, starchy part of the wheat, it is very light and soft. That's why a whole wheat piecrust is more substantial and somewhat less tender and flaky. It is, however, flaky enough to make a perfectly delicious pie. I think the robust flavor of whole wheat complements traditional pie fillings in a most pleasing way, and it almost goes without saying that these pies offer real nutritional value. To assure the tenderest possible crust, use whole wheat pastry flour (milled from soft wheat, low in gluten) rather than all-purpose whole wheat flour.

The coarser texture of whole wheat pastry makes it easier to handle than white flour pastry. In fact, you can even roll it out between two sheets of wax paper, which is by far the neatest method known. If you've always had trouble rolling out pastry, you'll like the difference that whole wheat pastry flour makes.

ALTERNATIVE PIECRUSTS

There are also delicious alternatives to basic pastry that are nice for a change of pace, or when you're in a hurry, since all of the alternatives are less exacting than the classic pastry we have been discussing.

Delectable meringue shells are just as easy as "whip and bake" and are especially nice filled with sweetened fresh fruit and topped with yogurt or whipped cream. They should be filled just before serving, but they can be made a day ahead.

Crumb crusts that you can put together in a few minutes are often used for cheesecakes (which are really cheese pies) and for some chiffon fillings.

Moist, chewy coconut crusts are wonderful filled with mousse or pudding, and they can be prepared a day ahead of time.

CRUSTS FOR TARTS

Tart crusts are a derivative of basic pastry, but more cookielike or cakelike, and the same preparation techniques apply. Baked tart shells are usually layered with pastry cream or jelly and finished with decorative glazed fruit. I like the artistic possibilities that tarts provide, and so I suggest choosing two or more contrasting colors of fruit and creating an interesting pattern with them. Definitely showy!

SERVING TIPS

Tarts and fruit pies are at their best served soon (one to five hours) after being made. An exception to this rule is mincemeat pie which often improves in flavor if it stands for a day before being eaten.

Cheesecake is a good choice if you want to make a dessert that can be held overnight.

When deciding what type of pastry to prepare, keep the occasion and circumstances in mind. I like to serve a hearty pie as a dessert after a light meal, such as a chowder supper, but after an opulent dinner, a tart is a better choice. Lattice-top pies and turnovers are good "travelers" to picnics and potluck dinners, while cream pies and cheesecakes must be kept chilled and are therefore best eaten at home. Certain fruit pies, such as fresh pineapple or grapefruit pie, make interesting additions to a brunch menu.

Basic Flaky Piecrust

3 tablespoons water
1 tablespoon lemon juice
1¼ cups whole wheat pastry flour
2 tablespoons vegetable oil
¼ cup cold butter, cut into chunks

Combine water and lemon juice in a small pitcher. Add 2 ice cubes.

Measure flour into a large bowl. Blend oil into flour. Cut in butter with a pastry blender until the largest pieces are the size of a small pea and the rest of the mixture resembles coarse meal. (This much can be done in a food processor using the steel blade and on/off turns of the motor, but the mixture must then be transferred to a large bowl and the pastry finished as follows.)

Add iced liquid, 1 teaspoon at a time, tossing with 2 forks to blend completely before adding more. Use just enough liquid so that the pastry will hold together in a ball when pressed, about 3 tablespoons. Roll out to fit an 8-, 9-, or 10-inch pie plate between 2 sheets of wax paper. Turn pastry often while rolling; and if wax paper wrinkles, remove it and lay it down over the pastry again so that it is smooth.

To prebake pastry for prepared filling: Preheat oven to 450°F. Remove 1 sheet of wax paper. Invert pastry over pie plate. Remove second sheet of wax paper, and fit pastry into plate without stretching it. Trim excess, and press rim with the tines of a fork. Prick bottom and sides of pastry with a fork. Place on top shelf of oven, and immediately reduce temperature to 425°F. Bake for 15 minutes, or until nicely browned. If pastry rises on bottom during cooking, prick the risen place with a fork. (This doesn't happen as often with whole wheat flour as it does with white flour.)

Cool completely in pie plate on a wire rack.

Makes 1

Coconut Crust

2 cups unsweetened flaked coconut
3 tablespoons butter, melted

Preheat oven to 350°F.

In a medium-size bowl, mix coconut and butter to blend completely. Press onto bottom and sides of a 9-inch pie plate. Bake on middle shelf of oven for 10 to 20 minutes, or until golden brown.

Cool completely before filling.

Makes 1

VARIATION

Coconut Crust for a 10-inch pie: Use 2½ cups coconut and ¼ cup butter, melted.

Ricotta Pie   Page 74

Tart Pastry 1

    1¼ cups whole wheat pastry flour
    ½ teaspoon baking powder
    ½ cup butter, cut into 8 pieces
    1 egg yolk
    1 teaspoon honey
4 to 6 tablespoons ice water

In a large bowl, sift together flour and baking powder. Add butter. With a pastry blender or 2 knives, cut in butter until the largest pieces are the size of a small pea. (Up to this point, the pastry can be prepared in a food processor fitted with a steel blade, but the following steps must be done by hand.)

Place egg yolk into a ¼-cup measure. Add honey and enough ice water to fill measure. Spoon the mixture, scraping out all the honey, into a small bowl, and beat it with a fork until well blended. Pour it over the flour mixture, and, with 2 forks, lightly toss until the liquid ingredients are incorporated into the dry ingredients. Add 1 to 2 tablespoons more ice water, until dough will hold together when pressed. On a flat surface, form the dough into a ball. Then flatten the ball into a 6-inch circle, wrap in plastic wrap, and chill.

When ready to bake, preheat oven to 450°F.

Roll out dough between 2 pieces of wax paper to a 12-inch circle. Carefully strip off 1 piece of the wax paper. Invert the dough over a 10-inch tart pan with a removable rim. Remove the second piece of wax paper, and fit pastry into pan without stretching it. Mend any tears. With the flat of your hand, press top of rim to remove excess pastry. With a fork, prick the inside of the pastry shell at ½-inch intervals.

Lay a 10-inch piece of aluminum foil over the bottom of the crust lightly, and form the edge of it into a 1-inch lip that does not touch the sides of the shell. Fill the foil with an even layer of rice or beans, about 1½ cups. (These can be saved and used many times for the same purpose.) Place pan on top shelf of oven. Reduce heat to 400°F. Bake for 7 minutes.

Take shell out of oven, and carefully remove foil and rice or beans. Return shell to oven and bake 7 minutes longer or until lightly browned all over. (If bottom of shell bubbles up, prick it with a fork.)

Cool on a wire rack.

After filling pastry shell, remove rim.

Makes 1

Tart Pastry 2

½ cup butter, softened
½ cup cream cheese, softened
2 tablespoons milk
1 teaspoon honey
1¼ cups whole wheat pastry flour

In a large bowl, cream together butter and cream cheese until soft, fluffy, and well blended. Blend in milk and honey. Gradually add flour to make a dough that is just firm enough to handle. Chill dough for at least 1 hour.

Preheat oven to 450°F.

To make tart shell, roll out dough between 2 sheets of wax paper. Carefully remove one sheet of wax paper, and invert pastry over tart pan with a removable rim. Remove the second sheet of wax paper, and fit pastry into pan without stretching it. (If pastry becomes too soft and difficult to handle, chill in refrigerator.) With a fork, prick pastry on the bottom and sides at ½-inch intervals. Place pastry shell on top shelf of oven, and reduce heat to 400°F. Bake for 15 to 20 minutes, or until lightly browned all over.

Cool on a wire rack.

After filling pastry shell, remove rim.

Makes 1

Meringue Pie Shell

3 egg whites
⅛ teaspoon cream of tartar
1 tablespoon honey
½ teaspoon vanilla extract

Preheat oven to 250°F. Butter and lightly flour a 9-inch pie plate.

In a large bowl, beat together egg whites and cream of tartar until foamy. Add honey and vanilla, and beat until stiff. Line bottom and sides of prepared pie plate with beaten whites, spreading mixture high on sides (crust will shrink during baking). Bake on middle shelf of oven for 30 to 35 minutes, or until golden brown.

Makes 1

Coconut Lime Cream Pie

pastry for 1 Basic Flaky Piecrust (page 57)
5 eggs, separated
¾ cup honey
⅓ cup lime juice
1 teaspoon vanilla extract, divided
⅛ teaspoon cream of tartar
1 cup unsweetened flaked coconut
1 cup heavy cream
2 tablespoons honey

Preheat oven to 350°F. Roll out pastry, and line a 9-inch deep-dish pie plate with it. Prick on bottom and sides, and bake on middle shelf of oven for 10 minutes.

Cool thoroughly.

In the top of a double boiler, beat egg yolks and ¾ cup honey. Mix in lime juice. Set over simmering water and cook, stirring constantly, until mixture coats the back of the spoon, about 10 minutes.

Add ½ teaspoon vanilla, and set aside to cool.

In a large bowl, beat together egg whites and cream of tartar until stiff peaks form. Fold in cooled egg yolks and then coconut. Turn into shell and bake on middle shelf of oven for about 20 minutes, or until lightly browned.

Cool and refrigerate.

Just before serving, whip together cream, 2 tablespoons honey, and ½ teaspoon vanilla until soft peaks form. Spread on top of pie.

Makes 1

Apricot Chiffon Tarts

pastry for 3 Tart Pastries 2 (page 59)
2½ cups dried apricots
2½ cups water
¼ cup orange juice
1 envelope unflavored gelatin
3 eggs, separated
½ cup honey
3 egg whites
⅛ teaspoon lemon extract
1 cup heavy cream
1 tablespoon honey

Preheat oven to 425°F.

Roll out pastry, and cut into 36 5-inch rounds. (To do this, you'll have to reroll scraps.) Line 3 12-cup muffin tins with pastry. Prick bottoms and sides with the tines of a fork, and bake on middle shelf of oven for 7 to 10 minutes, or until golden.

Cool.

In a large saucepan, simmer apricots in water for about 20 minutes, or until soft.

Pour orange juice into a cup, and sprinkle gelatin over orange juice. Set aside for 3 minutes to soften.

Puree apricots and cooking water in a blender or food processor.

In the top of a double boiler set over simmering water, whisk together egg yolks and ½ cup honey. Gradually add apricot puree, while stirring constantly, and continue cooking until mixture begins to thicken. Add gelatin and orange juice, and continue to cook until gelatin dissolves. Cool until thickened but not set.

In a medium-size bowl, beat egg whites until stiff, adding lemon extract as you beat. Fold into cooled apricot mixture. Turn into tart shells and refrigerate until set.

In a medium-size bowl, beat together cream and 1 tablespoon honey until soft peaks form. Top each tart with whipped cream before serving.

Makes 3 dozen

Cherry Currant Pie

This tasty pie relies entirely on the fruit for its sweetness.

    1 cup dried currants
      pastry for 2 Basic Flaky Piecrusts
      (page 57)
 1½ tablespoons cornstarch
    3 cups frozen sweet cherries,
      thawed and drained with juice
      reserved
  ⅛ teaspoon almond extract

Place currants in a medium-size bowl. Cover with warm water, and set aside to plump for 5 minutes.

Preheat oven to 425°F.

Roll out half of pastry, and line a 9-inch pie plate with it.

In a medium-size saucepan, dissolve cornstarch in ½ cup reserved cherry juice. Add cherries and drained currants. Bring to a boil over medium heat, stirring constantly, until thickened, about 10 minutes.

Remove from heat, and stir in almond extract. Turn into prepared pie plate.

Roll out remaining pastry. Cut several steam vents into top. Place pastry over filling and trim, crimping edges together with fingers. Bake on middle shelf of oven for 15 minutes. Reduce heat to 325°F, and continue to bake for about 15 minutes, or until pie is golden.

Makes 1

Strawberry Meringue Pie

- 2 cups small fresh strawberries
- ¼ cup Strawberry Jelly (page 273)
  pastry for 1 Basic Flaky Piecrust
  (page 57)
- 2 cups Pastry Cream (page 272)
- 3 egg whites
- 2 teaspoons honey
- 1 teaspoon lemon juice

Set aside about 6 berries for decoration.

In a small saucepan, melt jelly over low heat, stirring. Mix berries not reserved for decoration with jelly. Chill mixture.

Preheat oven to 425°F.

Roll out pastry, and line a 9-inch pie plate with it. Prick dough with a fork, and bake on top shelf of oven for about 15 minutes, or until lightly browned.

Cool on a wire rack.

Spread Pastry Cream in cooled pie shell. Spoon berry mixture over cream. Keep chilled.

Preheat oven to 375°F.

In a small bowl, beat egg whites until foamy. Gradually add honey and lemon juice, continuing to beat until stiff peaks form. Spead meringue over pie, touching all edges of the crust. Bake on top shelf of oven until golden brown. Decorate with reserved berries sliced in half lengthwise.

Makes 1

French Apple Cream Pie

pastry for Basic Flaky Piecrust
(page 57)
5 egg yolks
2 tablespoons cornstarch
⅓ cup honey
2 cups sour cream
1 teaspoon ground cinnamon
½ teaspoon vanilla extract
2½ cups peeled, cored, and chunked
apples

Fresh Grape Tart

¼ cup plus 1 tablespoon Ribier
Grape Jam (page 235)
1 baked Tart Pastry 2 (page 59)
1½ cups Pastry Cream (page 272)
about 1 cup Ribier grapes
about ½ cup seedless green
grapes

Spread jam in cooled tart shell.
Spoon Pastry Cream over jam, and
gently spread it in an even layer.

Cut grapes in half. Seed Ribier
grapes with the point of a paring knife.
Make a circle of Ribier grapes, cut-
sides down, around the rim of the tart.
Use about 7 more halves at the center.
Fill the area between with rows of
green grapes. Chill until serving time.

This tart is best if assembled about
1 hour before serving, but it can be
prepared earlier if necessary.

Makes 1

Preheat oven to 400°F.

Roll out pastry, and line a 9-inch
deep-dish pie plate with it.

In a large bowl, beat together egg
yolks and cornstarch. Add honey, sour
cream, cinnamon, and vanilla, beating
just to blend. Fold in apples. Turn into
pie shell, and bake on middle shelf of
oven for 15 minutes. Reduce heat to
350°F, and bake for 40 to 45 minutes,
or until a knife inserted in the center
comes out clean.

Cool before serving.

Makes 1

Easy Carob Pie

2 cups crumbs of Basic Honey
   Cookies (page 46)
6 tablespoons butter, melted
1 recipe Basic Carob Pudding
   (page 103), chilled
1 cup heavy cream
1 tablespoon honey
1 teaspoon vanilla extract or
   ½ teaspoon rum extract

In a medium-size bowl, combine cookie crumbs and butter. Press firmly onto bottom and sides of a 9-inch deep-dish pie plate.

Whisk chilled pudding until smooth, and turn into pie shell.

In a medium-size bowl, beat together cream, honey, and flavoring until soft peaks form. Spread on top of pudding. Cover or wrap, and refrigerate.

Makes 1

Fresh Papaya and Kiwi Tart

This attractive tart is a nice addition to a brunch menu as well as a lovely dessert.

½ cup Apricot Preserves (page 276)
1 Tart Pastry 1 (page 58) baked in 10-
   inch tart pan with removable rim

¼ cup Apple Jelly (page 274)
2 kiwi fruit
1 ripe papaya

Spread Apricot Preserves over inner surface of cooled tart shell.

Place Apple Jelly in a small saucepan and heat over low heat, stirring often, until it melts. Keep warm.

Peel and slice kiwi into rounds. Reserve 3 whole rounds, and slice the others into half rounds.

Cut papaya in half lengthwise. Scoop out seeds, and peel halves. Slice into 3- to 4-inch pieces, ½ inch thick.

Lay papaya slices, like spokes of a wheel, as close together as possible over preserves. Use half rounds of kiwi to make a border. Arrange the 3 reserved rounds in the center. With a pastry brush, brush fruit with Apple Jelly until all pieces are evenly coated. Remove rim of tart pan, and place tart on serving dish.

This tart is best if served less than 1 hour after assembly, but it can wait longer if necessary.

Makes 1

VARIATION

Peach and Kiwi Tart: Substitute 4 ripe peaches for papaya. Use either Apricot Preserves or Peach Preserves (page 276) to coat shell.

Deep-Dish Apple Pie with Molasses

14 to 16 baking apples
1 tablespoon cornstarch
½ teaspoon ground cinnamon
½ cup honey
2 tablespoons molasses
2 tablespoons butter
  pastry for 1 Basic Flaky
  Piecrust (page 57)

Preheat oven to 450°F.

Peel, core, and quarter apples. Cut them into uniform slices, fitting them into a 2-quart casserole, which can be either deep and round or oblong. When casserole is full of slices, remove apples to a large bowl, and mix them with cornstarch and cinnamon until these additions are well distributed throughout. Stir in honey, and return apples to casserole. Drizzle molasses on top, and dot with butter.

Roll pastry between 2 sheets of wax paper to fit casserole top. Remove top sheet of wax paper, invert pastry onto casserole, and remove the second sheet. Trim edges of pastry, and press them down with the tines of a fork. Cut steam vents into top. Place casserole on middle shelf of oven, and reduce heat to 350°F. Bake for 50 minutes, or until apples are tender (test by probing through vent with a fork), and pastry is golden brown.

Serve warm or at room temperature.

French Vanilla Ice Cream (page 131) makes a delicious accompaniment.

8 servings

Fresh Bosc Pear Pie

pastry for 2 Basic Flaky Piecrusts
  (page 57)
5 cups sliced peeled ripe Bosc pears
  (about 6 large pears)
½ cup honey
3 tablespoons cornstarch
½ teaspoon ground ginger
1 tablespoon lemon juice
2 teaspoons molasses
2 tablespoons butter

Preheat oven to 425°F.

Roll out half of pastry, and line a 9-inch pie plate with it.

Place the sliced pears into a large bowl, drizzle with honey, and sprinkle them with cornstarch and ginger. Mix gently and thoroughly with 2 forks. Turn the mixture into the pie plate. Sprinkle with lemon juice. Drizzle molasses over all. Dot with bits of butter.

Roll out remaining pastry and place it on top of pie. Press edges with tines of a fork to seal the 2 crusts. Cut vents into top crust for steam to escape. Place pie on top shelf of oven, and bake for 15 minutes. Reduce heat to 350°F, and continue baking for 40 minutes longer.

Cool on a wire rack.

Makes 1

Fresh Fig Pie

This sumptuous dessert is very rich and should be served in small slices.

>   pastry for 1 Basic Flaky Piecrust
>   (page 57)
>   8 fresh figs
>   3 eggs
>   1 cup honey
>   ¼ cup butter, melted and cooled
>   1 tablespoon molasses
>   1 tablespoon flour

Preheat oven to 450°F.

Roll out pastry, and line a 9-inch pie plate with it. Trim excess, and press rim with the tines of a fork.

Remove stems of figs, but don't peel them. Dice figs. (You should have 2 cups.) Spoon into pastry-lined pie plate.

Combine remaining ingredients in blender container, and process to blend completely (or beat by hand with a whisk). Pour mixture over figs. Place pie on middle shelf of oven, and reduce heat to 350°F. Bake for 1 hour, or until a knife inserted near the center comes out clean. During the last 20 minutes of baking, if the pie has browned, lay a sheet of aluminum foil loosely over the top to prevent overbrowning.

Cool completely before serving. Refrigerate leftovers.

Makes 1

Fresh Pineapple Pie

Making this pie begins with selecting good, ripe, fresh pineapple. A rich aroma indicates ripeness. Another test is to pull a leaf from the center of the crown; it should come out easily if the pineapple was picked at the proper time. Pineapples do not ripen further after picking.

>   4½ to 5 cups cubed fresh pineapple
>   (1 large pineapple or
>   2 small to medium)
>   ⅓ cup honey, to taste
>   3 tablespoons cornstarch
>   ¼ cup water
>   pastry for 2 Basic Flaky
>   Piecrusts (page 57)

Combine pineapple, honey, cornstarch, and water in a medium-size saucepan. Bring to a boil, stirring constantly. Reduce heat, and simmer, stirring often, until fruit is tender, about 25 minutes. Chill filling.

Preheat oven to 450°F.

Roll out half of pastry, fit it into a 9-inch pie plate without stretching, and trim edges. Spoon filling into pie shell. Roll out second half of pastry into a 12-inch square. Cut the square into ¾-inch strips, and use them to make a lattice-top crust (see illustration on opposite page). Trim, and press edges with a fork to secure lattice. Place pie on top shelf of oven, and reduce heat to 400°F. Bake for 25 minutes, or until lightly browned.

Cool to room temperature before serving.

Makes 1

Fresh Peach Lattice Pie

Pastry for 2 Basic Flaky Piecrusts (page 57)
4 cups sliced peeled peaches
1 tablespoon lemon juice
1 teaspoon ground cinnamon
2 tablespoons quick-cooking tapioca
¼ cup honey (½ cup if fruit is tart)
1 egg yolk, beaten

Preheat oven to 375°F.
Roll out half of pastry, and line a 9-inch deep-dish pie plate with it. Roll out other half of pastry and cut into 1-inch strips.

In a large bowl, toss peaches with lemon juice, cinnamon, and tapioca. Add honey and toss again. Turn into prepared pie shell. Wet edges of pastry. Place strips on top, ½ inch apart. Make lattice pattern by placing remaining strips across those already in place at right angles. Press ends of strips into bottom pastry, and brush with egg yolk. Bake on middle shelf of oven for

40 to 45 minutes, or until fruit is bubbly and pastry is golden.

Makes 1

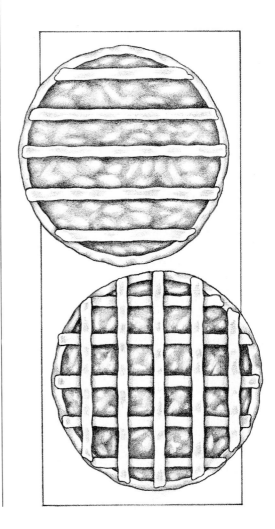

Fresh Strawberry Tarts with Pistachios

pastry for 1 Tart Pastry 2
(page 59)
2 cups sliced fresh strawberries
¼ cup honey, warmed slightly
1 cup heavy cream
¼ teaspoon vanilla extract
10 to 12 small fresh strawberries,
unhulled
½ cup chopped pistachio nuts

Preheat oven to 450°F.

Divide pastry into 2 portions. Roll out 1 portion between 2 sheets of wax paper into a 9 by 9-inch square. Remove 1 piece of wax paper. Cut dough into 3-inch squares. Fit each square into a 2½-inch fluted tart pan. Press edges to remove any overhang. Prick dough with a fork on bottom and sides. Repeat until first portion of dough has been used, rerolling scraps. Follow the same procedure with second portion of dough. If you don't have 18 tart pans, you can make tarts in batches, reusing pans. Place tarts on a large baking sheet. Reduce oven temperature to 400°F, and bake tarts on top shelf for 15 minutes, or until lightly browned.

Cool on wire racks until they can be handled easily. Invert on palm of hand and gently tap on bottom to remove tarts from pans. Finish cooling on wire racks.

Mix strawberries with honey, and refrigerate.

Whip cream, adding vanilla, then cover and refrigerate until needed.

Cut strawberries for decoration into halves, lengthwise, through hulls. Lay them cut-side down on a plate, and refrigerate.

Assemble when ready to serve. Sprinkle a little of the pistachios in each tart, using about half of them. Drain strawberries and divide among tart shells. Top with a dollop of whipped cream, the rest of the pistachios, and strawberry decoration.

Makes 1½ to 2 dozen

Glazed Apple-Pear Turnovers

3 cups whole wheat pastry flour
1 cup butter
1 cup sour cream
2 apples
2 pears
1 tablespoon lemon juice
¼ cup raisins, plumped
1 teaspoon ground cinnamon
½ teaspoon ground allspice
¼ cup honey
2 cups Vanilla Icing (page 268)

Sift flour into a large bowl. Cut butter into chunks, and then cut into flour with a pastry blender or in a food processor until mixture is crumbly. Mix in sour cream with a spoon. Wrap dough in plastic wrap and refrigerate for 1 hour. (If dough is chilled longer it may be too firm to roll.)

Peel, core, and chop apples and pears. Place them into a large bowl and cover with cold water. Stir in lemon juice.

Preheat oven to 400°F.

In 2 batches, roll out dough on lightly floured surface. Cut into 5-inch squares.

Thoroughly drain apples and pears. Stir raisins into fruit, and toss with cinnamon and allspice. Place about 2 tablespoons fruit mixture on one side of each piece of dough. Drizzle with 1 teaspoon honey. Fold dough over filling to form a triangle, firmly pressing edges together to seal. Prick top of each turnover with a fork. Place turnovers on a baking sheet, and bake on middle shelf of oven about 20 minutes, or until lightly browned.

Remove to a wire rack to cool. Frost cooled tarts with icing.

Makes 1 dozen

Fresh Plum Tarts

pastry for 1 Tart Pastry 2
  (page 59)
1½ cups Pastry Cream (page 272)
1½ cups pitted peeled purple plums
  (unsweetened canned plums
  may be substituted)
¼ cup Peach Preserves (page 276)

Preheat oven to 425°F.

Roll out pastry, and cut into 12 5-inch rounds. (To do this, you'll have to reroll scraps.) Line a 12-cup muffin tin with pastry. Prick bottom and sides with the tines of a fork, and bake on middle shelf of oven for 7 to 10 minutes, or until golden.

Cool thoroughly.

Place 3 tablespoons Pastry Cream into each cooled tart shell. Top with 3 tablespoons plums.

In a small saucepan, melt Peach Preserves. Brush over plums, and chill tarts until ready to serve.

Makes 1 dozen

Grapefruit Pie

This unusual pie is an Arizona favorite that can cause a mild sensation when served to the uninitiated.

¼ cup cornstarch
1¼ cups milk
½ cup honey
2 teaspoons molasses
¾ cup unsweetened grapefruit juice
1 cup unsweetened grapefruit
  sections, very well drained
1 baked Basic Flaky Piecrust
  (page 57)
3 egg whites
2 teaspoons honey
1 teaspoon lemon juice
  orange and grapefruit sections
  (optional)

In a small saucepan, stir cornstarch into milk until dissolved. Mix in ½ cup honey and molasses. Bring to a boil, stirring constantly. (Mixture will separate when cooking but will be smooth when done.) Remove from heat. Gradually add grapefruit juice, stirring. Return to heat and bring to a boil again, stirring constantly. Remove from heat and mix in grapefruit sections. Cool mixture slightly and spoon into pie shell.

Preheat oven to 375°F.

In a small bowl, beat egg whites until foamy. Gradually add 2 teaspoons honey and lemon juice, continuing to beat until stiff peaks form. Spread meringue over pie, touching all edges of the crust. Bake on top shelf of oven until golden brown.

Cool slightly, and then chill in refrigerator until firm.

If desired, decorate with orange and grapefruit sections.

Makes 1

Greek Yogurt Prune Pie

1½ cups ground walnuts
3 tablespoons butter, softened
2 tablespoons honey
8 ounces cream cheese, softened
3 tablespoons honey
   juice of 1 large lemon (about
      ¼ cup)
½ teaspoon ground cinnamon
1 cup yogurt
1 cup finely chopped prunes

Mix together walnuts, butter, and 2 tablespoons honey in a medium-size bowl. Press into bottom of a 9-inch pie plate, and chill until firm.

In another medium-size bowl, beat cream cheese and 3 tablespoons honey. Blend in lemon juice and cinnamon. Gently fold in yogurt and then prunes, separating prune pieces with a spoon. Turn into prepared shell, and chill for 8 to 10 hours before serving.

Makes 1

Homemade Mincemeat Pie

   pastry for 2 Basic Flaky Piecrusts
      (page 57)
3 apples
1 tablespoon cornstarch
1¾ cups Mincemeat "Lite" (recipe
      below)
¼ cup honey

Preheat oven to 450°F.
Roll out 1 piecrust, and line a 9-inch pie plate with it.
Peel, core, and dice apples. You should have about 2½ cups chopped apples. Place into a large bowl, and

toss with cornstarch. Mix in mincemeat and honey. Spoon mixture into prepared pie shell.

Roll out top crust, and place it over filling. Trim excess with about ½ inch to spare all around, and turn edges under. Press with tines of a fork to seal. Cut 2 steam vents into the center, and place on middle shelf of oven. Reduce heat to 425°F and bake for 15 minutes.

Reduce heat to 350°F, and bake for an additional 35 minutes, or until crust is golden brown and apples are tender. Test apples by inserting the point of a paring knife through the vents.

Makes 1

Mincemeat "Lite"

Though not as heavy, fatty, or dark as traditional mincemeat, this version is just as rich in spicy old-time flavor.

2½ pounds meaty veal breast or
      1¼ pounds stewing veal
2 cups apple cider or apple juice
2 cups golden raisins
½ cup honey
   juice of 1 lemon
   grated rind of 1 lemon (about 1
      tablespoon)
2 tablespoons cider vinegar
2 teaspoons ground cinnamon
2 teaspoons ground allspice

In a large pot, cover veal with water, bring to a boil, and simmer for 1½ hours, or until very tender (or cook in a pressure cooker for 25 minutes). Drain, cool, and finely chop meat, discarding fat, gristle, and bone. (Save liquid for the stock pot.) You should have about 2 cups meat. In the same pot, combine meat with remaining ingredients, and simmer, uncovered, over low heat for 45 to 60 minutes, stirring occasionally. Mixture should be quite thick.

Yields about 5 cups

Molasses Pecan Pie

The molasses in this pie adds a distinctive flavor to a classic dessert.

    1 pastry for Basic Flaky Piecrust
       (page 57)
    ¼ cup butter, softened
    ⅔ cup honey
    ¼ cup molasses
    4 eggs
    1 teaspoon vanilla extract
    1 cup coarsely chopped pecans

Preheat oven to 350°F.
Roll out pastry, and line a 9-inch pie plate with it.
In a large bowl, beat butter until fluffy. Beat in honey, molasses, and eggs in that order. Mix in vanilla and then nuts. Turn into prepared pie shell, and bake on middle shelf of oven for about 45 minutes, or until a knife inserted near the center comes out clean.

Makes 1

Jewel Fruit Tart

    1 recipe for Basic Honey Cookies
       (page 46)
    8 ounces cream cheese, softened
    2 tablespoons honey
    ½ teaspoon vanilla extract

    1 cup halved fresh strawberries
    1 cup halved seedless green grapes
    1 cup unsweetened mandarin orange
       segments
    ½ cup Apricot Preserves (page 276)

Preheat oven to 350°F. Butter a 12-inch pizza pan.
Press cookie dough into pan, trimming edges. Prick with a fork, and bake on middle shelf of oven for 15 to 20 minutes, or until lightly browned. Cool thoroughly in pan.
In a small bowl, beat together cream cheese, honey, and vanilla, and spread on cooled cookie crust. Arrange fruit on tart in an attractive design.
In a small saucepan, heat Apricot Preserves, and brush lightly on top of fruit. Chill before serving.

10 to 12 servings

Fresh Strawberry Tarts with Pistachios
Page 68

Irish Apple Dumplings

Along with being a great dessert, these dumplings (which remind me of big, friendly Irish spuds) are also quite welcome at a Sunday brunch. If one dumpling is too large a serving, it can be cut in half neatly from top to bottom and still hold its shape.

5 medium-size baking apples
2 tablespoons lemon juice
½ cup finely chopped walnuts
¼ cup honey
½ teaspoon grated lemon rind
¼ teaspoon ground cinnamon
pastry for 2 Basic Flaky Piecrusts (page 57)
ground cinnamon, for sprinkling

Core apples leaving a ½-inch plug at bottom to hold filling. Scrape out seeds with point of corer, and enlarge holes to 1-inch diameter.

Peel apples, placing them into a large bowl. Cover with cold water, and stir in lemon juice.

In a small bowl, mix together walnuts, honey, lemon rind, and ¼ teaspoon cinnamon until blended.

Preheat oven to 450°F.

Divide pastry into 4 portions. Roll out 1 portion large enough to cut evenly into a 7-inch square. (If apples are medium-large, you may need 8-inch squares.) Sprinkle square lightly with cinnamon. Take an apple out of the water and dry it with a paper towel. Spoon filling into hollow, and stand apple in the center of square of pastry. Bring up 4 corners to top of apple and fasten well by pressing with tines of a fork. Repeat with remaining apples, rerolling scraps of pastry to enclose fifth apple. Place apples on a large baking sheet or jelly-roll pan.

Reduce heat to 400°F. Bake apples in top third of oven for 15 minutes, and then reduce heat to 350°F. Continue baking for 30 minutes longer, or until apples are tender when pierced with a fork and pastry is nicely browned.

Place pan on a wire rack, and allow apples to cool. The dumplings may be served warm or at room temperature.

Makes 5

Kentucky Carob Pie

pastry for 1 Basic Flaky Piecrust (page 57)

1 cup milk carob chips (dark carob
　　chips may be substituted)
4 eggs, beaten
⅓ cup butter, melted
½ cup maple syrup
¼ cup honey
1½ teaspoons vanilla extract
1½ cups chopped walnuts
16 walnut halves (optional)

Preheat oven to 350°F.

Roll out pastry, and line a 9-inch deep-dish pie plate with it. Sprinkle carob chips on bottom.

In a medium-size bowl, combine eggs, butter, maple syrup, honey, vanilla, and chopped walnuts. Pour over carob chips. Decorate top with walnut halves, and bake for 40 to 45 minutes, or until knife inserted 1 inch from the center comes out clean.

Remove from oven and cool. Center will cook completely during this time. Serve either warm or cold.

Makes 1

Rhubarb Cheese Tarts

2 cups crumbs of Basic Honey
　　Cookies (page 46)
5 tablespoons butter, melted
16 ounces cream cheese, softened
3 eggs
½ cup honey
1 tablespoon lemon juice

1 teaspoon vanilla extract
1¼ cups cold water, divided
1½ envelopes unflavored gelatin
2 cups chopped rhubarb
¼ cup honey
½ cup Strawberry Jam (page 273)

Preheat oven to 375°F. Line 18 muffin cups with foil liners.

In a medium-size bowl, mix crumbs and butter with a fork. Divide among prepared muffin cups, pressing firmly onto bottoms with the back of a spoon. Bake on middle shelf of oven for 7 minutes.

Set aside to cool, and reduce heat to 350°F.

In a large bowl, beat cream cheese until fluffy. Beat in eggs, ½ cup honey, lemon juice, and vanilla. Divide equally among muffin cups, filling each about three-quarters full. Bake on middle shelf of oven for about 30 minutes, or until set.

Set aside to cool.

Pour ¾ cup water into a small bowl, and sprinkle gelatin on top. Set aside for a few minutes to soften.

In a medium-size saucepan, combine rhubarb, ¼ cup honey, and ½ cup water. Bring to a boil, reduce heat, and simmer for 10 minutes.

Remove from heat. Stir in gelatin until dissolved. Stir in Strawberry Jam, and refrigerate until thickened but not set. Divide among cooled cheese tarts. Refrigerate until set.

Makes 1½ dozen

Ricotta Pie *(Pizza Dolce)*

pastry for 1 Basic Flaky Piecrust
  (page 57)
1 egg white, beaten until foamy
3 cups ricotta cheese
3 eggs
½ cup honey
1 teaspoon grated lemon rind
2 teaspoons grated orange rind
¼ cup finely chopped dried figs
¼ cup finely chopped dried apricots
2 rounded tablespoons milk carob
  chips (optional)

Preheat oven to 450°F.

Roll out pastry, and line a 10-inch
pie plate with it. Trim excess, and press
edges with the tines of a fork. Brush
with beaten egg white. Refrigerate crust
until ready to fill.

In a large bowl, beat ricotta, eggs,
and honey until smooth and blended.
This can be done by hand, with an
electric mixer, or in a food processor
fitted with a steel blade. With a spoon,
mix in lemon rind, orange rind, figs,
and apricots. Add carob chips, if desired.
Pour filling into prepared crust, place
on middle shelf of oven, and reduce
heat to 375°F. Bake for 40 minutes, or
until crust is golden and filling is set.

Cool completely on a wire rack
before cutting.

Makes 1

VARIATION

Pizza Dolce Pronto: Prepare only the
filling, and pour it into a buttered
9-inch pie plate. Bake in a preheated
375°F oven for 40 minutes, or until
filling is set.

Sweet Potato Pie

4 medium-size sweet potatoes
  pastry for Basic Flaky Piecrust
  (page 57)
4 tablespoons butter, softened
¾ cup honey
3 eggs
1 cup milk
1 teaspoon ground cinnamon
½ teaspoon ground ginger
½ teaspoon ground nutmeg
3 tablespoons butter
3 tablespoons honey
½ cup ground walnuts

Peel sweet potatoes, and cook in
enough water to cover until tender.
Drain, and puree.

Preheat oven to 425°F.

Roll out pastry, and line a 9-inch
deep-dish pie plate with it.

In a medium-size bowl, beat 4
tablespoons butter until fluffy. Beat in
¾ cup honey and then eggs.

Place sweet potatoes into a large
bowl. Beat in butter mixture, then milk,
and spices. Turn into pie shell, and
bake on middle shelf of oven for 10
minutes. Reduce heat to 325°F, and
bake for 1 to 1½ hours, or until a knife
inserted into the center comes out clean.
Cool.

In a medium-size saucepan, melt
3 tablespoons butter. Add 3 tablespoons honey, and bring to a boil. Stir
in nuts, and pour on top of pie. Chill.

Makes 1

CHAPTER
4

Show~Off Pastries

Pastries are reserved for special occasions, to my mind, because they are so decorative and so rich. Prepare them for those events at which you want, ever so modestly, to shine as a superb pastry cook. But you really must practice the recipes beforehand so that you'll know just what to expect at every step of the procedures involved.

Cream puff pastry, also called *pâte à chou* or just *chou*, is the easiest of all the fancy pastry doughs to prepare at home. (I don't include filo dough, since most cooks buy this already prepared.) In fact, it's much easier to make than basic pie pastry. Although many traditional desserts made with cream puff pastry specify a cream filling of some type, there is no reason why they can't be filled with lightly sweetened fresh berries instead. Whatever you do with this versatile pastry, it always looks spectacular. For all these reasons, it is my favorite.

If you've never ventured into the world of haute cuisine pastry, I heartily recommend that you begin with cream puff pastry and its many variations: eclairs, profiteroles, pastry sculptures, miniature puffs, and even cakes made from this basic dough.

Correct baking is the only tricky step in preparing cream puff pastry. Like all pastries, it is supposed to be crisp, the better to contrast with some melt-in-the-mouth filling. To insure crispness, this pastry must be baked so that it's dry inside as well as out, and it must be filled just before serving time.

To make certain that the inside is dry, once the cream puff pastry is baked

Boston Cream Eclair Cake   Page 83

79

to a golden brown, in whatever form you choose, pierce the pastry on the sides where it won't show with the point of a paring knife. This allows the moist steam to escape. I let the pastry stand in the warm oven, with the heat turned off and the door ajar, while this is going on. Then the cooling is finished on wire racks.

One of the joys of cream puff pastry is that it can be made ahead and frozen. Just freeze the pastry shells in a single layer on a baking sheet, then pop them into a plastic freezer bag until needed. They defrost in a very short time. But they must be recrisped! A few minutes in a moderate oven (325° to 350°F) will do it.

The customary cream or custard-based pastry fillings are highly perishable, but since you're going to fill your pastries just before serving, the filling can and should be kept refrigerated until you're ready for this step. Leftover cream-filled pastries should be refrigerated.

Using a pastry tube to fill cream puffs or eclairs makes a much neater, prettier dessert, but it's not strictly necessary.

The other classic pastry dough is called puff pastry, and it's a version of piecrust only with even flakier layers. This is achieved by incorporating much more butter than is used in regular piecrust and by employing a technique of folding and chilling the dough several times to create many very thin layers. Although you can't see them, these layers of dough bake up into delightful flakes of tender pastry.

Puff pastry is used to make patty shells, French pastry tarts, Napoleons, and many of those beautiful layered pastries you may have admired in bakery showcases. Sad to say, the puff pastries from most bakeries look a lot better than they taste.

The puff pastry in this book is different from the bakery variety. First, it is made with whole wheat flour, which makes it sturdier. Second, I make a short-cut version which uses less butter than the classic recipe—but still uses more than regular pie pastry. Although it's rich, the ingredients are all wholesome. As the name "short-cut" implies, my version takes less time to prepare than classic puff pastry, and it's quite satisfactory for a number of impressive and tasty desserts.

Although whole wheat pastry flour is desirable for making pie pastry, for puff pastry it's better to use whole wheat bread flour, which has more strength to hold up many thicknesses of flakes. Puff pastry isn't rolled as thin as pie pastry—$\frac{3}{16}$ of an inch is about right for most pastry shells made with this type of dough.

Once you've rolled and cut the shapes you desire, freeze the uncooked dough before baking. When ready to bake, put it in the oven still frozen. This will produce a flakier pastry.

Not all the pastries in this chapter are made with cream puff pastry or short-cut puff pastry. Strudel and baklava, for instance, are made with filo dough, which may be purchased in many supermarkets. Filo dough is a very thin, almost transparent dough, difficult to make in home kitchens. By using many layers of this paper-thin dough and brushing each with melted butter, a flaky pastry is created for many popular European desserts.

The most important point to remember in working with filo dough is to keep the dough covered with a damp towel, taking out only the amount you are working with and keeping the rest well wrapped. Because they are so thin, when filo sheets are exposed to air they dry out quickly, become brittle, and crumble.

All of these kinds of pastry are used to make shells or layers, and their purpose is to hold cream, fruit, nut, or other fillings in delicate, airy cases. Often they're topped with a glaze or frosting. There's a delightful contrast, of course, between the flaky pastry and the soft filling, plus the extra-smooth sweetness of frosting, that makes these artful desserts among the most elegant a cook can create.

Basic Cream Puff Pastry (*Chou* Paste)

Of all the show-off pastries, this is the easiest for the novice cook to master, and yet it yields spectacular results.

¾ cup whole wheat pastry flour
¾ cup unbleached white flour
1¼ cups water
¾ cup butter, cut into chunks
5 eggs

Preheat oven to 400°F. Butter the number of baking sheets required by recipe.

In a medium-size bowl, sift together whole wheat pastry flour and unbleached white flour.

In a medium-size saucepan, combine water and butter. Heat until butter has melted, then bring to a full rolling boil. Add flour all at once, and stir with a wooden spoon until pastry forms a ball and comes away cleanly from sides of pan. Continue to cook 2 minutes longer over low heat, stirring constantly.

Spoon batter into large bowl of electric mixer or workbowl of food processor. Allow batter to cool slightly. Beat in eggs, 1 at a time.

Shape and bake according to recipe instructions. Place on top shelf of oven. If using more than 1 baking sheet, do not put them into oven at the same time, as the ones on the bottom will not brown properly. Instead, bake in batches.

When puffs are lightly browned, doubled in size, and firm, they are done. Pierce on each side with the point of a paring knife to allow steam to escape. Return to oven for a few minutes, and then cool on wire racks.

Fill puffs as close to serving time as possible to prevent them from getting soggy. Unfilled puffs freeze very well. Heat frozen puffs for a few minutes in a 350°F oven if they lose their crispness.

Makes about 12 large or 30 small cream puffs, or 20 eclairs

Short-Cut Puff Pastry

This is not the traditional puff pastry, but it is a good and speedy substitute that is much easier to make and uses a lot less butter. I've used this short-cut version for all recipes calling for puff pastry in this book.

¾ cup cold butter, cut into pieces
1 cup whole wheat flour
1 cup unbleached white flour
⅓ to ½ cup cold water
2 teaspoons lemon juice
1 egg, beaten

In a medium-size bowl, cut butter into whole wheat flour and unbleached white flour until pieces vary from the size of a large pea to the size of a rice grain. This can be done in a food processor, using on/off turns of the motor.

Place flour-butter mixture into a large bowl.

Pour ⅓ cup cold water into a cup. Add lemon juice and 2 ice cubes. Add 3 tablespoons lemon-water mixture to flour, tossing mixture with 2 forks until blended. Add 2 more tablespoons, and mix the same way. Add 1 tablespoon more. If necessary, add more water, 1 tablespoon at a time, until dough will hold together when pressed. Form dough into a ball, pressing lightly until ball is about 2 inches in diameter. If you have added enough water, all the flour will be incorporated when you do this. Wrap dough with plastic wrap, and chill for 1 hour.

Between 2 sheets of wax paper, roll out dough into a 12 × 6-inch rectangle. Fold into thirds as you would a sheet of letter paper. Place seam-side down, dust with flour, and roll again into a 12 × 6-inch rectangle between 2 fresh sheets of wax paper. Do this 2 more times—4 times in all. Chill dough.

When ready to bake, roll out and cut into shapes called for in your recipe. Pastry will puff more if you freeze it before baking. To glaze pastry, brush exposed surfaces with egg.

Makes about 1 pound

Boston Cream Eclair Cake

1 recipe for Basic Cream Puff Pastry
  (page 82)
    ground cinnamon, for sprinkling
½ recipe for Coconut Cream Frosting
  (page 267)

Carob Fudge Glaze (page 266)
unsweetened flaked coconut, for
  sprinkling
carob curls (optional)*

Preheat oven to 400°F. Butter 2 9- or 10-inch layer cake pans.

Divide Basic Cream Puff Pastry between pans, and spread with spatula, making sure to touch all edges. Sprinkle with cinnamon. Bake on middle shelf of oven for 20 minutes. With a spatula, press down any places on the surface of the layers that are higher than the rest.

Reduce heat to 375°F, and continue baking for an additional 20 minutes, or until layers are evenly golden and crisp.

Pierce layers with the point of a paring knife all around the edges and about 5 times near the center. Turn off heat, and leave layers in oven, with door ajar, to dry out for about 20 minutes longer.

Remove from pans, and cool completely on wire racks.

About 30 minutes to 1 hour before serving, spread Coconut Cream Frosting on 1 layer, top with second layer and spread Carob Fudge Glaze on top. If glaze becomes too stiff to spread, add a tablespoon or more of very hot water, and stir to blend. Sprinkle glaze with coconut, and decorate with carob curls, if desired. To serve, gently cut into wedges with a serrated knife.

8 servings

*To make carob curls, warm a bar of carob slightly. Using long strokes, shave carob into curls with a vegetable parer.

Blackberry-Raspberry Tart

1 recipe for Short-Cut Puff Pastry
    (page 82)
1 cup Pastry Cream (page 272)
1 cup fresh blackberries
1 cup fresh raspberries
½ cup Raspberry Jelly (page 273)
½ cup heavy cream (optional)

Roll out puff pastry to a ³⁄₁₆-inch thickness. Cut a 12 × 6-inch rectangle for base of tart, and place on a dampened baking sheet. Cut 4 strips of pastry 1½ inches wide to make sides of tart—2 strips will be 12 inches long and 2 will be 6 inches long. Dampen edges of pastry base, and lay strips in place. Pinch slightly to make them high rather than flat. With a fork, prick base of the tart shell at 1-inch intervals. Freeze tart shell on baking sheet.

Preheat oven to 375°F.

Bake frozen tart shell for 35 to 40 minutes, or until golden brown. If base rises in the center during baking, prick again with a fork.

Cool baked shell on baking sheet on a wire rack.

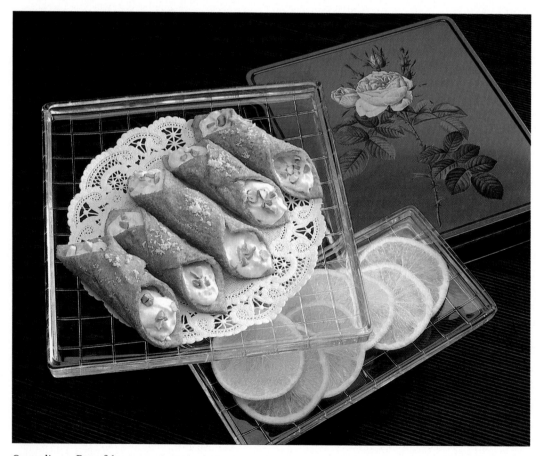

Cannoli   Page 86

When ready to assemble tart, spread Pastry Cream on bottom of shell. Make alternate diagonal stripes about 2 inches wide of blackberries and raspberries.

Spoon jelly into a small saucepan, melt over low heat, and brush liberally over berries. If desired, whip cream in a small bowl until soft peaks form, fill a pastry tube, and pipe puffs of whipped cream around border of tart just before serving.

6 to 8 servings

VARIATION

French Apple Tart: Instead of berries and heavy cream, use 3 cooking apples such as Cortland or Granny Smith. Core, halve, and peel them. Cut each half into thin slices without separating them. Place in a buttered baking dish, brush tops with butter, and sprinkle with cinnamon. Bake in oven while tart shell is baking. Cool in pan.
When ready to assemble tart, gently pick up each sliced half apple with a spatula, place it on layer of Pastry Cream, and fan out slices slightly so that the 6 half apples will fill base. Substitute Apple Jelly (page 274) for Raspberry Jelly, melt over low heat, and brush over apples.

High Tea Puffs

These delightful tidbits will disappear fast!

1 recipe for Basic Cream Puff Pastry (page 82)

FILLINGS
½ cup cream cheese
¼ cup chopped dates
1 small avocado
1 tablespoon lemon juice
½ teaspoon grated lemon rind
¼ cup shredded cheddar cheese
½ cup Apple Butter (page 278)

Preheat oven to 400°F. Butter 2 baking sheets.

Drop puff pastry batter onto prepared baking sheets by well-rounded tablespoonfuls, about 15 to each sheet. Bake on top shelf of oven for about 15 minutes, or until puffed and golden brown.

Pierce each puff on the side with the point of a paring knife to allow steam to escape. Return to oven with door ajar for a few minutes to dry out. Cool puffs on wire racks.

To make the fillings: Beat cream cheese in small bowl until fluffy. Beat in dates.

Peel and pit avocado. Place in another small bowl and mash. Beat in lemon juice and lemon rind.

In a medium-size bowl, stir cheddar cheese into Apple Butter.

Refrigerate fillings if they are not to be used within an hour. Bring to room temperature before using.

Fill each puff with one of the fillings just before serving. They look especially pretty on a 3-tiered cookie plate.

Makes about 30 2-inch puffs

ALTERNATE FILLINGS
Pineapple Filling (page 271)
Cranberry Filling (page 267)

Cannoli

Cannoli cylinders, which mold the dough into tubes for filling, are made of wood or aluminum. They can be bought in cookware departments, or you can make your own by cutting an old broomstick into 6-inch lengths, and sanding the wood smooth. You will need 8 of these cylinders. Cannoli traditionalists insist on the cheese filling given below, but others may prefer a filling of sweetened, flavored whipped cream or Pastry Cream (page 272). As you see, I am a traditionalist.

PASTRY
    1 cup sifted whole wheat pastry
        flour
    ¾ cup sifted unbleached white flour
    1 teaspoon ground cinnamon
    2 tablespoons butter
    3 tablespoons wine vinegar
    3 tablespoons water
    1 tablespoon honey, warmed
    1 egg, beaten
FILLING
    3 cups ricotta cheese
    ⅓ cup honey, or more to taste
    1½ teaspoons vanilla extract
    1 teaspoon grated orange rind

    1 egg white, slightly beaten
        vegetable oil, for deep frying
    1 tablespoon honey
    1 tablespoon Coconut Sugar
        (page xxii)
    ¼ cup chopped pistachio nuts

    To make the pastry: Sift together whole wheat flour, unbleached white flour and cinnamon into a medium-size bowl. Cut in butter until mixture resembles meal.

    In a small bowl, mix together vinegar, water, honey, and egg. Pour into flour mixture and blend until dough comes away from sides of bowl. If dough is too moist, add a little more flour. If too dry, add a little water. Knead dough until smooth, about 5 minutes. If desired, dough can be made in a food processor, in which case processing the dough for 30 seconds will substitute for kneading. Wrap dough with plastic wrap, and chill for 20 minutes.

    To make the filling: Mix together ricotta, ⅓ cup honey, vanilla, and grated orange rind in a medium-size bowl. Cover, and refrigerate until needed.

    Divide dough into fourths. Roll out one-fourth of the dough into an 8 × 8-inch square. Cut dough into 4 4-inch squares. Roll each square around a cylinder, beginning with a pointed end. Brush the final point with egg white before wrapping to seal it well. Repeat with another fourth of the dough.

    In a large heavy saucepan, heat 2 inches of vegetable oil to 375°F. Fry cannoli, 2 or 3 at a time, until golden on all sides. Drain on a wire rack over paper towels. When 8 are cooked, reduce heat under oil.

    When cannoli are cool enough to handle, wrap your hand around each one, and pull it off the cylinder. Place cannoli on another wire rack to cool completely.

    Roll and form the remainder of the dough the same way, using the same molds. Reheat oil, fry, drain, and unmold.

Just before serving, fill cannoli with cheese filling, using a demitasse spoon. Brush a little honey over the top of each, and sprinkle with Coconut Sugar. Dip each end into pistachio nuts.

Makes 16

Lemon Napoleons

1 recipe for Short-Cut Puff Pastry (page 82)
2½ cups Lemon Filling (page 272)
½ cup Vanilla Icing (page 268)
¼ cup milk carob chips
2 tablespoons butter

Preheat oven to 350°F.

Roll out puff pastry into 2 9 × 10-inch sheets. Cut each sheet of pastry lengthwise into 3 pieces, 3 × 10 inches each. Prick with a fork, and bake on an ungreased baking sheet for about 20 minutes, or until golden. Cool completely.

Whisk Lemon Filling in a medium-size bowl to make it smooth. Spread on 4 pieces of cooled pastry. Spread Vanilla Icing on the other 2 pieces of pastry.

In top of a double boiler set over hot water, melt together carob chips and butter. Drizzle in lines across Vanilla Icing. With the edge of a fork, make several lines from one end of pastry to the other through carob. This will make an attractive design.

Place one lemon-covered pastry on top of another lemon-covered pastry. Top with a frosted pastry. Repeat proce-dure with remaining pastries. Refrigerate for 1 hour.

With a serrated knife, cut each into thirds, crosswise.

Makes 6

Persimmon Puff Turnovers

2 large ripe persimmons
1 tablespoon cornstarch
2 tablespoons honey
1 recipe for Short-Cut Puff Pastry (page 82)
½ cup Apricot or Peach Jam (page 276)
1 egg, beaten

Peel and dice persimmons. Place into a medium-size bowl, and mix in cornstarch. Stir in honey.

Roll out puff pastry to a ³⁄₁₆-inch thickness. Cut into 4-inch squares. Spread about 1 tablespoon jam on each square of pastry, leaving a ½-inch margin at edges. Then place about 2 table-spoons (or 1 heaping tablespoon) persimmon filling on each square, and fold pastry into a triangle. Seal edges with tines of a fork. Cut 2 slashes in top for steam to escape. Place turn-overs on a baking sheet, and put into freezer until pastry is just frozen.

Preheat oven to 400°F.

Brush turnovers with egg, and bake for about 35 minutes, or until golden brown.

Remove from pan, and cool on wire racks.

Makes about 9

Swan Lake   Page 92

Rogelach

These are traditional pastry roll-ups stuffed with jam and nuts.

1 cup butter
8 ounces cream cheese
1 cup whole wheat pastry flour
1 cup unbleached white flour
1 cup Peach Jam (page 276)
1 cup ground walnuts
1 teaspoon ground cinnamon

In a food processor, combine butter and cream cheese just until smooth. Gradually add whole wheat pastry flour and unbleached white flour, using an on-off motion, until blended in. Divide dough (which will be soft) into 4 portions. Place each portion in the center of a piece of plastic wrap. Wrap and refrigerate until firm, about 3 hours.

Whisk jam in a small bowl to make it spreadable. In another small bowl, mix together walnuts and cinnamon.

Preheat oven to 350°F. Chill a baking sheet.

Roll dough out, 1 piece at a time, between 2 pieces of wax paper or plastic wrap, into a circle 7 to 8 inches in diameter. Spread ¼ cup jam over entire surface of circle. Sprinkle ¼ cup walnut mixture over jam.

Cut each circle into 8 pie-shaped pieces. Remove each piece from circle, and roll up from large end to point. If dough breaks when you roll it, it's too cold. Let it stand for a few minutes. If it is limp, it's too warm. Refrigerate it for a few minutes. This step is delicate and must be done when the dough is at just the right temperature.

Place rolls on chilled baking sheet, and bake on middle shelf of oven for 20 to 25 minutes, or until lightly browned.

Cool on wire racks.

Makes 32

Strawberry-Apple Strudel

3 apples
2 tablespoons lemon juice, divided
8 sheets filo dough
6 tablespoons butter, melted
1 cup ground walnuts, divided
1 cup quartered fresh strawberries
½ teaspoon ground cinnamon
1 tablespoon quick-cooking tapioca
2 tablespoons honey

Preheat oven to 375°F. Butter a baking sheet.

Peel, core, and coarsely chop apples, placing them into a large bowl. Cover with water, and stir in 1 tablespoon lemon juice.

Lay out 2 sheets of filo dough on a piece of wax paper. Brush with butter, and sprinkle with ⅓ cup nuts. Place 2 more sheets of filo dough on top. Repeat layers until 6 filo sheets have been used. Top with remaining filo sheets, and brush with butter.

Drain apples thoroughly. Toss with strawberries, 1 tablespoon lemon juice, cinnamon, and tapioca. Spread mixture on prepared filo, leaving a 1-inch margin at edges. Drizzle honey over filling.

Using wax paper as a guide, roll filo around filling, folding in ends after first roll. Place on prepared baking sheet, brush top with any remaining butter, and bake on middle shelf of oven for 20 to 25 minutes, or until golden.

Makes 1

VARIATION
Cranberry Strudel: Substitute 1 cup cranberries for strawberries. Boil until they pop, about 10 minutes, and drain well. Increase honey to ¼ cup.

Waikiki Nests

1 recipe for Short-Cut Puff Pastry (page 82) or 1 Basic Flaky Piecrust (page 57)
¼ cup chopped Macadamia nuts, divided
Pineapple Filling (page 271)
ground cloves, for sprinkling
powdered carob, for sprinkling

Preheat oven to 400°F.

Roll out pastry or piecrust into an 8 × 10-inch rectangle. Cut into 6 circles, 3½ to 4 inches in diameter (I use a large mug for cutting), rerolling scraps to make last circle.

Use an upside-down, 6-cup muffin tin to bake nests. Lay a circle of pastry over each cup, pressing to fit and secure it. Bake on top shelf of oven for 15 minutes, or until golden.

As soon as they can be handled, remove nests and cool completely, right side up, on wire racks.

Just before serving, sprinkle insides with 2 tablespoons nuts. Fill with Pineapple Filling. Sprinkle with remaining 2 tablespoons nuts, and top with a light dusting of cloves and carob.

Makes 6

into rings. Bake on middle shelf of oven for 10 minutes. Reduce heat to 375°F, and bake for another 15 minutes. Turn 2-inch rounds over. Continue to bake 15 minutes longer.

Cool on a wire rack. Remove 2-inch rounds. With a sharp knife, carefully cut out uncooked pastry from inside shells.

Just before serving, divide Pastry Cream among shells. Top with raspberries, Raspberry Sauce, and rounds.

Makes 6

Baklava

¾ cup butter, melted
2½ cups ground walnuts
1 tablespoon ground cinnamon
10 sheets filo dough
½ cup honey, warmed
¾ cup honey
1 teaspoon lemon juice

Preheat oven to 350°F. Brush bottom and sides of a 12 × 9 × 2-inch pan with a little butter.

In a medium-size bowl, mix together walnuts and 2½ teaspoons cinnamon.

Halve filo sheets crosswise. (There are now 20 sheets to work with.) Keep sheets wrapped in a slightly damp towel until you need them. Put 1 sheet on bottom of prepared pan, and brush with butter. Repeat until there are 7 layers of filo dough. Sprinkle 6 heaping tablespoons nut mixture over filo. Dribble 2 tablespoons warmed honey over nuts. Add 2 filo sheets, brushing each with butter. Repeat layers of nut mixture, honey, and 2 filo sheets until there are 4 layers of the nut mixture. Top with remaining 7 filo sheets, brushing each sheet with butter as you add it.

Raspberry *Vol au Vents*

1 recipe for Short-Cut Puff Pastry (page 82)
2 cups Pastry Cream (page 272)
1½ cups fresh raspberries
1½ cups Raspberry Sauce (page 271)

Preheat oven to 425°F.

Roll out puff pastry to a ³⁄₁₆-inch thickness. Cut 12 3-inch rounds from pastry. (You may have to reroll scraps to get 12 rounds.) Place 6 of them on a baking sheet. Cut 2-inch rounds out of centers of the remaining 6, and set aside. (You now have 6 rings.)

Place 3-inch rings on top of 3-inch rounds. With a sharp knife, cut an indentation into rounds, tracing around insides of rings. Using cold water, seal rings to rounds by molding both insides and outsides of rings together with wet fingers. Put 2-inch rounds back

With a sharp knife, cut through pastry to bottom of pan, dividing baklava into 12 equal pieces. Bake on middle shelf of oven for about 35 minutes, or until top is crisp and golden.

Combine ¾ cup honey, remaining ½ teaspoon cinnamon, and lemon juice in a small saucepan. Bring to a boil, and cook for 2 minutes, stirring constantly. Pour over baked baklava. Cool before serving.

12 servings

Profiteroles

1 recipe for Basic Cream Puff
  Pastry (page 82)
1 quart Lemon Ice Cream
  (page 123) or French Vanilla Ice
  Cream (page 131)
1¾ cups Apricot Sauce (page 269)

Preheat oven to 400°F.

Drop batter by heaping teaspoonfuls onto ungreased baking sheets. Bake on middle shelf of oven for about 20 minutes, or until lightly browned.

Cool on wire racks.

Split each profiterole crosswise with a sharp knife. Quickly fill each pastry with 1 to 2 tablespoons of Lemon or French Vanilla Ice Cream. Replace tops. Freeze on baking sheet.

When Profiteroles are firmly frozen, store in plastic bags in freezer.

When ready to serve, remove from freezer, and top with Apricot Sauce.

Makes about 3 dozen

Swan Lake

These swan-shaped cream puffs on a "lake" of blueberry sauce are both decorative and delicious.

1 recipe for Basic Cream Puff Pastry (page 82)
3 cups fresh blueberries
½ cup honey
½ teaspoon ground cinnamon
1 cup water
2 tablespoons cornstarch
2 cups heavy cream
2 tablespoons honey
1 teaspoon vanilla extract
¼ cup Coconut Sugar (page xxii), optional

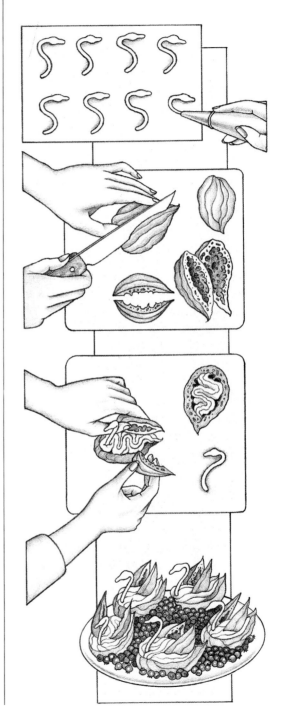

Preheat oven to 400°F. Butter 2 baking sheets.

To shape bodies, arrange 12 heaping tablespoons of batter on a baking sheet. Form with backs of 2 spoons into a tear shape (one end slightly pointed). Bodies should be a bit bigger than a large egg. Bake for 25 to 30 minutes on top shelf of oven, or until lightly browned, doubled in size, and firm.

Prick both sides with the point of a paring knife, and then return to oven for a few minutes. Remove from baking sheet, and cool completely on wire racks.

To make necks, fill a pastry tube half full of batter and fit with a plain round nozzle. Pipe 12 *s*-shapes on baking sheet, going back over them 3 times so that they are about as thick as a pencil. Pipe a bit extra at the top of each *s* for the swan head. The completed *s*-shapes should be about 3 inches long. Bake for 18 minutes on top shelf of oven, or until lightly browned and crisp.

Cool completely on wire racks.

To make blueberry "lake," combine blueberries, ½ cup honey, and cinnamon in a medium-size saucepan. Pour water into a cup, and stir in cornstarch until dissolved; then pour mixture into pan. Cook over medium-high heat, stirring constantly, until mixture bubbles and thickens. Continue to cook for 2 minutes. Remove from heat, and chill. (Sauce may be pureed, if desired.)

Whip cream in a chilled medium-size bowl until soft peaks form. Beat in 2 tablespoons honey and vanilla. Keep refrigerated until ready to use.

To assemble, cut swan bodies in half crosswise. Cut top halves of bodies in half lengthwise. Fill bottoms with cream, heaping in a mound. Place top halves on each side to resemble wings. Tuck s-shapes into cream, head-sides up, to complete swans. Spoon sauce on a large platter or on individual plates, and float swans on top. Sprinkle with Coconut Sugar, if desired.

Makes about 12

CHAPTER
5

The Proof
of the Pudding

I must admit that puddings are among my favorite desserts. There's something down-home, basic, and appealing about them, and so many good puddings can be made with no fuss that they're obvious choices for busy-day treats.

You can use whole eggs, egg yolks, cornstarch, arrowroot, or flour as a thickener for puddings, depending on the type you're making and the thickness you wish to attain. I seldom use flour in puddings since it requires additional cooking to avoid a raw taste, and it's higher in calories than either cornstarch or arrowroot, which I use instead.

If you're converting a recipe from flour to another liaison, remember that the thickening power differs with each one. Two teaspoons of cornstarch does the thickening job of 1 tablespoon of flour; and 1 teaspoon of arrowroot replaces 2 teaspoons of cornstarch.

CUSTARDS

Among the loveliest of many delightful desserts, custard, which can be cooked on top of the stove or baked in the oven, is the base for many other types of puddings. It's usually made with egg yolks (but whole eggs can be used) and either milk or cream. A sweetener and a flavoring are added. When I'm dieting, I use whole eggs and milk to make the pudding because they have less fat and fewer calories.

The ratio for a medium-thick custard is one egg or two egg yolks for every cup of milk. If you prefer a firmer custard, or if the pudding is to

Peaches 'n' Cream Molded Pudding with
  Honey Almonds   Page 108

97

be molded, use more eggs and a tea-spoon of cornstarch to stabilize and thicken it.

To make custard, beat the eggs or egg yolks just until they're mixed, never to the frothy stage. Then add milk or cream. Do this gradually if the milk has been scalded first, a procedure that cuts down on the cooking time considerably when a custard is to be baked. If the mixture is stringy or has unpleasant pieces of egg floating in it, strain it before proceeding with the recipe.

Fill the dish in which you're going to bake custard two-thirds to three-quarters full. To prevent the eggs from curdling, place the dish of custard into a slightly larger pan, then add water to the pan to just slightly above the depth of the custard mixture. This provides a buffer against the heat while still al-lowing the custard to cook.

Custard is gently cooked in a slow oven. The time varies, depending on the number of eggs used (the more eggs the shorter the cooking time), whether the milk was scalding when it was mixed with the eggs, and the size of the custard. Individual custards, of course, take considerably less baking time. Custard is done when there's just a small pool of liquid visible in the center. This liquid will cook after you've removed the custard from the oven.

Boiled custard (also called stirred custard or stove-top custard) isn't boiled, but rather slowly cooked, usually in the top of a double boiler, over (but not in) simmering (not boiling) water.

When boiled custard just coats a metal spoon, it should be removed from the heat. It will thicken substantially as it cools.

If custard curdles or has a "tough" texture, chances are it's either overcooked or was cooked too rapidly at too high a temperature. Overcooking may also make a boiled custard lumpy or cause a baked custard to become porous and watery.

BREAD PUDDINGS

These long-favored members of the pudding family are made with fresh or stale bread, toasted or untoasted, crum-bled or broken into chunks. You can dress them up with meringues or sauces, or serve them plain. You may want to make a bread pudding that's filled with succulent fruit or you may prefer it flavored with just a dash of cinna-mon or some other spice.

Bread pudding is a form of custard. The basic ingredients are bread, egg, milk or cream, sweetener, and flavoring. But the dish in which bread pudding is baked is placed directly on an oven shelf to cook, rather than in a pan of water, because the bread soaks up much of the custard during baking and acts as a buffer between the heat and the delicate egg mixture.

I usually bake bread pudding in a glass casserole so I can observe whether the bottom and sides are browning evenly as well as the top. If you do this, lower the oven temperature by 25 degrees. When a knife inserted in the center of a bread pudding comes out clean, the pudding should be done to perfection. I usually serve bread pudding warm or hot for maximum flavor, but when there's leftover pudding, I enjoy it chilled, adorned with whipped cream or ice cream.

TRIFLES

I always serve these exquisitely handsome desserts in a glass bowl so that their beautiful layers can be appreciated. Trifles are made from layers of cake, occasionally preserves, fruit, and pudding. First the cake (usually a plain yellow cake) is arranged on the bottom of the dish and sprinkled with some kind of liquid (generally a bit of fruit juice). A layer of jam, preserves, or puree may then be spread on the cake. This is followed by a layer of fruit and finally one of pudding or custard. The layers are repeated until the dish is full. The trifle is then chilled.

Trifles are usually served with whipped cream topping and sometimes decorated with fruit or nuts. These quite simple puddings are impressive desserts.

SOUFFLÉS

There are two types of soufflés, and they have little in common but a name. The cold, or gelatin-based soufflé

is discussed in the chapter on chilled and frozen desserts. The hot soufflé is really a pudding. I've seen experienced cooks wince at the very mention of a hot soufflé, yet it's not a difficult dish to master.

Two things will make the difference between a successful hot soufflé and a flop. First, you must beat the egg whites until peaks form. Second, you must fold the beaten whites into the other ingredients (as shown on page xiii) quickly and efficiently so that the air you've beaten in won't be released. Do these two things right, and your soufflé will rise to magnificent heights.

There are a few hot soufflés that require a soufflé collar, but for the most part, if the pan is filled about three-quarters full of batter, the soufflé will rise just enough to take it about an inch above the rim of the dish.

Soufflé dishes are available in many sizes ranging from a pint to several quarts. If you don't have one, an ordinary ovenproof glass dish or casserole will do nicely. If you use a glass dish, though, lower the oven temperature about 25 degrees.

A soufflé must be served at once, for it is quick to deflate after baking.

RICE PUDDINGS

Rice combined with milk and eggs (a custard base) and a few other ingredients to make a pudding is just another wonderful use for this basic food.

If you make rice pudding on the top of the stove, it should be just thick enough to mound when you spoon it into a dish. The ovencooked renditions should be thicker. I sometimes blend a teaspoon of softened gelatin into a stove-top rice pudding, and then mold and chill it. It looks attractive when it's unmolded and topped with fruit or whipped cream.

Rice puddings aren't light in texture. Their substantial character makes them good choices to end light meals.

TAPIOCA PUDDINGS

Old-fashioned tapioca puddings are made with pearl tapioca. They take a little longer to prepare because the tapioca must be soaked for at least two hours before it's added to the rest of the ingredients, while the instant tapioca, although not instant as its name implies, can be added to the ingredients after just five minutes of soaking. Pearl tapioca is coarser than the more modern, instant variety and produces a thicker pudding.

This stove-top pudding can be made fluffy by adding one stiffly beaten egg white after the pudding has cooled.

COBBLERS

These deep-dish dessert puddings feature a fruit and a biscuit dough cooked in layers. In some recipes the fruit goes in first; in others the dough is put on the bottom of the pan. Whatever the sequence, cobblers are at their best served warm with a sauce, nut butter, whipped cream, or ice cream topping.

STEAMED PUDDINGS

To make a steamed pudding, you need at least one mold, a cover for the mold (I use buttered wax paper and foil), a trivet or rack on which to place it, and a large, heavy, covered pan in which to steam the pudding. Butter the inside of the mold and sprinkle it with ground nuts or coconut sugar to prevent sticking.

After combining the ingredients, fill the mold two-thirds full. Put the wax paper (butter-side down) over the top of the mold. Place the foil over the wax paper, and tie it in place with a piece of string. Put the trivet or rack in the large pan; place the filled mold on the trivet; and add boiling water to a level halfway up the sides of the mold. If you're steaming more than one pudding at a time, be sure to allow space between the molds for the steam to circulate.

A steamed pudding is started on high heat and kept at that temperature for about 30 minutes, then the heat is reduced and the pudding gently cooked to a delicious tenderness. After about three hours, the pudding should be done. Take it out of the large pan, remove the cover from the mold, and let the pudding stand for about ten minutes. This will allow the steam to escape and make unmolding easier.

Steamed puddings have a very heavy texture and so are served in small amounts.

A HELPFUL HINT

Cooked puddings, especially those of the custard type, often form a skin as they cool. There are two ways to avoid this: You can pour a very thin layer of milk over the top of the pudding while it's still hot. Then just before serving, stir this topping in well. Or you can cover the pudding with a piece of plastic wrap that just touches the top of the pudding, removing it at serving time.

Basic Rice Pudding

2 eggs
⅓ cup honey
2 cups milk
1 teaspoon vanilla extract
2 cups cooked brown rice
½ cup raisins, plumped
½ teaspoon ground cinnamon

Preheat oven to 325°F.

In a 2-quart casserole, beat together eggs and honey. Beat in milk and vanilla. Stir in rice, raisins, and cinnamon. Bake on middle shelf of oven for about 1 hour and 10 minutes, or until a knife inserted near the center comes out clean.

Serve warm or chilled.

6 servings

VARIATIONS

Pineapple Rice Pudding: Mix in ½ cup well-drained unsweetened crushed pineapple along with raisins.
Carob Chip Rice Pudding: Substitute ½ cup milk carob chips for raisins, and omit cinnamon.

Basic Tapioca Pudding 1

¼ cup quick-cooking tapioca
3 cups milk
¼ cup honey
1 egg, beaten
1½ teaspoons vanilla extract

In a large saucepan, combine tapioca, milk, honey, and egg. Set aside for 5 minutes.

Bring milk mixture to a boil over medium heat, stirring constantly.

Remove from heat, and add vanilla. Cool for 20 minutes.

Stir well, and turn into a medium-size bowl. Chill if not serving immediately.

6 servings

VARIATIONS

Orange Tapioca: Substitute 1 teaspoon orange extract for vanilla extract. Fold 1 peeled, seeded, chunked orange into slightly cooled pudding.
Cinnamon Raisin Tapioca: Stir 1 teaspoon ground cinnamon into pudding while cooking. Stir ½ cup raisins into slightly cooled pudding.

Basic Tapioca Pudding 2

¾ cup small pearl tapioca
3 cups milk
4 eggs, separated
½ cup honey
1½ teaspoons vanilla extract
⅛ teaspoon cream of tartar

Place tapioca in a small bowl, and soak in enough water to cover for 2 hours, or according to directions on package.

Drain well, and mix with milk in top of double boiler set over hot water. Cover, and cook for 1½ hours.

Remove from heat, and allow to cool slightly.

In a medium-size bowl, beat together egg yolks, honey, and vanilla. Mix into cooked tapioca, return to heat, and cook ½ hour longer.

In another medium-size bowl, beat egg whites and cream of tartar until stiff peaks form.

Preheat oven to 350°F.

Alternate layers of tapioca mixture and beaten egg whites in a 2½-quart baking dish, beginning with tapioca and ending with egg whites. Bake on middle shelf of oven for 20 to 25 minutes.

6 servings

Basic Vanilla Pudding

¼ cup cornstarch
2½ cups milk, divided
¼ cup honey
1 egg yolk, beaten
2 teaspoons vanilla extract

In a small bowl, dissolve cornstarch in ½ cup milk, stirring until smooth.

In a medium-size saucepan, combine 2 cups milk, honey, and cornstarch mixture. Bring to a boil over medium heat, stirring constantly.

Place egg yolk into a small bowl. Gradually pour ¼ cup hot mixture into egg yolk, whisking as you do so. Return to saucepan, and simmer for 2 minutes, stirring constantly.

Remove from heat, and mix in vanilla. Chill before serving.

4 servings

VARIATIONS
Dieters' Vanilla Pudding: Use skim milk, and omit egg.
Basic Carob Pudding: Omit egg yolk,
reduce vanilla to 1 teaspoon, and add 2 tablespoons Basic Carob Syrup (page xviii) along with vanilla.

Apple Tapioca

2 cups milk
3 tablespoons quick-cooking tapioca
2 apples
⅓ cup water
1 egg, separated
⅓ cup honey, slightly warmed
¼ teaspoon ground cinnamon
½ teaspoon vanilla extract

Pour milk into a medium-size bowl, and stir in tapioca. Let stand while peeling and dicing apples.

Combine apples and water in the top of a double boiler. Over direct heat, bring apple mixture to a boil. Cook over medium heat, stirring often, for 5 minutes, or until apples are tender and water has evaporated.

Add egg yolk, honey, and cinnamon to milk mixture, and beat until well blended. Pour into apples. Set pan over simmering water, and cook for 15 minutes, or until thickened, stirring often.

Remove from heat, and stir in vanilla. Let mixture cool slightly.

In a small bowl, beat egg white until stiff peaks form. Fold egg white into warm pudding until well blended. Chill pudding before serving.

5 to 6 servings

Blueberry Flummery

This dessert is equally good served warm with a spoonful of lemon sherbet on top or chilled with a topping of lemon-flavored whipped cream.

3½ cups fresh or unsweetened frozen
    wild blueberries (1 pound)
¾ cup water, divided
¼ cup honey
1 tablespoon lemon juice
½ teaspoon ground cinnamon
3 tablespoons cornstarch

Place blueberries into a medium-size saucepan. Add ½ cup water, and cook over medium heat, while stirring, until berries yield their juice, about 5 minutes.

Add honey, lemon juice, and cinnamon. Simmer 2 minutes longer. (At this point, berries can be pureed in a blender, if desired. It's best to do this in 2 batches, since hot mixtures splatter. Return berry puree to saucepan.)

Combine ¼ cup water with cornstarch in a cup. Stir until cornstarch is dissolved. Add to blueberries, and cook, while stirring, until mixture bubbles and thickens. Simmer over low heat for 2 minutes.

Spoon into dessert dishes.

5 to 6 servings

VARIATION
Blue Angel Parfaits: Alternate layers of cooled Blueberry Flummery with cooled Basic Vanilla Pudding (page 103) in parfait glasses. Top with whipped cream and whole blueberries or a ripe sweet cherry with stem.

10 servings

Butter Pecan Pudding

¼ cup cornstarch
2 cups milk
⅓ cup honey
3 tablespoons butter, melted and
    cooled
1 egg yolk
2 teaspoons molasses
½ cup chopped pecans
1 teaspoon vanilla extract
5 pecan halves

In a medium-size bowl, stir cornstarch into milk until completely dissolved. Add honey, butter, egg yolk, and molasses, and beat with egg beater or electric mixer until well blended. Pour into a medium-size saucepan, and cook over medium heat, stirring constantly, until mixture bubbles and thickens.

Remove from heat, and stir in pecans and vanilla. Spoon pudding into 5 sherbet glasses. Top each serving with a pecan half, and chill.

5 servings

Carob Custard
with Orange Topping

2½ cups milk
¼ cup honey
2 tablespoons Basic Carob Syrup
    (page xviii)
5 eggs
1 teaspoon vanilla extract
2 cups Orange Topping (page 272)

Preheat oven to 350°F.

In a medium-size saucepan, heat milk, honey, and carob syrup to scalding. Remove from heat.

In a medium-size bowl, beat eggs well. Stir in vanilla. Add 1 cup of the scalded milk mixture, a little at a time, whisking constantly. Return to pan, stirring constantly. Turn into a 1½-quart casserole. Place in a pan of hot water, and bake on middle shelf of oven for about 1 hour and 10 minutes, or until a knife inserted near the center comes out clean.

Cool completely, and chill. Serve with Orange Topping.

8 servings

Nesselrode Pudding

There are many kinds of Nesselrode Pudding. Each of them contains some kind of chopped cookie, nuts, and fruit with a creamy filling. The version I've developed is one of the easiest to make, and yet it comes off as an elegant company dessert.

    2 cups chopped Minute Macaroons
      (page 219)
    1 cup halved and pitted fresh sweet
      cherries
    ½ cup chopped pecans or pecan
      halves
    ¼ cup cold water
    1 envelope unflavored gelatin
    2 cups milk
    ½ cup honey
    2 eggs, beaten
    1 teaspoon vanilla extract
      fresh sweet cherries (optional)

Place macaroons, cherries, and pecans into a 1½ or 2-quart mold.

Pour cold water into a cup, and sprinkle gelatin on top. Let stand for a few minutes to soften.

Heat milk and honey in top of a double boiler set over simmering water.

Slowly pour hot milk mixture into beaten eggs while whisking or beating. Return mixture to double boiler, and cook, stirring constantly, until custard thickens and coats the back of the spoon.

Remove from heat, and stir in vanilla and gelatin. Pour custard over cookies, cherries, and pecans, and stir just to mix. Chill pudding until firm about 4 hours.

Unmold onto a plate. If desired, decorate with additional cherries.

6 to 8 servings

Cranapple Kissel   Page 112

Cherry Pineapple Cobbler

3½ cups pitted frozen sweet cherries
　　(1 pound), thawed and drained
　　with juice reserved
　1 can (8 ounces) unsweetened
　　crushed pineapple, drained with
　　juice reserved
　⅓ cup water
　4 teaspoons cornstarch
　2 tablespoons honey
　½ teaspoon vanilla extract
1¼ cups whole wheat flour
　1 teaspoon baking soda
　¼ teaspoon ground cinnamon
　1 tablespoon butter, melted
　2 tablespoons honey
　⅓ cup half-and-half
　1 egg
　　heavy cream (optional)

Preheat oven to 375°F. Lightly butter an 8 × 8 × 2-inch baking dish.

Combine cherry juice, pineapple juice, and water in a jar with a tight-fitting lid. Add cornstarch, and shake until blended. Pour into a medium-size saucepan. Add cherries, pineapple, and 2 tablespoons honey. Cook over medium heat until bubbly and thick. Add vanilla.

In a medium-size bowl, sift together flour, baking soda, and cinnamon. Add butter, 2 tablespoons honey, half-and-half, and egg, and blend just until dry ingredients are moistened.

Pour cherry-pineapple mixture into prepared baking dish. Place 6 even spoonfuls of dough over fruit, and bake for about 25 minutes, or until topping is lightly browned.

Serve warm topped with cream.

6 servings

Crème Brulée

10 egg yolks
　⅓ cup honey
　2 tablespoons vanilla extract
　1 quart milk
　¼ cup maple syrup or date sugar

Preheat oven to 325°F.

In a large bowl, beat egg yolks until lemon colored. Beat in honey and vanilla.

In a medium-size saucepan, heat milk to scalding. Slowly pour milk into egg yolks, whisking constantly. Pour mixture into a 1½-quart casserole.

Place casserole in a pan, then place in oven, and fill pan with water halfway to top of casserole. Bake for about 2 hours, or until custard is firm in center.

Remove from oven and cool. Refrigerate to chill.

Brush top of chilled pudding with maple syrup or date sugar. Place directly under broiler for 1 to 3 minutes. Chill.

6 servings

Floating Island

CUSTARD BASE
2 cups half-and-half
2 tablespoons honey
6 egg yolks
1 teaspoon vanilla extract
MERINGUES
3 egg whites
⅛ teaspoon cream of tartar
2 tablespoons honey

To make the base: In a medium-size saucepan, heat half-and-half and honey until scalding.

In a medium-size bowl, whisk egg yolks. Gradually add half-and-half mixture, whisking constantly. Cook in top of double boiler set over, but not touching, simmering water, stirring constantly, until mixture thickens and coats the back of the spoon.

Remove from heat, and stir in vanilla. Turn into a shallow dish. Cover, and chill for at least 2 hours.

To make the meringues: In a medium-size bowl, beat together egg whites and cream of tartar until foamy. Add honey, and continue to beat until stiff peaks form.

In a large skillet, simmer enough water to allow egg whites to float easily without touching bottom. Divide beaten egg whites into 6 portions. Slide 3 portions into simmering water, and cook for 5 minutes, turning once.

Remove with slotted spoon, and drain on paper toweling. Place on top of chilled custard base, and repeat with remaining 3 portions of egg white. Chill, or serve immediately.

6 servings

German Red Fruit Pudding

If desired, this pudding can be pureed, although I prefer it chunky style.

2 cups water, divided
½ cup quick-cooking tapioca
2 cups ripe fresh red currants (blueberries may be substituted)
2 cups fresh raspberries
½ cup honey, or to taste

Pour 1 cup water into a small bowl. Add tapioca, and let stand a few minutes to soften.

Combine fruit with remaining 1 cup water in a large saucepan. Bring to a simmer. Stir in tapioca mixture, and cook, stirring constantly, until mixture bubbles and thickens. Remove from heat, and stir in honey. Chill.

Red Fruit Pudding can be served alone or with Custard Sauce (page 268). It can also be used as a topping for plain cakes or ice cream.

Yields about 1½ quarts

Peaches 'n' Cream Molded Pudding with Honey Almonds

    3 large ripe peaches (6 un-
       sweetened canned peach halves
       may be substituted)
 1½ cups water
   ½ cup honey
   ½ cup orange juice
   2 envelopes unflavored gelatin
   1 cup sour cream or yogurt
   ½ teaspoon almond extract
   2 tablespoons butter
   ⅓ cup sliced almonds
   2 tablespoons honey

    Peel and halve peaches. Remove pits. Place peaches into a medium-size saucepan. Add water and ½ cup honey. Simmer, uncovered, for 45 minutes, or until peaches are tender when pierced with a knife. (If using canned peaches, reduce time to 20 minutes.) Drain peaches, reserving liquid.

    Pour orange juice into a cup and sprinkle gelatin on top. Set aside for a few minutes to soften.

    Measure poaching liquid; if less than 1½ cups, add water to make up the difference.

    Dice 1 peach (2 halves), and spoon into a 1½-quart mold. Puree remaining peaches in a blender or food processor.

    Add, one at a time, poaching liquid, gelatin mixture, sour cream or yogurt, and almond extract. Process until blended. Pour into mold over diced peaches. Chill for 4 hours, or until quite firm.

    Unmold onto serving plate.

    In a small skillet, melt butter. Add almonds, and stir constantly over low heat until just golden. Do not brown them. Add 2 tablespoons honey, and continue stirring over low heat for 2 minutes.

    Decorate top of pudding with almonds. Keep chilled until ready to serve.

6 1-cup servings

Molded Peach Bread Pudding with Raspberry Sauce

 1½ cups chunked peaches, peeled
   4 cups Custard Sauce (page 268)
   6 cups whole grain bread cubes
     (about ½ inch) with crusts
   2 cups Raspberry Sauce (page 271)

    Drain peaches thoroughly.

    Preheat oven to 350°F. Generously butter a 2½-quart mold. Cover bottom with wax paper.

In a medium-size bowl, mix together peaches and Custard Sauce. Place a layer of custard/peach mixture on bottom of prepared mold, and top with bread cubes. Continue layering until both custard/peach mixture and bread cubes have been used, ending with custard. Place mold in a baking pan, and fill pan with enough boiling water to almost reach top of mold. Bake on middle shelf of oven for 1 hour and 15 minutes.

Remove from oven and from boiling water. Allow to cool for 1 hour.

Run a knife around edge to free pudding. Turn out onto platter, and pour 1 cup of Raspberry Sauce over pudding. Pass remaining sauce at the table for use on individual servings.

6 servings

Peanut Butter Soufflé

This particularly easy soufflé packs a protein boost. Like all hot soufflés, it must be served the minute you take it out of the oven.

> 2 tablespoons finely chopped
>   peanuts
> 10 egg whites
> ½ teaspoon cream of tartar
> ¾ cup peanut butter
> ½ cup honey

> ¼ teaspoon vanilla extract
> 1 to 1½ cups Carob Fudge Sauce
>   (page 269)
>   chopped peanuts, for
>   sprinkling

Preheat oven to 350°F. Butter a 1½- to 2-quart soufflé dish, and scatter 2 tablespoons peanuts over bottom and sides of dish.

In large bowl of an electric mixer, beat egg whites until foamy throughout. Sprinkle with cream of tartar, and continue beating until stiff peaks form. Do not underbeat. Remove bowl and cover with a plate.

In a large bowl, blend together peanut butter, honey, and vanilla until smooth. Whisk in 1 cup beaten egg whites to lighten mixture, using a wire whisk. Fold in remaining egg whites until just blended, using a rubber spatula. Spoon mixture into prepared soufflé dish, and smooth top. If there are any peaks, they will tend to over-brown. Bake on middle shelf of oven for 45 minutes, or until soufflé has risen, browned, and cracked. The crack should appear dry.

To serve, spoon 2 to 3 tablespoons Carob Fudge Sauce onto bottom of each dessert dish. Top with soufflé, and sprinkle with remaining peanuts.

6 to 8 servings

Deep-Dish Blueberry Pudding

This easy pudding is a delightful base for a scoop of vanilla ice cream.

  3 cups fresh, or frozen and thawed
     blueberries
  ¼ cup honey
  1 tablespoon cornstarch
  ½ cup orange juice
2½ cups soft whole grain bread crumbs
  ½ teaspoon ground allspice
  ½ cup butter, melted

Preheat oven to 375°F.

In a medium-size saucepan, combine blueberries and honey.

In a small bowl, dissolve cornstarch in orange juice. Add to blueberry mixture, and cook over high heat until bubbly and thick, stirring constantly. Set aside.

In a medium-size bowl, mix together bread crumbs, allspice, and butter.

Turn half of the blueberry mixture into an 8 × 5 × 3-inch pan, and top with half of bread mixture. Repeat layers. Bake on middle shelf of oven for 15 minutes.

Serve warm.

6 to 8 servings

Sultana Pudding with Hard Sauce

  ¼ cup ground nuts
  ⅓ cup butter
  ½ cup honey
  3 eggs
  1 teaspoon vanilla extract
2⅓ cups whole wheat pastry flour

  2 teaspoons baking powder
  ½ cup milk
  1 cup golden raisins
  1 cup Hard Sauce (page 270)

Butter the inside of a 2-quart heatproof mold, and sprinkle with nuts.

In a large bowl, beat butter until fluffy. Beat in honey, eggs, and vanilla.

In a medium-size bowl, sift together flour and baking powder. Mix with a fork or whisk to blend. Beat flour mixture and milk alternately into butter mixture, ending with flour. Fold in raisins, and turn into prepared mold, pushing down to fill all corners of mold. Cover with a piece of buttered wax paper, butter-side down, and a piece of foil. Secure with string and steam on top of stove for 2 to 2½ hours, following directions on page 100.

Serve warm with Hard Sauce.

6 to 8 servings

Bartlett Bread Pudding with Meringue

2 cups diced peeled Bartlett pears
1 tablespoon lemon juice
2 cups milk
2 tablespoons butter
1 egg
2 eggs, separated
¼ cup honey
1 teaspoon ground cinnamon
½ teaspoon vanilla extract
5 cups whole grain bread cubes
1 tablespoon honey

Place pears into a medium-size bowl. Cover with cold water, and stir in lemon juice. Set aside.

Preheat oven to 350°F. Butter a 2½-quart casserole.

In a medium-size saucepan, heat milk and butter until milk is hot and butter has melted.

In a large bowl, beat together egg, 2 egg yolks, and ¼ cup honey. Mix in cinnamon, vanilla, bread cubes, drained pears, and milk mixture. Bake in prepared casserole on middle shelf of oven for about 1 hour, or until golden.

In a medium-size bowl, beat egg whites until foamy. Add 1 tablespoon honey, and continue to beat until stiff but not dry. Spread on top of pudding, covering surface to sides of dish. Broil 4 to 5 minutes, or until lightly browned.

8 servings

Old-Fashioned Grapenuts Pudding

⅓ cup butter, softened
½ cup honey
3 eggs, separated
¼ cup lemon juice
1½ teaspoons grated lemon rind
1½ cups milk
3 tablespoons whole wheat flour
⅓ cup plus 1 tablespoon Grapenuts cereal
nutmeg, for sprinkling.

Preheat oven to 325°F. Butter a 2-quart casserole, and place it in a baking pan that will hold it with room on all sides.

Cream butter in a large bowl. Blend in the following ingredients in the order given: honey, egg yolks, lemon juice, lemon rind, milk, flour, Grapenuts. (Mixture may look curdled.)

In a medium-size bowl, beat egg whites until stiff, and then fold into pudding mixture. Spoon pudding into prepared casserole, and sprinkle with nutmeg. Place on middle shelf of oven, and fill baking pan with enough hot water to almost reach top of casserole. Bake for 1 hour, or until top springs back when lightly touched.

This pudding makes its own sauce. Serve warm or chilled.

8 servings

Rice Tart *(Torte di Riso)*

Brown rice gives this pudding a rich caramel color.

3 cups milk
¼ cup brown rice
⅓ cup honey
2 tablespoons butter
1 teaspoon vanilla extract
½ teaspoon almond extract
3 eggs
½ cup sliced almonds

Pour milk into top of a double boiler. Add rice. Set over simmering water, and cook for about 2½ hours, or until rice is quite tender.

Remove from heat. Stir in honey, butter, and vanilla and almond extracts.

Preheat oven to 325°F. Butter a 9- or 10-inch quiche pan.

In a large bowl, beat eggs until frothy and well blended. Add hot milk and rice mixture in a slow stream while beating with a whisk. Stir in almonds. Pour mixture into prepared pan, and bake for 30 minutes.

6 to 8 servings

Strawberry Trifle

1 recipe for Ladyfingers (page 10)
3 cups frozen strawberries, thawed
  with juice
3 cups Creamy Cake Filling
  (page 273)
1 cup heavy cream
1 tablespoon honey
½ teaspoon vanilla extract
8 fresh strawberries (optional)

Line bottom and sides of an 8-cup dish with Ladyfingers. Add 1 cup thawed strawberries and then 1 cup Creamy Cake Filling. Continue layering, ending with Creamy Cake Filling. Chill.

Just before serving, whip cream with honey and vanilla in a medium-size bowl. Arrange whipped cream in scoops on top of pudding. Decorate with fresh strawberries.

8 servings

Super Vanilla Pudding

2 cups milk, divided
2 envelopes unflavored gelatin
1 piece vanilla bean, 4 inches long,
  split
⅓ cup honey
4 eggs
1 cup heavy cream
  fresh fruit (optional)

Pour ½ cup milk into a small bowl. Sprinkle gelatin on top, and set aside for a few minutes to soften.

In a medium-size saucepan, heat 1½ cups milk, vanilla bean, and honey over medium heat until milk is scalding, stirring often. Add softened gelatin, and stir until dissolved. Strain mixture.

In a medium-size bowl, beat eggs until foamy. Slowly pour about ½ cup milk mixture into eggs, stirring constantly. Pour eggs into remaining milk mixture, whisking well. Place in refrigerator until slightly thickened, about 1 hour, stirring every 10 minutes.

Whip cream, in a medium-size bowl, and gently fold into thickened egg mixture. Cover, and refrigerate until set.

If desired, decorate with fruit just before serving.

8 servings

Cranapple Kissel

Tartness is the traditional characteristic of this Russian dessert so rhubarb and cranberries are common ingredients, though apricots and strawberries are delightfully acceptable alternatives even to purists.

2 cups chunked apples (2 large
  apples)
1½ cups fresh cranberries
1¼ cups water
½ cup honey, or more, to taste
¼ cup cornstarch
¼ teaspoon ground cinnamon
1 cup heavy cream

Combine apples, cranberries, and water in a medium-size saucepan. Bring to a boil, and simmer, uncovered, for 10 minutes.

Cool slightly, and then puree mixture in a food processor or blender. Add honey, cornstarch, and cinnamon, and process until well blended. Return to saucepan and bring to a simmer, stirring constantly. Cook for about 2 minutes. Taste to correct seasoning;

add more honey if too tart. Place pan in a bowl of ice water to cool quickly, whisking occasionally.

In a medium-size bowl, whip cream until soft peaks form. Fold 1 cup whipped cream into cooled pudding. Divide pudding among dessert dishes, and top with remaining cream. Refrigerate until ready to serve.

6 to 8 servings

Maple Walnut Pudding Cake

When baked, this pudding forms a cake on top with a sauce beneath.

½ cup milk
2 egg yolks
¾ cup maple syrup
¼ teaspoon maple extract (vanilla extract may be substituted)
1 cup minus 2 tablespoons whole wheat flour
2 teaspoons baking powder
3 tablespoons butter, melted and cooled
1 cup finely chopped walnuts
1⅔ cups hot water

Preheat oven to 350°F. Butter a 2-quart casserole.

Blend together all ingredients except walnuts and hot water. If you wish, you can use a food processor to do this, adding the ingredients in the order given. Pour mixture into prepared casserole, sprinkle walnuts on top, and pour hot water over all. Bake for 35 minutes, or until a cake tester or food pick inserted in the center of the upper portion, the cake part of the pudding, comes out clean.

Serve warm. French Vanilla Ice Cream (page 131) or Lemon Ice Cream (page 123) makes a nice topping.

6 to 8 servings

CHAPTER
6

Ice Cream Parlor Frozen and Chilled Desserts

The Italians claim to have invented ice cream. So do the French and the English. This dessert is so popular, it seems that everyone wants credit for creating it. Dolley Madison introduced this frozen favorite to the United States when she served it at the White House. Since then it has become as American as the apple pie with which it's often served.

Homemade ice cream, correctly prepared, is the queen of desserts. It's relatively easy to make, and lends itself to all manner of innovations. If you have a favorite flavor that has been neglected by ice cream manufacturers, who must cater to the mass taste, you can soon learn to develop your own ice cream specialty. But first, try your hand at some of the recipes in this chapter to get the hang of it.

If you're an ice cream lover, and they are legion, I suggest you invest in an ice cream maker. Briefly, these can be divided into three categories.

First, there is the kind of ice cream maker that contains its own refrigerator unit, so that you don't have to be bothered with ice and salt. It has the disadvantages of being heavy, filling significant counter space, and costing hundreds of dollars. A second type of ice cream maker uses your own kitchen refrigerator freezer as the freezing unit. The capacity of either of these ice cream makers is disappointing; some only make a pint of ice cream at a time.

A third type of ice cream maker requires crushed ice (which *you* have to crush) and rock salt (which you then have to dispose of). But it does come in sizes large enough to make as much as a gallon at one time. Of course, that big a machine presents a storage problem, especially if you have a small kitchen.

I have found a machine that uses ordinary ice cubes and table salt to achieve its freezing capability, is quite inexpensive, and makes about 1½ quarts. It is the Waring Ice Cream Parlor. This is the one I heartily recommend. It makes lovely ice cream.

Several classifications commonly accepted under the umbrella name "ice cream" include: French ice cream which has a custard base enriched with many egg yolks; American ice cream which also has a custard base but uses fewer eggs; and Philadelphia ice cream which contains no eggs at all.

Sherbets have a large proportion of pureed fruit or fruit juices, with some milk or half-and-half added. Sometimes egg whites or gelatin are included as binders. "Sorbet" is the French name for sherbet; however, a sorbet is supposed to be more concentrated than a sherbet, containing a higher proportion of pureed fruit and sweetener and no binders. Ices contain no milk or cream at all; they are not quite as sweet and a bit "icier" than sorbets. That's why ices are especially delightful in the summer, light and refreshing. Granitas (or granités, from the word "grain") are like ices, but with a more granular texture. Originally, they were frozen solid and then scraped with a fork into a serving dish. The impracticality of that soon led to a modification by which they are prepared much like ices and are virtually indistinguishable from them, except that granitas

tend to be made in trendier flavors, such as tangerine or pink grapefruit.

Since ice cream is often a topping on or an ingredient in other desserts, you may find there are times when you want to use store-bought ice cream. If so, I urge you to read the ingredients list on the package carefully, as I always do. The ingredients list doesn't tell the whole story, but it tells a lot. With a little diligent package reading you can find the ice cream manufacturers who use natural flavoring, milk, cream, and fresh fruit. There are even some who are experimenting with honey instead of white sugar and carob instead of chocolate. Except for these departures, however, I think they show very little imagination.

Once a package of store-bought ice cream has been opened, it may pick up flavors from other foods in the freezer and develop ice crystals that spoil its fine texture. To prevent this, place the opened package in a heavy-duty freezer bag and close it tightly.

Homemade ice cream may be made with cream, heavy or light, half-and-half, milk, or any combination of these. A flavoring, frequently fruit, is added, and a sweetener—in this book, honey. Surely a very wholesome dish! Because cream and milk are good mediums for the growth of bacteria, care must always be taken to have all containers, dashers, covers, and so on, absolutely clean. Before beginning to make ice cream, wash all equipment in hot, soapy water, and rinse well in very hot water.

Ice cream is churned while being frozen to give it a smooth texture and to aerate it. If you don't have an ice cream maker, you can achieve almost the same effect by allowing the mixture to freeze to a slush, then beating it smooth, refreezing, rebeating, and so forth. Directions are given at the close of this section.

There are a few kinds of ice cream that needn't be stirred in the making. Generally they contain cream that has been whipped, such as in a frozen mousse.

Salt is added to ice in the freezing of ice creams and sherbets because salt makes ice melt faster thus producing a colder temperature than can be achieved by ice alone. The more salt you use, the faster the ice cream will freeze and the larger will be the ice crystals within the cream. But it takes fine ice crystals to get the smoothest texture, so I suggest you use the least amount of salt that your particular ice cream maker allows, according to manufacturer's instructions. It will take longer to freeze the ice cream, but the finished product will be more velvety.

Of course, ice cream makers that have a built-in refrigerator unit or fit into your freezer eliminate this consideration.

When making a custard-based ice cream, you'll be cooking some of the ingredients. After cooking, the mixture should be thoroughly chilled in the refrigerator before the freezing process is attempted.

Ice cream expands as it freezes, so 1 quart of liquid increases to about 1½ quarts of ice cream, depending on which sort of ice cream maker you use. (Some aerate the mixture more than others.) When filling the container in the ice cream maker, always allow room for this expansion.

If you like pieces of fruit in your ice cream, it's best to add these just after the mixture is frozen so that the particles of fruit do not turn into ice cubes.

After freezing, the ice cream or sherbet is still quite soft and must be stored in the freezer for a few hours to harden, or "ripen."

HOW TO MAKE ICE CREAM WITHOUT A MACHINE

Set the freezer at its coldest setting. Pour the chilled ice cream mixture (using any ice cream or sherbet recipe given in this chapter) into a metal pan of a size so that mixture will be 1½ to 2 inches deep, and freeze. As soon as the mixture becomes slushy, spoon it into a bowl and beat it until smooth. Pour the mixture back into the pan, and repeat the previous steps. Beat three or four times in all. After the last beating, allow the mixture to freeze until almost firm. If there are any chunky ingredients, such as pieces of fruit, fold them in at this point. Smooth the top with a table knife, cover with foil, and let ripen for one hour or more before serving.

Homemade frozen desserts, because they contain no preservatives, are best if eaten within a few days of preparation. You'll find this no hardship at all.

CHILLED DESSERTS

These wonderful gelatin-based desserts can be molded into all sorts of fancy shapes and so look very elegant when served. However, little effort is required to make them. A gelatin dessert can be as simple as fruit juice and sweetener, with pieces of fruit folded in when the mixture has almost set. It can be whipped when half-set to produce a delightfully airy dessert, or whipped cream can be folded in to make a rich mousse. There are countless possibilities, bounded only by the limits of your imagination.

One envelope of unflavored gelatin holds a scant tablespoon, which will jell about 2 cups of liquid. It should be softened in a small amount of liquid before being added to other dessert ingredients. To be certain that it has dissolved completely, which is most important, it's stirred over low heat until the mixture is no longer grainy. I often do this in the top of a small double boiler set over barely simmering water.

Some cooks find a problem in unmolding gelatin desserts. If you lightly oil the interior of the mold with a bland vegetable oil before filling it, the dessert will slide out easily.

When ready to unmold, make certain that the dessert is completely set. The top should be firm to the touch and when jiggled should not slip to one side.

Wet the serving plate on which the dessert is to be unmolded. This will make it easier to center the dessert should it unmold to one side.

Dip a paring knife in warm water, and slip it around the top edge of the mold to a depth of about 1 inch. Then dip the whole mold to within 1 inch of the top in a dishpan of warm (not hot) water. Hold it there for about ten seconds.

Invert the serving plate over the mold, then turn them both so that the mold is on top and the plate below. You should be able to lift off the mold, leaving the dessert on the serving plate. If the dessert does not free itself from the mold, try dipping the mold again in warm water for ten seconds and then inverting it. If necessary, center it on the plate.

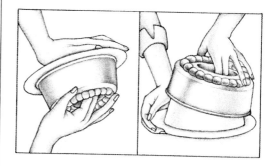

Certain gelatin-based desserts require special techniques for their characteristic look.

A soufflé collar is used on cold soufflés to simulate the puffed appearance of hot soufflés. You can also use a collar for a hot soufflé if you like to help it rise evenly above the dish. To construct the collar, cut a piece of foil

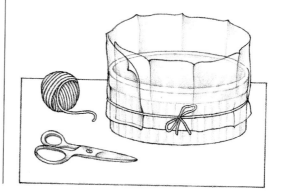

10 inches wide and long enough to encircle the soufflé dish you're using plus 2 inches overlap. Fold the foil lengthwise so that it is doubled (5 inches wide). Secure it around the dish with kitchen twine so that the collar is 3 inches above the top of the dish and 2 inches below. Tape the top of the seam together at the overlap. When you butter or oil the inside of the soufflé dish, do the same for the inside of the collar.

HOW TO MAKE PLAIN FRUIT GELATIN

Use 2 cups fruit juice other than lemon or lime. Sprinkle 1 envelope gelatin over ¼ cup juice. When the gelatin has softened, stir the mixture into the remaining juice. Dissolve gelatin completely by stirring over very low heat. If the juice is tart, add 2 to 3 tablespoons honey and blend well. To make lemon or lime gelatin, you'll have to dilute the juice with water, ½ cup juice to 1½ cups water, using honey to taste, about ⅓ cup. Pour the mixture into a lightly oiled mold or unoiled individual serving dishes.

If desired, fresh fruit and/or nuts can be added, up to 1½ cups. Fold them in when the gelatin is about half-set. Fresh pineapple, figs, and papayas should not be used because they contain an enzyme that inhibits jelling. However, this enzyme is not present in canned pineapple and dried figs or dried papaya, which can be used successfully in gelatin desserts.

For a layered look, prepare one flavor of gelatin and allow it to set until firm in a mold or in individual serving dishes. Then prepare a second mixture using a contrasting color of fruit juice, chill it, and pour it while still liquid over the first mixture. Finally, chill the dessert until the top layer is firm.

If you wish to enhance the natural color of the fruit juice base, one or two drops of natural food coloring may be added.

Chilled desserts look very pretty with a simple decoration of whipped cream or fresh fruit around the edges of the serving plate.

After-Dinner-Mint Ice Cream

2 cups milk
½ cup honey
2 eggs
¼ cup sifted powdered carob
1 tablespoon cornstarch
1½ teaspoons peppermint extract
1 cup half-and-half
1 cup light cream

In a blender container, combine milk, honey, eggs, carob, and cornstarch, and process until well mixed. Pour into a large saucepan, and cook over medium-high heat, while stirring constantly, until mixture bubbles and thickens slightly. Remove from heat, and stir in peppermint extract. Chill mixture in refrigerator.

When chilled, mix in half-and-half and light cream. Pour mixture into an ice cream maker, and freeze according to manufacturer's instructions. If not using an ice cream maker, follow directions for making refrigerator ice cream on page 119.

Yields 1 quart

Ginger-Melon Ice Cream

With its pretty pale orange color and gingery "bite," this ice cream makes the perfect conclusion to an Oriental dinner.

2 cups cubed cantaloupe, loosely packed
1 cup honey
2 teaspoons ground ginger
½ teaspoon grated peeled ginger root, or more, to taste
2 cups light cream

Puree cantaloupe in a food processor or food mill. Transfer to a larger bowl and add the remaining ingredients in the order given. Stir until well blended. Taste to assure that ginger flavor is to your liking; because taste buds are chilled by ice cream, ginger should be pronounced in order to insure a flavorful result. Pour mixture into an ice cream maker, and freeze according to manufacturer's instructions. If not using an ice cream maker, follow directions for making refrigerator ice cream on page 119.

Yields about 5 cups

Hazelnut Ice Cream (Gelato alla Nocciola)

The hazelnuts or filberts required for this recipe are available in many natural foods stores if you can't find them in your supermarket.

1 cup shelled hazelnuts or filberts
2 cups milk
1½ cups light cream
4 eggs
½ cup honey
2 teaspoons vanilla extract

Preheat oven to 350°F.

Arrange nuts in a baking dish in a single layer, and bake for 10 minutes.

Remove from oven, and turn them out onto a rough towel. Rub them together in the towel while still warm to remove dark skins. This is called blanching, although no water is used.

In a blender or food processor, grind the nuts, ½ cup at a time, to a fine powder. Reserve in a small bowl.

Combine milk and cream in top of a double boiler. Set over simmering water, and scald the mixture.

Place eggs into blender container, and whip them. Take off removable part of blender cover, and, with motor running, add half of hot milk mixture and the honey in a slow stream. Pour egg-milk mixture back into top of double boiler, stirring into remaining hot milk. Set over simmering water, and cook, stirring constantly, until mixture thickens and coats the back of the spoon. Remove from heat, and stir in vanilla and ground nuts. Chill.

When chilled, pour mixture into an ice cream maker, and freeze according to manufacturer's instructions. If not using an ice cream maker, follow directions for making refrigerator ice cream on page 119.

Yields about 1 quart

Lemon Ice Cream

2 eggs
½ cup honey
1 cup milk
1 cup heavy cream
¼ cup lemon juice, strained
½ teaspoon lemon extract

In a large bowl, beat together eggs and honey. Add milk, cream, lemon juice, and lemon extract. Beat for 1 minute. Place in freezer until almost firm, 2 to 3 hours.

Remove from freezer, and beat until smooth. Return to freezer for 1 hour.

Remove from freezer, and beat again until smooth. Pour into an 8 × 6½ × 2½-inch pan, and freeze until firm. Cover tightly until ready to serve.

Yields about 1 quart

Strawberry 'n' Banana Ice Cream

The strawberries must marinate overnight, so plan accordingly when making this dessert.

2 cups sliced fresh strawberries
⅓ cup honey
2 ripe bananas
2 cups heavy cream
1 cup light cream
¼ cup honey

Mix strawberries and ⅓ cup honey in a small bowl. Cover, and refrigerate overnight.

Mash strawberries and strain, reserving both juice and pulp separately.

In a medium-size bowl, mash bananas.

Mix in strawberry juice, cream, and ¼ cup honey. Pour mixture into an ice cream maker, and freeze according to manufacturer's instructions. If not using an ice cream maker, follow directions for making refrigerator ice cream on page 119.

When ice cream is finished but still soft, add reserved strawberry pulp, and allow the dasher to distribute pulp throughout.

Yields about ½ gallon

Beautiful Baked Alaska

A handsome dessert that you'll want to make for company. Even though the final preparation must be done just before serving, it takes only a few minutes. When served, the meringue will be warm and the ice cream cold, a triumph of timing!

   3 cups French Vanilla Ice Cream
      (page 131)
   3 cups After-Dinner-Mint Ice Cream
      (page 122)
   5½ × 9½ × 1-inch slice of Italian
      Sponge Cake (page 10)
   5 egg whites
   ¼ teaspoon cream of tartar
   2 tablespoons honey
   ½ teaspoon vanilla extract

Soften French Vanilla Ice Cream. Spread in a layer in an 8½ × 4½ × 2½-inch loaf pan, and freeze solid.

Soften After-Dinner-Mint Ice Cream, spread over the first layer, and freeze solid.

Trim layer of sponge cake to size, wrap, and reserve. Cut a piece of brown paper of the same size, and set it aside.

In a medium-size bowl, beat egg whites until foamy throughout. Sprinkle with cream of tartar, and continue beating until stiff peaks form. Beat in honey and vanilla. Remove beaters, cover bowl with a plate, and refrigerate egg whites until ready to assemble cake. If possible, do this no more than an hour before serving.

When ready to complete recipe, preheat oven to 450°F.

Wet a bread board on both sides, and shake off excess water. Place brown paper on board, and lay cake on top. Unmold ice cream by dipping loaf pan for a few seconds in a pan of warm water, and place loaf of ice cream on cake. (Ice cream must be a solid brick.) Quickly frost ice cream and cake with beaten egg whites, taking care to cover completely.

Bake immediately in top third of oven for 5 minutes, or until meringue is golden.

Remove board from oven, and slip the dessert onto a serving platter. Serve at once, sliced.

6 to 8 servings

Frozen Carob Chippers

A favorite snack for youngsters and some who are not so young.

   2½ cups French Vanilla Ice Cream
      (page 131)
   1 cup milk carob chips
   24 Good Old Butter Cookies (page
      48)

Place ice cream into a medium-size bowl, and allow to soften until it can be stirred. Stir in carob chips. Spread about 3 tablespoons ice cream between 2 cookies to form a sandwich. Repeat with the rest of the cookies. Place on a baking sheet, and freeze until firm. Then wrap each sandwich in foil, and place them all into a plastic bag. Freeze.

Makes 1 dozen

Ice Cream Pie in a Coconut Crust   Page 126

Frozen Ladies

A delicious make-ahead dessert for a balmy summer evening.

  1½ cups milk carob chips
   ½ cup butter
  12 Moist Carob Cupcakes (page 22)
   1 quart French Vanilla Ice Cream
     (page 131), softened

Line a 12-cup muffin tin with paper liners.

In top of a double boiler set over hot water, melt together carob chips and butter. Cool slightly.

While carob mixture is cooling, cut cupcakes in thirds crosswise. Place about 2½ tablespoons of softened ice cream between each layer, and put cupcakes back together. Place into prepared muffin tin. Frost with carob mixture, and freeze.

Makes 1 dozen

125

Frozen Carob Sponge

6 eggs, separated
¼ teaspoon cream of tartar
3 tablespoons honey
2 teaspoons vanilla extract, divided
2 tablespoons Basic Carob Syrup
　(page xviii)
1 cup sifted whole wheat pastry
　flour
1½ cups Peach Preserves (page 276)
½ cup ground walnuts
1½ quarts French Vanilla Ice Cream
　(page 131), frozen in a block
1 cup heavy cream
1 tablespoon honey

Preheat oven to 350°F. Butter and flour an 11½ × 17 × 1-inch pan.

In a medium-size bowl, beat together egg whites and cream of tartar until stiff peaks form.

In a large bowl, beat egg yolks until lemon colored. Add 3 tablespoons honey, 1 teaspoon vanilla, and carob syrup, and beat for another 5 minutes.

In another medium-size bowl, sift flour and then fold into egg yolk mixture. Fold in egg whites. Spread batter in prepared pan, and bake on middle shelf of oven for about 10 minutes, or until cake springs back when lightly pressed with fingertips.

Cool in pan for 10 minutes, and then turn out onto a lightly floured towel to cool completely. Cut off edges of cake, and cut cake into quarters (once across and once lengthwise).

Place preserves into a small bowl, and whisk to make them spreadable. Spread each bottom side of 3 pieces of cake with one-quarter of the preserves. Sprinkle with nuts, using all of them. Place remaining cake on a large piece of foil.

Remove ice cream from freezer, and slice into ½-inch pieces, cutting them to fit cake layers. Place a layer of ice cream slices on cake on foil. Place another piece of cake, preserve-side down, on top of it, followed by another layer of ice cream. Continue until all cake layers are in place, ending with cake. Wrap in foil, and place in freezer.

Just before serving, whip together in a medium-size bowl cream, 1 tablespoon honey, and 1 teaspoon vanilla until soft peaks form. Spread remaining preserves on cake. Top with whipped cream. For an extra-special touch, pipe whipped cream through a pastry bag onto top and sides of frozen sponge. Slice with a sharp knife.

6 to 8 servings

Ice Cream Pie in a Coconut Crust

2½ cups Strawberry 'n' Banana Ice
　Cream (page 123)
2½ cups Blueberry Ice Cream (page
　130)
1 Coconut Crust for a 10-inch pie
　(page 57)
1 cup heavy cream
1 tablespoon honey
½ teaspoon vanilla extract

Place each kind of ice cream into a separate bowl, and allow to soften at room temperature until ice cream can be stirred with a spoon but is still frozen.

Spread a layer of the Strawberry 'n' Banana Ice Cream in the Coconut Crust. Top with a layer of Blueberry Ice Cream. Place pie in freezer.

In a medium-size bowl, whip cream until it forms soft peaks when beater is lifted. Whisk in honey and vanilla.

Remove pie from freezer. Use a pastry decorator or a spoon to arrange cream in an attractive pattern on pie. Return pie to freezer and freeze solid, at least 8 hours. Then cover with plastic wrap. When ready to serve, let pie stand at room temperature until it can be cut with a knife, 5 to 10 minutes. Do not let it get too soft.

Makes 1

Fresh Strawberry Sorbet

A delicious answer to, "What will I do with all these strawberries?"

    4 cups quartered fresh strawberries
    ¾ cup honey (½ cup if strawberries
      are sweet)
    ½ tablespoon lemon juice
    1 cup cold water

In a large bowl, mix together strawberries and honey, and allow to stand for 30 minutes to soften berries.

In a food processor, puree berry mixture in 2 batches. Strain into a large bowl. Stir in lemon juice and

water, and freeze until firm, about 2½ hours.

Remove from freezer, and beat until smooth. Freeze until firm, about 1½ hours.

Remove from freezer, and beat again until smooth. Turn into a 4- or 5-cup container, cover, and freeze.

Yields about 1 quart

Grape Granita

    3 cups red grape juice
    ¼ cup honey
    2 cups water
    1 teaspoon lemon extract
    8 to 10 seedless white grapes, halved

Pour grape juice into a medium-size bowl. Mix honey into grape juice thoroughly. Stir in water and lemon extract. Pour into an 11½ × 9 × 3½-inch metal pan, and freeze until ice crystals begin to form, about 1½ hours.

Remove from freezer, and stir well to break up crystals. Freeze for another 5 hours, breaking up crystals every 30 minutes.

Serve in champagne glasses decorated with grape halves.

8 to 10 servings

VARIATION

Lemon Granita: Use ¾ cup honey, 1½ cups lemon juice, and 3½ cups water. Omit grape juice and lemon extract. Decorate with whole strawberries instead of grape halves.

Orange Ice Cups

A cherry on top of each serving adds a tasty and decorative touch.

3½ cups water, divided
1 envelope unflavored gelatin
8 to 10 oranges
1 cup honey
¼ cup lemon juice

Pour ½ cup water into a small bowl, and sprinkle gelatin on top. Set aside for a few minutes to soften.

Cut oranges into halves, and squeeze until you have 3 cups juice. Set aside. Reserve orange shells.

In a large saucepan, combine 3 cups water and honey. Bring to a boil, and boil for 1 minute.

Remove from heat, and stir in gelatin mixture, mixing until dissolved. Pour into a large bowl. Mix in orange juice and lemon juice, and allow to cool.

Turn into 2 medium-size metal bowls, and place in freezer for 1 hour.

Remove from freezer, and beat. Return to freezer, removing every hour to beat until mixture has been beaten 4 times. Cover, and freeze until firm.

Serve in reserved orange shells.

Yields about ½ gallon or 8 to 10 servings

Frozen Peach Yogurt

3 cups sliced peeled peaches
    (peeled apricots may be
    substituted)
¼ cup honey
½ teaspoon vanilla extract
2 cups yogurt

In a food processor, puree peaches and honey. Strain into a large bowl through a coarse strainer.

Stir in vanilla and yogurt just until blended, and then freeze until just firm.

Remove from freezer, and beat until smooth. Turn into a 6-cup container, cover, and freeze.

Yields 4 to 4½ cups

Lemon and Lime Snow

A light, refreshing dessert that's especially nice for hot summer days.

½ cup cold water
2 envelopes unflavored gelatin
1 cup boiling water
¾ cup honey
½ cup lemon and lime juice
    combined (about 1 lemon and
    3 limes)
2 egg whites
¼ cup sour cream or yogurt
½ teaspoon grated lemon rind
    frozen seedless green grapes
    (page 209), optional

Pour water into a large bowl, and sprinkle gelatin on top. Let stand for a few minutes to soften. Pour in boiling water, and stir until gelatin is completely dissolved. Stir in honey until blended and then lemon and lime juice. Chill in refrigerator until syrupy.

In a small bowl, beat egg whites until stiff but not dry. Fold into chilled gelatin mixture using a whisk. (A spatula will not work well on this mixture.)

Mix sour cream or yogurt with grated lemon rind and fold into pudding. Chill in refrigerator until half-set. Remove and beat until fluffy. Chill until firm.

Spoon into sherbet glasses and, if desired, decorate with frozen grapes.

About 8 servings

Apricot Yogurt Whip

The tangy, slightly tart flavor of this dessert makes it a perfect ending for a rich meal.

½ cup apple juice
1 envelope unflavored gelatin
3 cups halved peeled apricots
2 tablespoons honey
1 teaspoon vanilla extract
1 cup yogurt

Pour apple juice into a small saucepan, and sprinkle gelatin on top. Set aside for 5 minutes to soften.

Puree apricots in a blender or food processor.

In a large bowl, stir together apricot puree, honey, and vanilla.

Heat apple juice until gelatin is dissolved. Cool, and then add to apricot mixture. Beat with an electric beater for 3 minutes. Fold in yogurt, mixing well. Turn into 4 dessert cups and chill until set, about 2 hours.

4 servings

Fancy Peach Mousse

¾ cup orange juice
2 envelopes unflavored gelatin
4 eggs, separated
1½ cups milk
½ cup honey
1 tablespoon light molasses
1 teaspoon rum extract (optional)
⅛ teaspoon cream of tartar
2 tablespoons honey
1 cup heavy cream
20 Ladyfingers (page 10)

Pour orange juice into a small bowl, and sprinkle gelatin on top. Set aside for 5 minutes to soften.

In a medium-size saucepan, beat egg yolks. Add milk, ½ cup honey, and molasses. Cook over low heat, stirring constantly, until mixture begins to thicken and coats the back of the spoon. Mix in gelatin, and stir to dissolve. Add rum extract, if desired. Pour into a large bowl, and chill until thickened but not set, stirring often.

In a medium-size bowl, beat together egg whites and cream of tartar until foamy. Add 2 tablespoons honey, and continue to beat until stiff peaks form.

In another medium-size bowl, beat cream until soft peaks form.

Line a 9-inch springform pan with Ladyfingers.

Fold egg whites, whipped cream, and peaches into gelatin mixture in that order. Turn into prepared pan, and chill until set, about 4 hours.

Remove sides of pan, invert, and remove bottom.

10 to 12 servings

Cranberry-Orange Ripple Sherbet

1 cup Jellied Cranberry Sauce (page 273)
1 teaspoon grated orange rind, divided
1 cup orange juice
1 envelope unflavored gelatin
¾ cup honey
2½ cups half-and-half

Mash cranberry sauce in a small bowl, blending in ½ teaspoon orange rind. Refrigerate until needed.

Pour orange juice into top of a double boiler. Add remaining ½ teaspoon orange rind. Sprinkle gelatin on top. Set over hot water, and stir until gelatin is dissolved. Blend in honey. Stir in half-and-half. Pour mixture into an ice cream maker, and freeze according to manufacturer's instructions. If not using an ice cream maker, follow directions for making refrigerator ice cream on page 119.

When ice cream is frozen but still soft, fold in reserved cranberry mixture so that it forms ripples throughout. Do not blend completely.

Yields about 1½ quarts

Blueberry Ice Cream

2 cups fresh blueberries
½ cup honey
½ cup water
½ teaspoon ground cinnamon
2 cups half-and-half
1 cup light cream
¼ cup honey

In a medium-size saucepan, combine blueberries, ½ cup honey, water, and cinnamon. Bring to a boil, while stirring, and simmer, uncovered, for 5 minutes. Strain, reserving both berries and juice separately. Cool.

Combine blueberry juice, half-and-half, light cream, and ¼ cup honey, stirring to blend well, and pour mixture into an ice cream maker. Freeze according to manufacturer's instructions. If not using an ice cream maker, follow directions for making refrigerator ice cream on page 119.

When ice cream is finished but still soft, add reserved blueberry pulp, and allow the dasher to distribute pulp throughout.

Yields about ½ gallon

French Vanilla Ice Cream

1 cup milk
1 piece vanilla bean, 4 inches long,
    split lengthwise
1 cup light cream
½ cup honey
    about 1½ cups half-and-half,
    divided
8 egg yolks
    vanilla extract, to taste, up to 2
    teaspoons (optional)

In a blender container, combine milk and vanilla bean. Blend until bean is reduced to bits. Vanilla bean can also be crushed using a mortar and pestle and then stirred into milk. Strain mixture, through a tea strainer into top of a double boiler. Add light cream, honey, and 1 cup half-and-half. Set over boiling water, and cook until mixture is scalding, stirring to blend in honey.

Place egg yolks into a cup measure. Add enough half-and-half to make 1 cup. Pour this mixture into blender container, and blend until well mixed. Remove insert in blender cover and, with motor running, pour hot cream mixture into egg yolk mixture in a slow, steady stream. (Transferring hot cream to a pitcher first makes this step easier.) Cream and eggs can also be combined gradually using a whisk or egg beater.

Return mixture to top of double boiler. Set over boiling water, and reduce heat so that water only simmers. Cook until mixture thickens and coats the spoon, while stirring constantly, about 8 minutes.

Remove from heat, and chill thoroughly in refrigerator.

When ready to freeze, taste to correct seasoning. If desired, blend in vanilla extract to taste. Pour custard into an ice cream maker, and freeze according to manufacturer's instructions. If not using an ice cream maker, follow directions for making refrigerator ice cream on page 119.

Raspberry Sauce (page 271) makes a nice accompaniment to this popular ice cream.

Yields 1½ quarts

Fresh Nectarine Mousse with Strawberries

½ cup cold water
2 envelopes unflavored gelatin
½ cup milk
5 to 6 ripe nectarines
⅓ cup honey
2 egg whites
1 cup heavy cream
1 cup thickly sliced fresh
    strawberries
    unhulled whole fresh
    strawberries

Pour water into a small bowl, and sprinkle gelatin on top. Let stand for a few minutes to soften.

Warm milk in top of a double boiler set over hot water. Add gelatin to milk, and stir over hot water until completely dissolved.

Peel nectarines, and slice them into a 2-cup measure, packing tightly, until it is filled. Chop nectarine slices in a food processor or blender. Add honey. Blend but do not puree. There should be small pieces of fruit in the mixture. Place chopped nectarines into a large bowl, and stir in gelatin.

Beat egg whites in a small bowl until stiff but not dry. Fold into fruit.

In a medium-size bowl, whip cream until soft peaks form. Fold into fruit. Pour into an oiled 2-quart mold. Fold in sliced strawberries, and chill until firm.

Unmold onto serving dish. Decorate top of mousse and rim of plate with unhulled strawberries.

8 servings

Piña Colada Soufflé

¼ cup cold water
2 envelopes unflavored gelatin
1 can (20 ounces) unsweetened
    crushed pineapple
½ cup honey
5 egg whites
¼ teaspoon cream of tartar
1 cup yogurt
2 cups unsweetened flaked coconut,
    divided
1 teaspoon rum extract
    fresh cherries (optional)

Construct a soufflé collar (page 120), and secure it around a 1½-quart soufflé dish. Oil inside of dish and collar.

Pour water into a small bowl, and sprinkle gelatin on top. Let stand for a few minutes to soften.

Drain pineapple, reserving juice and pulp separately.

In a small saucepan, combine pineapple juice and honey, and stir over low heat until blended and hot. Remove from heat. Stir in gelatin mixture until completely dissolved.

In a medium-size bowl, beat egg whites until foamy. Sprinkle with cream of tartar, and continue beating until stiff.

In a large bowl, combine pineapple pulp with yogurt, stirring until blended. Reserve 2 tablespoons coconut, and stir the rest into pineapple. Add rum extract. Gradually add juice-gelatin mixture, stirring until well blended. Fold in egg whites. Spoon mixture into prepared soufflé dish, and sprinkle top with reserved coconut. Chill until set, 6 to 8 hours.

To serve, remove collar and decorate soufflé with cherries, if desired.

8 servings

Strawberry Soufflé with Raspberry Sauce

    3 cups fresh strawberries
    1 cup cold water
    3 envelopes unflavored gelatin
   10 eggs, separated
    ⅔ cup honey
    2 cups heavy cream
    ¼ teaspoon cream of tartar
    1 cup Raspberry Sauce (page 271)

Prepare a 2-quart soufflé dish with a collar (page 120).

Puree strawberries in a food processor.

Pour water into a small bowl, and sprinkle gelatin on top. Set aside for a few minutes to soften.

Beat egg yolks and honey in top of a double boiler set over hot (not boiling) water for 5 minutes. Remove from heat.

In a small saucepan, heat gelatin over low heat until dissolved. Whisk a little of the beaten egg yolk into gelatin. Return to egg yolk mixture, whisking constantly. Stir in strawberry puree, and then pour into a large, chilled bowl. Set aside to cool slightly.

In another large bowl, beat cream until soft peaks form. Fold into cooled strawberry mixture.

Grape Granita   Page 127

In a medium-size bowl, beat egg whites until foamy. Add cream of tartar, and continue beating until stiff. Fold into strawberry whipped cream mixture. Turn into prepared soufflé dish, and chill for about 4 hours.

Remove collar, and serve with Raspberry Sauce.

6 to 8 servings

VARIATION

Lemon Soufflé: Omit strawberries. Substitute 1 cup freshly squeezed lemon juice for 1 cup water. Add 2 teaspoons lemon extract to whipped cream. Use a 1½-quart soufflé dish instead of a 2-quart soufflé dish.

Pashka

This is a classic Russian Easter treat, but don't wait until that holiday comes to enjoy this fruited, nutted version which is my favorite.

⅔ cup milk
1 envelope unflavored gelatin
3 cups ricotta cheese
⅓ cup honey
½ cup diced dried papaya
½ cup chopped dates
½ cup chopped pistachio nuts

Pour milk into top of a double boiler. Sprinkle gelatin on top, and let stand for a few minutes to soften. Set over hot water, and warm mixture until gelatin is completely dissolved.

In a large bowl, beat together ricotta and honey until blended and smooth. Fold in gelatin mixture, then papaya, dates, and nuts. Spoon into a lightly oiled 1- or 1½-quart mold, and chill until firm.

To serve, unmold the pudding or spoon it out from the mold.

6 servings

Italian Mousse Café in a Coconut Crust

1 cup cold water
1 envelope unflavored gelatin
2 teaspoons decaffeinated instant coffee
¼ cup honey
½ teaspoon anise extract
1 cup heavy cream
1 Coconut Crust (page 57)
cinnamon, for sprinkling

Pour water into a small saucepan, and sprinkle gelatin on top. Let stand for a few minutes to soften. Stir mixture over very low heat until gelatin dissolves. Add coffee, and stir until dissolved. Blend in honey. Remove from heat, and stir in anise flavoring. Chill until mixture is syrupy, about 1 hour.

In a large bowl, whip cream until soft peaks form. Whisk in cold gelatin mixture. Spoon into Coconut Crust. Sprinkle top lightly with cinnamon. Chill until firm, at least 3 hours.

Cut into wedges to serve.

6 servings

CHAPTER
7

Company
Waffles, Pancakes, and Dessert Crepes

Waffles, pancakes, and their more sophisticated sisters, crepes, are the basis of many wonderful desserts. Pancakes have been a familiar pleasure for thousands of years, stemming from an early Hebrew bread that was baked on stone slabs made hot by the sun. Waffles were a later embellishment, and crepes are a modern rendition.

Butter, eggs, flour, and a liquid are the basic ingredients of most waffles, pancakes, and crepes. Eggs are sometimes the only leavening, although it's more common to use some baking powder or baking soda in waffles and pancakes. Yeast is occasionally used as a leavener.

The thickness of the finished product depends on the amount of liquid you use in proportion to the flour. Waffle and pancake batters are similar. To make them, mix all dry ingredients together, then all liquid ingredients, and combine the two, mixing just until the dry ingredients are well moistened. If you're using melted butter in the batter, allow it to cool slightly so that it won't congeal when it comes in contact with the other, cooler, ingredients. The batter will be lumpy, but don't overbeat it or the texture of the waffles or pancakes will be tough and heavy. Refrigerating the batter for 30 minutes before cooking adds to the delicacy of waffles and pancakes by relaxing the gluten in the flour. This step isn't necessary, however, if your batter contains yeast or beaten egg whites.

Ideally, pancakes are cooked on a heavy griddle or skillet that's been properly seasoned. However, any heavy pan will do if you heat it until a drop of water sizzles and disappears, then grease the surface lightly with unsalted butter. If the surface is the correct temperature, the pancakes should form a disc as soon as the batter hits the heated griddle. Cook pancakes on one side until bubbles appear on the surface. Then turn them before the bubbles break or the pancakes will be dry. The second side will cook more quickly, usually in about half the time it took for the first side, but it won't brown as evenly as the first side. Check the undersides, and remove the pancakes from the pan when they're golden brown.

Most waffle irons sold today are electric and have nonstick surfaces. But if you're using an older waffle iron, season it before cooking on it.

A waffle iron should be heated until a few drops of water dropped on the bottom half of the grid sputter and evaporate in a second or two. Then brush the top and bottom grids with melted butter, and pour the batter on the center of the bottom grid (I use a large measuring cup for this), allowing it to spread until the grid is almost covered. Then quickly close the top, and cook the waffle just until the iron stops steaming, about five minutes. Carefully raise the top. If it sticks, close it, and continue cooking the waffle until the top lifts freely. Should the waffle be thinner than you desire, use more batter for the next one; should it be too thick, use less batter.

For a warm dessert, serve waffles piping hot—right off the griddle as fast as you can assemble the dessert. If they're to be used for a cold dessert, allow the waffles to cool on wire racks so that they won't lose their crisp texture.

While pancake and waffle batters should be mixed with a light hand, crepe batters are beaten until smooth. You can do the job with an electric beater, a blender, a food processor, or, if you prefer to mix by hand, a wire whisk. The batter benefits greatly by resting, covered, for an hour or two in the refrigerator before it's cooked. Since the flour absorbs liquid during this resting period and crepe batter should be thin, you may have to whisk in a bit more liquid before cooking.

Crepe pans are convenient, but not really necessary. I always use a Teflon-lined skillet with sloping (never straight) sides. Unlike a crepe pan, a skillet can be used for other purposes.

To cook the crepes, first melt enough butter, about two teaspoons, to thoroughly coat the bottom of the pan. When the butter is bubbly, pour in a thin layer, about three tablespoons, of batter, tipping the pan from side to side so that the batter will cover the bottom evenly. Cook the crepe over medium heat for about 1 minute, or until it slides easily when you move the pan. Slide the crepe onto a plate, and flip it back into the pan on the uncooked side. Continue to cook it for about 30 seconds, or until the crepe slides freely in the pan. Don't overcook crepes or they'll break when you fold or roll them.

Hot crepes that you're going to use right away can be stacked. But if you're going to either reheat them or use them cold, place a piece of wax paper between each one as you stack them. For lengthy storage, the whole stack can be wrapped in plastic wrap and then in foil. Once the crepes are cool, they can be frozen.

The side of a crepe that's cooked first will be the best looking, so put your filling on the other side.

There are several ways to use crepes:

To make a roll, cover all of the crepe to within ¼ inch of the edge with filling. Roll it up as you would a jellyroll.

For a two-fold crepe, spoon the filling in a line along the center of the crepe. Fold one side over the filling, then fold the second side over the first.

A blintz is made by spooning the filling onto the center of a crepe, and folding one side over three-quarters of the filling. The other side is then folded over the filling and part of the crepe. Finally, the top and bottom are folded to the center.

Crepes Suzette are made by spreading the filling over the crepes, leaving a ¼-inch border, then folding the crepes in half, and the halves into quarters. They resemble triangles with one arched side.

To stack filled crepes, I spread the filling on all but one crepe to within ¼ inch of the edges. Then I stack them, putting the plain crepe on top. Some people prefer to spoon the filling on each crepe as it's put in place.

The fillings and toppings are, of course, what makes these delicacies into desserts. I sometimes use just the good, natural sweetness of fruit and a cream topping to create a mouth-watering dish. But at other times, I fill the cooked batter with delicate whipped puddings, homemade jams, or other tasty ingredients.

The following are some of my favorite recipes for waffles, pancakes, and dessert crepes.

Sweet Crepe Batter

4 eggs
1 cup whole wheat pastry flour
1 tablespoon honey
1 cup milk
¼ cup butter, melted
½ teaspoon vanilla extract

Mix all ingredients together in a blender. Refrigerate for 1 hour before using. Cook according to directions on page 140.

Makes 12 to 15 crepes

Dessert Pancakes

1 cup milk
1 tablespoon vinegar
1 egg
1 tablespoon butter, melted and cooled
½ teaspoon vanilla extract
2 tablespoons honey
1¼ cups whole wheat flour
1 teaspoon baking powder
½ teaspoon baking soda
1 tablespoon butter

Mix together milk and vinegar in a small bowl. Set aside for 10 minutes to sour.

In a large bowl, beat egg, adding soured milk, melted butter, vanilla, and honey, and beating again briefly.

Sift together flour, baking powder, and baking soda in a medium-size bowl.

Mix into liquid ingredients just enough to moisten. Refrigerate for 1 hour before using.

To cook, heat butter in a large skillet until bubbly.

Drop about ¼ cup batter into skillet for each pancake. Allow to cook undisturbed until bubbles form on top surface. Turn, and cook for about 30 seconds. Stack on plate, and keep warm in oven until all pancakes are cooked.

These pancakes are delicious served with Cherry Sauce (page 270).

Makes 10 to 12 pancakes

Blinchiki with Cottage Cheese and Cherry Sauce

1 tablespoon butter
1 recipe for Dessert Pancakes (see recipe on this page)
1½ cups creamed cottage cheese
1 tablespoon honey
½ teaspoon grated lemon rind
Cherry Sauce (page 270)

Melt butter in a large skillet. When butter bubbles, drop pancake batter by the tablespoonful onto skillet. Cook until bubbles form on top. Turn, and continue cooking until blinchikis are browned on bottom.

While blinchikis are cooking, quickly blend cottage cheese, honey, and lemon rind in a medium-size bowl.

Serve hot blinchikis with prepared cottage cheese and Cherry Sauce.

Makes about 2 dozen tiny pancakes

Basic Blintzes

2 eggs
1 tablespoon vegetable oil
1 cup milk
1 tablespoon honey
¾ cup whole wheat pastry flour
½ tablespoon butter

Mix together all ingredients, except butter, in a blender, food processor, or electric mixer. Cover, and refrigerate for 1 hour.

Melt butter in a 7-inch skillet over medium heat. Add 2 to 3 tablespoons batter, and tip pan to distribute batter evenly. Cook until browned on bottom and slightly dry on top. Place on wax paper, cooked-side down. Continue to cook until all the batter is used, replenishing butter as needed.

Makes 8 to 10 blintzes

Wonderful Waffles

3½ cups whole wheat flour
1 tablespoon baking powder
¼ teaspoon baking soda
4 eggs
⅓ cup honey
¼ cup butter, melted and cooled
4 cups buttermilk
1 teaspoon vanilla extract
¼ cup butter, melted

Sift together flour, baking powder, and baking soda into a large bowl.

In a medium-size bowl, beat eggs. Beat in honey and ¼ cup melted and cooled butter. Stir in buttermilk and vanilla. Add to dry ingredients, mixing just enough to moisten.

Heat a waffle iron, and brush with ¼ cup melted butter. Pour on just enough batter to fill waffle iron. Close, and cook until steaming stops. Repeat until all the batter is used.

Makes 10 to 12 waffles

VARIATION
Coconut Waffles with Fresh Mango Sauce: Fold 1 cup freshly grated coconut into batter before baking waffles. (Unsweetened flaked coconut may be substituted.) Serve with Fresh Mango Sauce (page 269).

Carob Pancakes with Raspberry Sauce
Page 144

143

Carob Pancakes with Raspberry Sauce

Here is an extraordinary centerpiece for that special brunch which can be served either warm or cold.

½ cup whole wheat flour
¾ cup unbleached white flour
1 teaspoon baking powder
½ teaspoon baking soda
1 egg
1 cup buttermilk
1 tablespoon butter, melted
3 tablespoons honey
2 tablespoons Basic Carob Syrup
   (page xviii)
½ teaspoon vanilla extract
2 cups Raspberry Sauce (page 271)
1 cup heavy cream (optional)
1 tablespoon honey (optional)
   carob shavings (optional)

In a food processor or blender, combine whole wheat flour, unbleached white flour, baking powder, baking soda, egg, buttermilk, butter, 3 tablespoons honey, carob syrup, and vanilla. Process until just mixed. Refrigerate for at least 1 hour, and then cook according to directions on page 139.

Stack on individual plates, pouring a little Raspberry Sauce between pancakes.

If desired, beat cream in a medium-size bowl, adding 1 tablespoon honey, until soft peaks form. Spread on top of each stack, decorate with carob shavings, if desired, and serve.

Makes 12 to 16 pancakes

Folded Mandarin Crepes

1 recipe for Sweet Crepe Batter
   (page 142)
⅓ cup butter
3 tablespoons honey
1¼ cups orange juice, divided
1 teaspoon lemon juice
1½ tablespoons cornstarch
1 tangarine, peeled and separated
   into sections
¼ cup Coconut Sugar (page xxii)

Cook crepes according to directions on page 140. Fold as shown in illustration, remove to plate, and place in warm oven.

In a medium-size saucepan, combine butter, honey, 1 cup orange juice, and lemon juice.

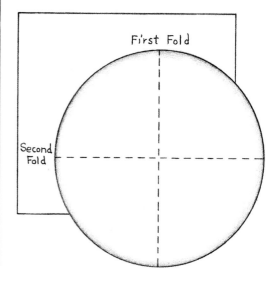

First Fold

Second Fold

Stir cornstarch into ¼ cup orange juice until dissolved. Add to saucepan. Heat, stirring constantly, until butter has melted and sauce is boiling. Continue cooking, stirring constantly, for about 2 more minutes.

Arrange crepes in chafing dish. Pour sauce over crepes. Top with tangarine sections, and sprinkle with Coconut Sugar.

Makes 12 to 14 crepes

Crepes South of the Border

    1 fresh mango, peeled, pitted,
        and diced
    1 fresh papaya, peeled,
        seeded, and diced
    2 kiwi fruit, peeled and diced
10 to 12 Sweet Crepes (page 142)
    1 cup cream cheese, softened
        and whipped
    3 tablespoons honey
        Coconut Sugar, for sprinkling
        (page xxii)

Preheat oven to 350°F.

Combine fruit in a large bowl.

Spread the centers of crepes with cream cheese. Divide fruit among crepes. Fold into packages. Place packages in a baking dish, and drizzle honey over all. Bake for 20 minutes.

Sprinkle with Coconut Sugar, and serve immediately.

Makes 10 to 12 crepes

Blueberry Blintzes

    1 recipe for Basic Blintzes (page 143)
    4 ounces cream cheese, softened
    4 ounces creamed cottage cheese
    1 teaspoon butter, softened
    1 egg yolk
    1 tablespoon honey
    1 teaspoon vanilla extract
    ½ tablespoon butter
    2 cups Blueberry Honey Sauce
        (page 269)
    1 cup sour cream or yogurt

Prepare blintzes according to directions on page 141.

In a medium-size bowl, beat together cream cheese, cottage cheese, softened butter, egg yolk, honey, and vanilla. Place about 2 tablespoons cheese mixture on cooked side of each blintz. Roll up, leaving ends open.

In a large skillet, melt butter. Sauté blintzes, seam-side down, until browned. Turn, and continue cooking until all sides are browned.

Serve immediately topped with Blueberry Honey Sauce and sour cream or yogurt.

Makes 8 to 10 blintzes

Swedish Rice Pancakes with Rhubarb Sauce

½ cup whole wheat pastry flour
¾ teaspoon baking soda
1 cup yogurt
2 egg yolks, slightly beaten
2 tablespoons milk
2 tablespoons butter, melted
1 tablespoon honey
1 cup cooked brown rice, cooled
2 egg whites, beaten until stiff peaks form
1 tablespoon butter
Rhubarb Sauce (page 271), warmed

Sift together flour and baking soda into a large bowl.

In a medium-size bowl, beat yogurt, egg yolks, milk, melted butter, and honey until blended. Add liquid ingredients to dry ingredients, and stir to blend. Mix in rice. Stir in about one-quarter of the egg whites to lighten batter; then fold in the rest.

Heat a griddle, and then melt butter until bubbly.

Use a serving spoon (about 2 tablespoons) to measure batter. Bake pancakes 2 inches apart until golden on both sides.

Serve warm with Rhubarb Sauce.

Makes about 20 pancakes

Scottish Oatcakes with Citrus Marmalade

1½ cups rolled oats, imported from Scotland or Ireland, or American uncooked quick oats briefly processed in a blender or food processor
⅛ teaspoon baking soda
1 tablespoon butter, melted
¼ cup hot water, or more as needed
1 tablespoon butter
Citrus Marmalade (page 274)

Mix oats with baking soda in a medium-size bowl. Stir in melted butter and ¼ cup water to make a stiff dough. If necessary, add a bit more water.

Turn dough out onto a surface well dusted with flour. Knead just until smooth. Roll out as thin as possible, adding more flour as necessary, and patching edges if they split. (This does take practice, but oat cakes will taste good even if they aren't perfectly shaped.) When dough is ⅛ inch thick, cut into wedges.

Heat a griddle, and then melt butter until bubbly. Cook until edges curl. Turn, and cook until lightly colored on the other side. Serve immediately with butter and marmalade.

3 to 4 servings

Plum *Clafouti*

This classic French peasant dessert lends itself to the addition of scoops of vanilla or lemon ice cream.

     4 cups quartered, peeled purple
         plums
     2 tablespoons honey
     1 teaspoon lemon extract
   1¼ cups milk
     1 cup whole wheat pastry flour
     ¼ cup honey
     1 egg
     ¼ teaspoon ground cinnamon
     1 tablespoon butter
     ¼ cup date sugar

Drain plums thoroughly.

Preheat oven to 350°F. Butter a 13 × 9 × 2-inch ovenproof dish.

In a medium-size bowl, toss together plums, 2 tablespoons honey, and lemon extract.

In a blender, combine milk, flour, ¼ cup honey, egg, and cinnamon. Pour half of mixture in bottom of prepared dish, and bake on middle shelf of oven for about 10 minutes, or until set. (If dough bubbles up, push it down with back of large spoon.)

Remove from oven, and spread fruit over cooked batter. Pour remaining batter over fruit. Dot with butter, sprinkle with date sugar, and return to oven for 25 to 30 minutes, or until a knife inserted into the center comes out clean. Serve warm.

8 servings

Pears Hélène Crepes

     4 ripe pears
     ¼ cup honey
     2 teaspoons lemon juice
     ½ teaspoon ground cinnamon
         Carob Fudge Sauce (page 269)
     8 Sweet Crepes (page 142)

Peel, core, and dice pears. Place into a medium-size bowl, and mix with honey, lemon juice, and cinnamon. Refrigerate until ready to assemble.

Warm Carob Fudge Sauce in top of a double boiler set over simmering water.

Place crepes on individual dessert dishes. Divide pear mixture among crepes, and fold crepes over. Top with Carob Fudge Sauce, and serve immediately.

Makes 8 crepes

VARIATION

Peach Melba Crepes: Substitute ½ teaspoon vanilla extract for cinnamon and substitute Raspberry Sauce (page 271) for Carob Fudge Sauce.

Scottish Oatcakes with Citrus Marmalade   Page 146
Potato Pancakes with Blueberry Honey Sauce   Page 148

Potato Pancakes with Blueberry Honey Sauce

    6 medium-size potatoes, peeled
    3 eggs
    ¼ cup whole wheat flour
    2 teaspoons baking powder
    1 teaspoon vegetable oil
    1 tablespoon butter
      Blueberry Honey Sauce (page 269)
      or applesauce

Grate potatoes into a large bowl using fine side of hand grater. Stir in eggs, flour, baking powder, and oil, blending well.

Heat a griddle, and then melt butter until bubbly. Drop batter by the heaping tablespoonfuls onto griddle, and brown pancakes on both sides.

Serve warm with Blueberry Honey Sauce or applesauce.

Makes about 24 pancakes

Strawberry Cream Crepe Cake

    3 cups whole fresh strawberries
    ⅓ cup honey
    1 tablespoon cornstarch
    1 recipe for Pastry Cream (page
        272)
  8 to 9 Sweet Crepes (page 142)

Reserve a few pretty berries for decoration. Slice remaining strawberries into a medium-size bowl. Stir in honey. Refrigerate for several hours.

Drain juice from berries into a small saucepan. There should be about 1 cup. If necessary, add enough water or orange juice to make that amount. Stir cornstarch into juice until there are no lumps. Cook over medium heat, stirring constantly, until mixture bubbles and thickens. Add strawberries, and cook just until mixture bubbles again. Chill in refrigerator.

On a cake plate, spread Pastry Cream between crepes, forming them into a stack. Pour strawberry sauce over top. Decorate with reserved berries. To serve, cut into wedges.

6 servings

CHAPTER
8

Easy~Does~It Breads, Muffins, and Coffee Cakes

For brunch or tea time or an evening snack, there is a wide range of rich breads and coffee cakes that, while not exactly desserts, are perfect for providing just the sweet note that's wanted. Homemade muffins and biscuits, too, add the special touch that makes an ordinary breakfast a festive event, a meal that no one would want to skip.

Almost without exception, these sweet but hearty treats freeze well, which solves one important problem for cooks who want to "keep 'em home for breakfast" without having to begin preparations at dawn. I like to keep my freezer well stocked with these tooth-some treats in serving-size portions. A few minutes in a warm oven restores them to just-baked appeal. And when unexpected company arrives, I am never at a loss for something homemade and delicious to serve with tea or coffee.

Breads and their derivatives, muffins and biscuits, may be divided into two categories according to how they are leavened: yeast breads and so-called quick breads. The requirements of one kind are different—sometimes completely opposite—from those of the other kind, so this is an important division to understand. Yeast breads need to be toughened up (which does not mean that the result will be a tough loaf), and quick breads need to be treated tenderly. Yeast breads require time for kneading and rising, and quick breads, as the name implies, need to be mixed and baked without delay. As is so often the case with cooking (like love), it is all a matter of chemistry.

153

YEAST BREADS

Yeast is a living organism that grows when it is provided with an environment that's nourishing, moist, and warm. Cold retards its growth; really high temperatures kill it. When yeast is combined with flour and a liquid in a warm place, it not only grows, it gives off carbon dioxide which raises the dough, providing the dough is strong enough not to collapse in the process. That's where gluten comes in. Gluten is a protein present in wheat that gives it the strength to endure being puffed up with carbon dioxide. Hard wheat is rich in gluten; soft wheat has some gluten, but not a lot. Soft wheat is used for pastry flour, to make it tender. Hard wheat is used for bread flour. All-purpose flour is a combination of soft wheat and hard wheat, supposed to be suitable for either pastry or bread.

Kneading strengthens or develops the gluten in flour, and so it's a necessary step in most yeast bread making. You can knead bread by hand, a process I personally find most satisfying; you can knead in an electric mixer that's equipped with dough hooks, in half the time; or you can knead in a food processor in about a minute. Many food processors, however, only have room in the work bowl for enough dough for one loaf, so you must knead in batches if you are making more than that.

Kneading by hand consists of folding, pressing, and turning the dough for about ten minutes, until it loses its stickiness and becomes elastic, meaning that when you press it down it bounces back as if it had a will of its own.

With so much depending on that hardy little collection of fungi, yeast, it's important to know if the yeast you're working with is alive and well. To find that out, I always "proof," or test, the yeast. Put a small amount of very warm (90° to 110°F) liquid (whatever the recipe calls for) in a cup and sprinkle the yeast on top, if it's dry yeast, or mash it in, if it's fresh yeast, and stir in a teaspoonful of honey. In five to ten minutes, the yeast should bubble up and grow. If this doesn't occur, the yeast is no longer active and should not be used.

Dry yeast comes in a little packet and is dated for best use. Fresh yeast is sold in cake form and must be refrigerated. Well wrapped, it will keep for about three weeks. They are equivalent and used interchangeably in recipes.

When the dough has been mixed and kneaded, it's allowed to rise in a warm place, 70° to 75°F. The first rising takes anywhere from one to two hours or more. The richer the dough (with eggs, milk, honey, and other such things) the slower it will rise.

This wait isn't always convenient, of course, but yeast doesn't care anything about your busy schedule. If you want to make yeast dough rise faster, you can put the bowl in an unlit oven with a pan of hot water underneath, which will heat the oven to about 100°F. The pilot light in a gas oven will do the same thing. When I am forced to rush the yeast this way, I always use an oven thermometer to make certain the oven is not warmer than 100°F. Should the oven get too warm, simply open the door.

On the other hand, if you have to go out and want to retard the growth of the yeast, you can put the dough in a cool place (about 60°F, not refrigerator-cold) to slow things down.

Once the dough has accomplished its first rising, punch it down, and refrigerate it if you really want to stop the process. To start again later, the dough will have to stand at room temperature for about three hours.

You punch down the dough after the first rising to eliminate all the gas bubbles, which returns it to its original size, and to distribute the yeast more evenly. Then the dough is formed into loaf, cake, biscuits, or whatever, and allowed to rise again (depending, of course, on the recipe you're using).

No harm will be done if you are not ready to form the dough and you punch it down and let it rise a second time. This merely creates a finer texture in the finished product. In fact, bread dough is usually allowed to rise twice. What will cause harm, however, is to allow the dough to overrise in either the first or second rising. (The dough has risen enough when it has doubled in size. If you gently poke it with your finger, the indentation should remain.) Should it overrise and collapse in the bowl during the first rising, it will never rise again. If you let it overrise in the second rising, it may very well collapse while baking.

During baking, the yeast gives off more carbon dioxide, raising the loaf still more, and then it is spent, leaving behind a light, fragrant loaf, strong enough to stand on its own.

The test for doneness in a yeast loaf or biscuit is to tap it on the bottom. I usually do this by raising the bread (very gingerly) with a pancake turner and tapping it with a metal spatula. However, if the bread is in a loaf pan, it's necessary to invert the pan and free the loaf to tap it. The bottom crust should sound hollow rather than emit a dull thud. Testing when the bread is risen, brown, and near the end of the baking time given in the recipe will not cause the loaf to fall. If it's not ready, simply put it back in the oven for a few minutes more.

When baked, remove the loaf from the pan right away. It should come out quite easily. If left in the pan, the moisture would cause it to become doughy in texture. Cool the loaf completely on a wire rack. Otherwise, it won't slice properly. If you like a soft crust, cover the top of the loaf loosely with a tea towel.

QUICK BREADS AND MUFFINS

Whether for muffins, biscuits, or loaves, any dough or batter made with baking soda (or baking powder, which is a derivative of baking soda) produces what is called a quick bread. You don't have to knead it, except for two or three turns if you are forming biscuits, and you don't have to wait for it to rise.

Because you're working with a different chemistry here, the techniques are different, too. To understand baking soda, just think of what happens when you stir it into water. It immediately fizzes up, no waiting. And after a few minutes, the fizzing subsides. Obviously, if you want to take advantage of the action, you have to work fast. So with quick breads, you get all the dry ingredients ready in one bowl and all the liquids in another, then combine them at the last possible moment before baking. Stir only enough to blend them. Don't be concerned if there are a few lumps; these will bake out. If you overbeat a quick bread, your baked goods will be neither as high nor as tender as they should be.

Baking soda is an alkaline substance that has an undesirable soapy taste. To neutralize that taste, recipes using baking soda always have an acid among the ingredients—such as sour milk, sour cream, or buttermilk. (Sweet milk can be soured for this purpose. See page xxiv.) Acid also helps baking soda to produce the carbon dioxide that causes the batter to rise.

Baking powder meets the requirement for acid by including an acid ingredient, cream of tartar. Since it has a less volatile temperament than baking soda, it doesn't need critical timing in getting the batter into the oven.

Because they don't depend on gluten to strengthen the loaf as it is rising, in quick breads you can use grains that contain little or no gluten, such as cornmeal, oats, and barley. These are sometimes used in yeast breads, but the proportion is limited by the need for gluten, so wheat flours predominate in yeast-based recipes. In quick breads, you are able to use grains without gluten in any proportion you desire.

A loaf of quick bread usually develops a crack on top as it is baking, which is part of its characteristic look. When testing a quick bread for doneness, it is wise to wait until the crack has developed and no longer appears moist before piercing it with a cake tester or food pick. If tested this way too early in the baking, the bread could fall.

A quick bread loaf is crumbly; allow it to cool completely for neat slicing. Muffins are crumbly, too, but since you don't have to worry about slicing them, by all means serve them warm. They are most delicious fresh from the oven with a bit of sweet butter melting inside.

BREADS

Boston Brown Bread

This steamed bread is easily mixed, and it can be kept frozen until needed. Serve it warm.

2 cups milk
1 tablespoon vinegar
1 cup cornmeal
1 cup rye flour
1 cup whole wheat flour
1½ teaspoons baking soda
½ cup molasses
1 cup raisins

In a medium-size bowl, mix together milk and vinegar. Let mixture stand at room temperature for 15 minutes to sour milk.

In a large bowl, blend dry ingredients together with a spoon.

Add molasses and raisins to milk, and then add mixture to dry ingredients. Beat until blended. Divide batter between 2 well-buttered 1-pound coffee cans or other cans of 5-cup capacity. Cover with dome-shaped rounds of aluminum foil, buttered on the down side, and secure around cans with rubber bands. Stand cans on a rack in a large kettle. Add enough hot water to reach three-quarters of the way up can molds but not enough to make them float. Cover kettle and simmer water for 2 hours to steam breads.

Remove breads from kettle, and let stand on wire rack until cool enough to handle, then remove from molds. Serve warm.

To reheat, wrap in aluminum foil, stand on rack in kettle, add hot water to level *below* rack, and simmer for 30 minutes.

Makes 2

Cinnamon Swirl Bread

2 tablespoons dry yeast
¼ cup warm water
1 teaspoon honey
¾ cup milk
⅓ cup butter
¾ cup honey
2 eggs
2¼ cups whole wheat flour
2¼ cups unbleached white flour
1 teaspoon ground cardamom
2 cups raisins
2 cups walnuts
2 teaspoons ground cinnamon
3 tablespoons butter, softened
1 egg, beaten
ground cinnamon, for sprinkling

Sprinkle yeast over warm water in a cup, and stir in 1 teaspoon honey. Let stand until mixture bubbles up, 5 to 10 minutes.

Heat milk and ⅓ cup butter together in top of a double boiler set over boiling water until butter melts. Remove from heat, and stir in ¾ cup honey. Cool mixture until just warm.

Beat 2 eggs in a medium-size bowl, and then slowly beat in milk mixture. Stir in yeast mixture.

Sift together whole wheat flour, unbleached white flour, and cardamom into a large bowl. Pour in milk-egg mixture, and mix to form a dough.

Turn out onto a floured surface, and knead for 10 minutes, or knead with dough hooks for 5 minutes. To use a food processor, divide dough into 2 portions, and process 1 portion at a time for about 1 minute, or until an elastic ball of dough is formed. Shape the 2 balls into 1.

Place the dough into a large well-oiled bowl, and turn to coat all sides. Cover, and let rise in a warm place until doubled in bulk, about 1½ hours.

Coarsely chop raisins and walnuts, and blend in 2 teaspoons cinnamon.

Punch down dough, and roll out on a lightly floured surface into a 12 × 18-inch sheet.

Spread sheet of dough with 3 tablespoons butter, and sprinkle raisin-walnut mixture over top to within 1 inch of edges. Roll up like a jellyroll. Place loaf on a buttered baking sheet, and pat it into a horseshoe shape. With scissors, cut slashes ½ inch deep into the top at 1-inch intervals to expose filling. Let rise in a warm place until doubled in bulk, about 1¼ hours.

Preheat oven to 375°F. Brush loaf with beaten egg, and sprinkle with cinnamon. Bake for 35 minutes, or until loaf sounds hollow when tapped on bottom.

Remove from baking sheet, and cool completely on a wire rack.

Makes 1

Cranberry Nugget Bread

Colorful chunks of jellied cranberry sauce give this sweet bread a festive appearance.

    2¾ cups whole wheat pastry flour
    2¼ teaspoons baking powder
     ¼ teaspoon baking soda
      2 tablespoons butter, softened
      1 cup honey
      1 egg
     ¾ cup cranberry juice or orange
        juice
      1 cup diced Jellied Cranberry
        Sauce (page 273)

Cinnamon Swirl Bread   Page 158
Currant Scones   Page 168
Glazed Strawberry Muffins   Page 164

Preheat oven to 325°F. Butter an 8½ × 4½ × 2½-inch loaf pan, and line the bottom with wax paper cut to fit.

In a medium-size bowl, sift together whole wheat pastry flour, baking powder, and baking soda.

Cream butter and honey together in a large bowl until well blended. Beat in egg. Add dry ingredients alternately with juice to creamed mixture, beginning and ending with dry ingredients. Gently fold in diced cranberry sauce, taking care not to mash the pieces. Spoon batter into prepared pan. Bake for 50 to 55 minutes, or until a cake tester or food pick inserted into the center comes out dry and clean.

Cool in pan on a wire rack for 10 minutes. Remove from pan, and cool completely on a wire rack. Remove wax paper.

Makes 1

159

Glazed Orange Bread

1 tablespoon dry yeast
¼ cup warm water
1 teaspoon honey
⅓ cup honey
2 eggs, beaten
½ cup sour cream or yogurt
¼ cup butter, melted and cooled
    slightly
2 tablespoons grated orange rind
    (about 2 oranges)
1 teaspoon ground cardamom
2 cups whole wheat flour (not
    pastry flour)
1¾ cups unbleached white flour
1 cup raisins
⅓ cup Orange Marmalade
    (page 274)

Sprinkle yeast over warm water in a cup; stir in 1 teaspoon honey. Let stand until mixture bubbles up, 5 to 10 minutes.

In a large bowl, beat ⅓ cup honey into eggs, then add sour cream or yogurt, butter, orange rind, and cardamom, in that order. Blend well.

In a medium-size bowl, blend the whole wheat and unbleached white flour with a fork. Add flour to egg mixture to make a soft dough. Turn out onto a floured surface, and knead for 10 minutes, or knead with dough hooks for 5 minutes. It is not advisable to use a food processor for this mixture, as it is so sticky that it will slow down the blade.

Place dough into a large well-oiled bowl, and turn to coat all sides. Cover, and let rise in a warm place until doubled in bulk, about 2 hours.

Turn dough onto a floured surface, and knead raisins into it. Form into a ball with raisins inside. If any raisins show, poke them into dough, or they will overbrown when bread is baked. Place ball of dough in a buttered 9- or 10-inch pie pan, and let rise in a warm place until doubled in bulk, about 1½ hours.

Preheat oven to 375°F.

Bake bread for 35 minutes, or until it sounds hollow when tapped on bottom. If bread gets brown too early in cooking time, cover it loosely with a sheet of aluminum foil.

Remove bread from pan. Place on a wire rack positioned over a sheet of wax paper. Heat Orange Marmalade in a small saucepan to soften it, and brush over hot loaf. Cool completely.

Makes 1

Hawaiian Nut Bread

½ cup butter, softened
½ cup honey
2 eggs
⅓ cup buttermilk
1¾ cups whole wheat flour
1½ teaspoons baking powder
1 teaspoon baking soda
½ cup well-drained, unsweetened
    crushed pineapple
½ cup chopped pecans

Preheat oven to 375°F. Butter the bottom of a 9 × 5 × 3-inch loaf pan, and line it with parchment paper.

In a large bowl, beat butter until fluffy. Beat in honey and then eggs. Mix in buttermilk.

Sift together whole wheat flour, baking powder, and baking soda into a medium-size bowl. Stir with a fork, or whisk to blend. Stir flour mixture into wet ingredients. Fold in pineapple and nuts. Turn into prepared pan, and bake on middle shelf of oven for 35 to 40 minutes, or until a cake tester or food pick inserted into the center comes out clean.

Cool 10 minutes, then turn out onto a wire rack. Remove parchment paper. Cool completely before cutting.

Makes 1

Hot Cross Buns

¾ cup dried currants
2 tablespoons dry yeast
½ cup warm milk
1 tablespoon honey
½ cup milk
¼ cup butter
⅓ cup honey
4 to 5 cups whole wheat flour
2 eggs, beaten
1 egg white, slightly beaten
½ cup Almond Glaze (page 266)

Place currants into a small bowl, cover with boiling water, and set aside to plump for 15 to 20 minutes.

Sprinkle yeast over warm milk in a cup. Stir in 1 tablespoon honey, and let stand until mixture bubbles up, 5 to 10 minutes.

In a small saucepan, heat ½ cup milk, butter, and ⅓ cup honey until butter is melted and milk is warm, stirring often. Allow to cool.

Sift flour. Measure 2 cups into a large bowl. Stir in milk-butter mixture and proofed yeast mixture, beating with an electric beater. Add eggs and ½ cup more flour. Beat for 2 minutes. Stir in enough of the remaining flour to make a firm dough. Turn out onto a floured surface, and knead by hand for 10 minutes, or until dough is elastic. Dough may also be kneaded in a food processor in 2 batches for about 1 minute each or until each batch forms an elastic ball of dough, or with dough hooks for 5 to 7 minutes.

Oil the inside of a medium-size bowl. Roll dough into a ball and place in bowl, turning to coat both sides. Cover loosely with plastic wrap, and allow to rise in a warm place until doubled in bulk, about 1 hour.

Butter 2 8-inch round cake pans.

On a floured surface, punch down dough. Drain currants thoroughly, and work into dough. Divide dough into 16 pieces. Shape into buns, and place into prepared pans. Set in a warm place to rise for 1 hour.

Preheat oven to 375°F.

Brush tops of buns with egg white, and bake on middle shelf of oven for 15 to 20 minutes, or until golden.

Cool thoroughly, and then make crosses with Almond Glaze.

Makes 16

Italian Fried Doughboys

These doughboys, pan-fried rather than deep-fried, are much like pancakes. In Italian households, they are served for holiday breakfasts.

   1 tablespoon dry yeast
   1 cup warm water
   1 tablespoon honey
1¾ cups whole wheat flour (not
     pastry flour)
1½ cups unbleached white flour
   ¼ teaspoon white pepper
   2 tablespoons butter, melted and
     cooled slightly
     vegetable oil
     Honey Butter or Cinnamon Honey
     Butter (page 237)

In a small bowl, sprinkle yeast over warm water. Stir in honey, and let stand until mixture bubbles up, 5 to 10 minutes.

Combine whole wheat flour and unbleached white flour with pepper in a large bowl. Stir with a fork to blend. Pour in yeast mixture and butter. Mix to form dough. Turn dough out onto a floured surface, and knead for 10 minutes, or knead with dough hooks for 5 minutes, or process in a food processor for about 1 minute—until dough is firm, elastic, and no longer sticky. If necessary, 2 or 3 more tablespoons of flour may be added.

Place 1 tablespoon oil in a large bowl, and turn dough in oil to coat all sides of bowl and dough. Cover with plastic wrap, and let rise in a warm place until doubled in bulk, 1½ to 2 hours.

Turn dough out onto a lightly floured surface, and form into a cylinder 2 inches in diameter. Cut off pieces 1 inch thick. Press each slice with palm to flatten. Let rest 10 minutes, and then roll slices out with a rolling pin until they are ovals about 6 × 3 inches. Lay ovals on wax paper, and let rise until doubled in depth about 30 minutes.

Cover the bottom of a skillet with a thin coat of oil. Heat oil, and fry doughboys over medium heat until golden brown on both sides. Don't rush them. Add more oil to the pan as needed. Serve doughboys warm with Honey Butter or Cinnamon Honey Butter.

Makes about 18

Special Savarin

This lovely dessert bread should be made in a 9½-inch savarin mold; but if you don't have one, a 10-inch springform tube pan can be used.

   1 cup golden raisins
  ⅔ cup milk
   2 tablespoons honey
   1 tablespoon dry yeast
1⅓ cups sifted whole wheat flour
1⅓ cups sifted unbleached white
     flour
  ⅔ cup butter, softened
  ⅓ cup honey
   4 eggs
   1 cup honey
  ½ cup water
  ½ teaspoon rum extract
     (optional)
   1 cup heavy cream

2 tablespoons honey
2 cups sliced peeled peaches,
 nectarines, or halved peeled
 apricots

Place raisins into a small bowl, cover with boiling water, and set aside to plump for 15 to 20 minutes.

In a small saucepan, heat milk and 2 tablespoons honey to about 110°F. Pour into a large bowl. Add yeast, stirring with a fork. Allow to stand until mixture bubbles up, 5 to 10 minutes.

Sift together whole wheat flour and unbleached white flour into a medium-size bowl, mixing with a fork to blend.

In a medium-size bowl, beat butter until fluffy. Beat in ⅓ cup honey and then eggs, 1 at a time.

Alternately beat flour and butter-egg mixture into yeast mixture. Cover with plastic wrap, and let rise in a warm place until doubled in bulk, about 2 hours.

Butter a savarin mold.

Stir down dough. Mix in drained raisins. Turn into prepared pan, cover with plastic wrap, and let rise in a warm place until doubled in bulk, about 1 hour.

Preheat oven to 350°F.

Bake savarin on middle shelf of oven for about 45 minutes, or until golden.

In a large saucepan, boil 1 cup honey and water to soft ball stage (234° to 238°F on a candy thermometer).

Remove from heat, and add rum extract, if desired. With a skewer, make deep holes in top of savarin. Pour honey syrup over top and down sides.

In a medium-size bowl, beat cream and 2 tablespoons honey until soft peaks form. Place in pastry bag, and pipe onto savarin. Arrange fruit in center and around edges.

10 to 12 servings

Tutti-Frutti Loaf

1½ cups finely chopped mixed dried
 fruit
¾ cup butter, softened
½ cup honey
2 eggs
2 tablespoons milk
½ teaspoon vanilla extract
1¾ cups sifted whole wheat flour
2 teaspoons baking powder
1 teaspoon baking soda

Place fruit into a medium-size bowl, and plump in enough water to cover for 15 minutes. Drain well.

Preheat oven to 350°F. Butter a 9 × 5 × 3-inch loaf pan.

Beat together butter and honey in a large bowl. Beat in eggs, milk, and vanilla. Stir in fruit.

Sift flour, baking powder, and baking soda into wet ingredients, mixing well. Turn into prepared pan and bake on middle shelf of oven for about 45 to 50 minutes, or until a cake tester or food pick inserted into the center comes out clean.

Cool in pan about 10 minutes, and then turn out onto a wire rack.

Makes 1

MUFFINS

Glazed Strawberry Muffins

   2 eggs, separated
2½ cups sifted whole wheat flour
   1 tablespoon baking powder
   1 cup buttermilk
   ⅔ cup honey, warmed slightly
   ¼ cup butter, melted and cooled
   1 cup diced fresh strawberries
  12 fresh strawberry halves (quarters
       if berries are large)
   ¼ cup Strawberry Jelly (page 273)

Preheat oven to 400°F. Line a
12-cup muffin tin with paper liners.

In a medium-size bowl beat egg
whites until stiff but not dry.

Sift flour and baking powder
together 3 times. Place into a large
bowl.

In another medium-size bowl, beat
together egg yolks, buttermilk, honey,
and butter until blended. Pour liquid
ingredients into dry ingredients, stirring until just blended. Stir in diced
strawberries. Fold in egg whites with a
spoon. (Batter is too heavy for a wire
whisk.)

Divide batter among muffin cups;
they will be almost full. Lightly press
strawberry halves or quarters on tops.
Bake on top shelf of oven for 25 minutes,
or until dry inside when pierced with
a cake tester or food pick.

While muffins are baking, melt
jelly (to be used as glaze) by placing it
in a Pyrex cup in a small saucepan of
simmering water, stirring occasionally.

Turn muffins out onto wire racks
over a sheet of wax paper. With a pastry brush, lightly brush glaze over tops.
Let cool about 20 minutes before serving.

These muffins are also good when
served at room temperature.

Makes 1 dozen

Yum-Yam Nut Muffins

   1 small baked yam
2¼ cups whole wheat pastry flour
   1 teaspoon baking soda
   1 teaspoon baking powder
   ½ teaspoon freshly grated nutmeg
       (ground nutmeg may be
       substituted)
   ½ cup buttermilk or sour milk (page
       xxiv)
   ½ cup vegetable oil
   ½ cup honey
   1 egg
   2 teaspoons grated orange rind
   ½ cup chopped pecans (peanuts or
       walnuts may be substituted)

Preheat oven to 375°F. Butter a 12-cup muffin tin, or line it with paper liners.

Mash yam well in a medium-size bowl. Whip with a fork. Measure ½ cup to use in recipe.

In a large bowl, sift together flour, baking soda, baking powder, and nutmeg.

In another medium-size bowl, beat together buttermilk or sour milk, oil, honey, and egg. Beat in yam and orange rind. Empty liquid ingredients into flour mixture, and stir just enough to blend. Fold in nuts. Fill muffin cups about two-thirds full, and bake on top shelf of oven for 15 minutes, or until risen and browned. A cake tester or food pick inserted into the center of a muffin should come out clean and dry.

Remove muffins from pan, and cool on wire racks. Serve warm or at room temperature.

Makes 1 dozen

Hazelnut-Anise Muffins

2 eggs, separated
2½ cups sifted whole wheat pastry flour
1 tablespoon baking powder
1 cup buttermilk
⅔ cup honey
¼ cup butter, melted and cooled
½ teaspoon anise extract
1 cup coarsely chopped hazelnuts

Preheat oven to 400°F. Butter a 12-cup muffin tin, or line it with paper liners.

In a medium-size bowl, beat egg whites until stiff but not dry.

Sift flour and baking powder together 3 times. Place into a large bowl.

In another medium-size bowl, beat together egg yolks, buttermilk, honey, butter, and anise until blended. Pour liquid ingredients into dry ingredients, stirring until just blended. Stir in hazelnuts. Fold in egg whites with a spoon. (Batter is too heavy for a wire whisk.)

Divide batter among muffin cups; they will be almost full. Bake for 25 minutes, or until lightly browned on top and dry inside when pierced with a cake tester or food pick.

Turn out onto wire racks. Serve warm with butter.

Makes 1 dozen

VARIATION
Fig-Pecan Muffins: Sift ½ teaspoon ground allspice with dry ingredients. Omit anise. Substitute ½ cup figs snipped into small pieces and ½ cup chopped pecans for hazelnuts.

Maple Walnut Muffins

2 eggs, separated
2 cups sifted whole wheat flour
¼ cup soy flour
1 tablespoon baking powder
1 cup buttermilk
⅔ cup maple syrup
¼ cup butter, melted and cooled
½ cup coarsely chopped walnuts

Preheat oven to 400°F. Butter a 12-cup muffin tin, or line it with paper liners.

In a medium-size bowl, beat egg whites until stiff but not dry.

Sift flours and baking powder together 3 times. Place into a large bowl.

In another medium-size bowl, beat together egg yolks, buttermilk, maple syrup, and butter until blended. Pour liquid ingredients into dry ingredients, stirring until just blended. Stir in walnuts. Fold in egg whites with a spoon. (Batter is too heavy for a wire whisk.)

Special Savarin   Page 162

Divide batter among muffin cups; they will be almost full. Bake on top shelf of oven for 25 minutes, or until lightly browned on top and dry inside when pierced with a cake tester or food pick.

Turn out onto wire racks. Serve warm with butter.

Makes 1 dozen

Apple-Cheese Muffins

3 medium-size baking apples
1 tablespoon lemon juice
2 cups whole wheat flour
1 tablespoon baking powder
¼ teaspoon ground cinnamon
1½ cups cubed Colby or any medium-sharp cheese
¾ cup honey
1¼ cups buttermilk
2 eggs
¼ cup butter, melted

Peel, core, and cut apples into chunks, placing them into a large bowl. Cover with cold water, and stir in lemon juice.

Preheat oven to 400°F. Butter a 12-cup muffin tin.

Sift flour, baking powder, and cinnamon into another large bowl. Mix in cheese.

Drain apples. Place honey, buttermilk, eggs, butter, and apples into food processor. Process with on/off motion until apples are in small pieces. Pour into dry ingredients and mix just until moistened. Fill muffin tin three-quarters full, and bake for 20 minutes, or until a cake tester or food pick inserted into the center of a muffin comes out clean. Serve warm.

Makes 12 to 15

COFFEE CAKES

Blueberry Teacakes

2¼ cups fresh blueberries
2 cups sifted whole wheat pastry flour, divided
4 teaspoons baking powder
2 teaspoons ground cinnamon
1½ cups cornmeal
½ cup butter
1 cup honey
2 eggs
1½ cups milk
cinnamon, for sprinkling

Preheat oven to 350°F. Butter 3 9-inch pie plates.

In a medium-size bowl, mix blueberries with ¼ cup flour, and set aside. Sift remaining flour into another medium-size bowl together with baking powder and cinnamon. Stir in cornmeal, and blend thoroughly.

In a large bowl, cream butter until soft. Beat in honey and then eggs. Add flour mixture and milk in 3 to 4 portions, beginning and ending with flour. Fold in berries. Divide batter evenly among prepared pie plates. Sprinkle tops with additional cinnamon. Bake on middle and upper middle shelves of oven (stagger pans) for 35 to 40 minutes, or until cakes are golden on top and dry inside when tested with a cake tester or food pick.

Serve warm, or cool in pie plates on racks. Cut into wedges to serve.

If not needed, the extra cakes freeze well and are delightful to have ready for a Sunday breakfast.

Makes 3

Currant Scones

½ cup dried currants
1¾ cups sifted whole wheat flour
1 tablespoon baking powder
¼ cup butter
⅓ cup milk
3 tablespoons honey
1 egg, beaten

Preheat oven to 450°F. Butter a baking sheet.

Place currants into a small bowl, cover with boiling water and set aside to plump for 15 to 20 minutes.

Sift together flour and baking powder 3 times. Place into a large bowl. With a pastry blender or 2 knives, cut butter into flour until mixture has a mealy consistency.

Drain currants, and add to flour mixture, stirring to blend.

Pour milk into a small bowl. With a fork, beat in honey. Add to flour mixture, stirring just until moistened.

With floured hands divide dough into 4 equal parts. On a floured surface, pat each piece of dough into a 5-inch round. Place on prepared baking sheet, and cut each round into 4 pieces, as you would slice a pie, cutting all the way through, but not separating them.

Brush egg on top and sides of dough. Bake on middle shelf of oven for 10 minutes, or until golden.

Serve hot with butter.

Makes 16

Coffee Cake Supreme

1¼ cups milk
⅓ cup honey
1 tablespoon dry yeast
¼ cup butter
1 egg, beaten
4 to 4½ cups whole wheat flour
1 teaspoon ground cinnamon
½ cup butter, softened
½ cup honey
1½ cups ground walnuts
¾ cup golden raisins

Butter a large bowl.

In a small saucepan, heat milk and ⅓ cup honey until warm (about 110°F). Pour about ¼ cup of the warm milk into a small bowl, stir in yeast, and let stand until mixture bubbles up, 5 to 10 minutes.

Add ¼ cup butter to milk in saucepan, and return to heat until butter is melted. Set aside until just warm.

In another large bowl, mix together cooled butter-milk mixture and proofed yeast. Stir in egg.

Sift together flour and cinnamon into a medium-size bowl. Stir with fork to blend, and then add to liquid in large bowl, a little at a time, working in as much flour as it will accept.

Knead in food processor in 2 batches until each batch forms an elastic ball of dough, about 1 minute, or with dough hooks for 5 to 7 minutes, or by hand for 10 minutes. Place ball of dough into buttered bowl, turning to coat all surfaces. Cover with plastic wrap, and let rise in a warm place until doubled in bulk, about 2 hours.

Punch down dough on a lightly floured surface, and roll into an 11 × 18-inch rectangle.

Preheat oven to 375°F. Sprinkle flour lightly on baking sheet.

In a medium-size bowl, beat together ½ cup softened butter and ½ cup honey until fluffy. Mix in walnuts and raisins. Spread on dough all the way to the narrow ends, but leave about a 1-inch margin on the long edges. Roll up from the long side, jelly-roll style. Place, seam-side down, on prepared baking sheet. Pull dough around into a circle so that ends meet. Seal together, using a little water.

With a sharp knife, cut slashes in top of ring about 1 inch apart and 1 inch deep. (Don't cut too deep or butter filling will run out.) Bake on middle shelf of oven for 20 to 25 minutes, or until browned.

Cool, and cut on the diagonal.

Makes 1

Sour Cream Coffee Cake

2 cups ground walnuts, divided
2½ teaspoons ground cinnamon
¾ cup honey

¾ cup butter, softened
1 cup honey
3 eggs
2 cups sour cream
2 teaspoons vanilla extract
1½ cups sifted whole wheat pastry flour
1½ cups sifted unbleached white flour
2 teaspoons baking powder
2 teaspoons baking soda

Preheat oven to 350°F. Butter a 10-inch tube pan.

In a small bowl, combine 1½ cups walnuts, cinnamon, and ¾ cup honey.

In a large bowl, beat together butter and 1 cup honey. Beat in eggs, sour cream, and vanilla.

Sift whole wheat pastry flour and unbleached white flour, baking powder, and baking soda into another large bowl, and then add to sour cream mixture, beating just until blended. Spread half the batter in prepared pan. With a lightly oiled rubber spatula, spread walnut-honey mixture on batter. Top with the rest of the batter, and sprinkle with remaining ½ cup walnuts. Bake on middle shelf of oven for 50 to 60 minutes, or until a cake tester or food pick inserted into the center comes out clean.

Cool thoroughly in pan before removing.

10 to 12 servings

Prune Danish

3 tablespoons dry yeast
¾ cup warm water
1 tablespoon honey
¾ cup milk
⅓ cup honey
¼ cup butter
2½ cups sifted whole wheat flour (not pastry flour)
2½ cups sifted unbleached white flour
1 cup cold butter, cut into bits
Prune Filling (page 272)
1 egg, beaten

Sprinkle yeast over warm water in a small bowl. Stir in 1 tablespoon honey, and let stand for 5 to 10 minutes. Mixture should bubble up during that time.

Heat milk to scalding in a small saucepan. Stir in ⅓ cup honey and ¼ cup butter until butter is melted and mixture is blended.

Combine whole wheat flour and unbleached white flour in a large bowl, either sifting or stirring to blend. Add yeast mixture and milk, stirring to mix well.

Knead mixture for 10 to 12 minutes by hand, or for 5 minutes with dough hooks. If using a food processor, divide dough in half, and process each half for about 1 minute, or until an elastic ball of dough forms. Combine the 2 halves into 1 ball. Place dough into a well-buttered bowl, and turn to coat all sides. Cover with plastic wrap, and let rise in a warm place for 30 minutes.

Punch down dough and roll out into a 14 × 18-inch rectangle. Scatter half the cold butter bits over center of dough. Fold 1 side of dough over butter,

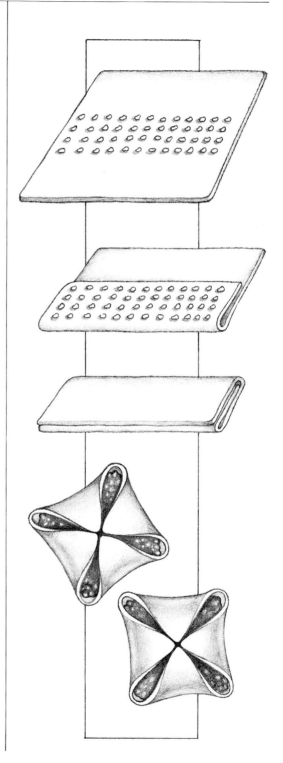

as if dough were a letter. Scatter remaining cold butter bits over folded section. Fold remaining side of dough over butter. Press to seal all butter in.

Again roll dough into a 14 × 18-inch rectangle. Fold like a letter, as before. Do this one more time, then cover dough with plastic wrap, and chill overnight or for at least 5 hours.

Butter 3 baking sheets. Divide dough in half. Keep half refrigerated, and roll out the other half ¼ inch thick. Cut into 4-inch squares. Spread a square with 1 tablespoon Prune Filling, leaving a 1-inch margin on all sides. Pick up each point of the square and fold it to the middle. Press down center points to seal. Repeat with all squares. Roll the other half of the dough, and fill as before. Place squares on prepared baking sheets, and brush with egg. Let the pastries rise until doubled in bulk, about 1 hour.

Preheat oven to 350°F.

Bake pastries 1 sheet at a time, for 15 to 20 minutes, or until golden brown.

Cool on wire racks.

Makes about 16

VARIATIONS

Cheese Danish: Use Ricotta Cheese Filling (page 271) instead of Prune Filling.

Jam Crescents: Cut dough into triangles instead of squares. Place 1 heaping teaspoon jam (any kind you desire) on large end of triangle. Roll up, starting at large end. Curve ends to make crescents.

Makes about 24

Peach Kuchen

1½ cups sifted whole wheat pastry flour
2 teaspoons baking powder
1 teaspoon baking soda
½ teaspoon ground cinnamon
½ cup butter
2 eggs
⅓ cup honey
¼ cup milk
3 cups sliced peeled peaches

Preheat oven to 375°F. Butter an 8-inch cake pan.

Sift together flour, baking powder, baking soda, and cinnamon into a large bowl. Cut in butter with a pastry blender or 2 knives until mixture is crumbly.

In a small bowl, beat together eggs and honey. Beat in milk. Stir into flour mixture just until moistened. Turn into prepared pan, arrange peaches on top, and bake on middle shelf of oven for 30 to 35 minutes, or until a cake tester or food pick inserted into the center comes out clean. Serve warm.

6 to 8 servings

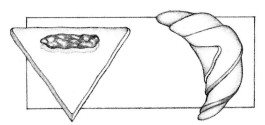

Polish Coffee Cake *(Babka)*

Easily mixed, these raisin-studded coffee cakes require no kneading. Baking the loaves in brioche pans gives them a festive appearance.

             1 cup milk
          ¼ cup butter
          ¾ cup honey
          ½ cup warm water
             2 tablespoons dry yeast
    4 to 4¼ cups whole wheat flour,
               divided
             4 eggs, at room temperature
             1 teaspoon grated lemon rind
          1½ teaspoons ground cinnamon
             1 cup raisins
          ½ cup slivered blanched
               almonds

Scald milk in a medium-size saucepan. Stir butter into milk to melt it. Stir in honey. Cool milk mixture until warm, not hot.

Pour warm water into a cup. Sprinkle yeast on top, and stir. Let stand until mixture bubbles up, 5 to 10 minutes.

In a large bowl, combine milk mixture with yeast.

In another large bowl, beat 1 cup of the flour into milk mixture. Beat in eggs, 1 at a time. Add lemon rind and cinnamon. Add 3 more cups of flour, 1 cup at a time, beating with a spoon after each addition to blend well. Cover bowl with plastic wrap, and let dough rise in a warm place until doubled in bulk, about 2 hours.

Mix raisins and almonds with remaining ¼ cup flour.

Punch down dough, using a spoon. (The dough is too sticky to do this by hand.) Stir in raisins and almonds until evenly distributed. Divide dough into 2 portions. Place each portion into a well-buttered 6-cup brioche pan. Let rise until dough just reaches the tops of the pans, about 1½ hours.

Preheat oven to 350°F.

Bake loaves on lowest shelf for 45 minutes, or until they sound hollow when tapped on the bottom. If they brown too deeply on top before being cooked through, cover tops loosely with sheets of aluminum foil.

Turn out of pans, and cool on wire racks. Serve warm, not hot, with butter and Orange Marmalade (page 274) or jam.

Makes 2

CHAPTER
9

Festive Holiday Specials

I can't imagine holiday time without the aroma of baked goods coming from the kitchen. I bake festive holiday desserts for family and company. I send cookies and fruit cakes to friends as a reminder that I'm thinking of them and wish they were with me to celebrate. We even use cookies and candies as ornaments on our Christmas tree. (Sometimes these mysteriously disappear.) When I'm expecting guests I like to put out a plate of goodies. Cookies or cupcakes are a perfect Halloween treat, especially if they're decorated with pumpkins, witches, or cats. And Thanksgiving, of course, calls for very special pies.

While some desserts, such as plum pudding and pumpkin pie, are associated with specific holidays, it's the shapes and presentations that make other desserts holiday fare. Fourth of July Cake (page 185), for instance, is a gloriously showy cake that, sans the stars-and-stripes decoration, makes a scrumptious dessert for any occasion. Just about any pie, cake, or cookie can be cut or decorated to represent a specific holiday.

One of my favorite forms of holiday entertaining is a dessert party. The table looks lovely laden with an assortment of treats. I usually invite my guests to arrive at about eight o'clock when dinner hour is well over, and they're hungry for dessert. I serve hot drinks and often a fruit punch to complement the sweets.

Progressive parties have become a popular way to celebrate holiday seasons. I usually offer to have the dessert part of the meal. It's really the easiest. All the desserts I plan can be made ahead of time. I just pop them on the table when the party arrives at our house, and I'm able to enjoy this part of the meal just as much as I did the other courses.

When I'm planning a really ambitious holiday party, I make the cakes and pies ahead of time and freeze them. This cuts way down on those frantic feelings a hostess often experiences when she has to assemble and cook everything just prior to the time company is scheduled to arrive.

There's no need to resort to colored sugars and other sweet doodads to make desserts look festive. To dress desserts up in their holiday finest, I use the natural food coloring that's available in most natural foods stores. I also add special garnishes of fresh or dried fruits (either whole or cut up); chopped, sliced, or ground nuts; coconut or Coconut Sugar (page xxii); carob chips; frozen seedless grapes (page 209); fruit leathers; and a variety of candies. And then there are desserts that are elegant in their simplicity and are knockouts without any frills or trimming, such as Pumpkin Cake Roll (page 201).

I make a Holiday Cookie Cottage (page 194) every year, and it has become the traditional centerpiece on my holiday table. Other spectacular desserts can be used as centerpieces, too. Try the Easter Bunny Cake (page 183) to dress up your Easter feast or the Strawberry Valentine (page 204), which is admired by lovers of all ages, as a table decoration for your Valentine's Day meal.

Children consider their birthdays holidays, so I've accommodated them by including cakes made in shapes that should tickle the fancy of any youngster. They're easy to make, and kids love them. When you cut a cake into shapes, you'll find that frosting the cake is easier if you allow the pieces to set long enough so the cut edges harden just a trifle. Should you frost the cake when it's first cut, crumbs will get into the frosting as you work, and you'll have a difficult and messy job.

When you're planning a number of desserts to serve after a big holiday meal, remember, not everyone will want every dessert. Also, your guests are apt to ask for smaller than usual portions. If you don't want lots of leftovers, plan accordingly.

Holidays offer the opportunity to be original in designing desserts. Let your imagination take over. You'll find it fun, and the appreciation and admiration of your guests will provide an extra reward for your creative endeavors.

Blueberry Meringue Torte

6 egg whites, at room temperature
¼ teaspoon cream of tartar
½ cup honey
3 teaspoons vanilla extract, divided
1 cup heavy cream
2 tablespoons honey
2½ cups fresh or frozen blueberries, thawed and drained
2 cups Custard Sauce (page 268)

Preheat oven to 275°F. Butter and flour 1 large and 1 small baking sheet. With a saucepan cover measuring about 7 inches, trace 2 circles on the large sheet and 1 on the small one.

In a large bowl, beat egg whites and cream of tartar together until soft peaks form. Gradually beat in ½ cup honey and 1 teaspoon vanilla until whites are very stiff. Divide mixture evenly among circles on baking sheets, spreading to edges of circles. Bake on middle shelf of oven until lightly browned, 40 to 45 minutes. (After about 25 minutes, reverse positions of baking sheets.)

Remove from oven and cool on baking sheets.

In a medium-size bowl, whip together cream, 2 tablespoons honey, and 2 teaspoons vanilla.

To assemble, place 1 meringue on serving plate, top with one-third of the whipped cream, one-third of the berries, and about ⅓ cup Custard Sauce. Top with second meringue, and repeat the process—one-third of the whipped cream, one-third of the berries, ⅓ cup Custard Sauce. Top with final meringue, remaining whipped cream, about 1 cup Custard Sauce (it will run down sides),

topping off with remaining berries. Reserve the remaining Custard Sauce to serve on the side. Cover lightly and store in refrigerator.

Cut with serrated knife when ready to serve.

Serves 8 to 10

Carob Crinkle Cups

This unique dessert is served in an edible dish.

1½ cups milk carob chips
6 tablespoons butter
1 quart French Vanilla Ice Cream (page 131) or Fresh Strawberry Sorbet (page 127)
1½ cups Custard Sauce (page 268)
½ cup unsweetened flaked coconut

Line a 6-cup muffin tin with foil liners.

In top of a double boiler set over simmering water, melt carob chips and butter together. Remove from heat, and cool until thick enough to coat the back of a spoon. Divide mixture among foil liners. Spread up sides and on bottoms of liner with the back of a spoon. Do this in layers until carob is thick on sides as well as on bottom. Refrigerate until hard.

Remove from muffin tin, and carefully peel off foil liners. To serve, fill each carob cup with a scoop of ice cream or sorbet. Top with Custard Sauce and coconut, and serve immediately.

6 servings

Amsterdam Easter Bread

This bread is as traditional in Holland as tulips and wooden shoes.

> ¾ cup lukewarm water
> 2 tablespoons honey, warmed
> 1 tablespoon dry yeast
> ½ cup milk
> 2 tablespoons butter
> 1 egg, beaten
> 4 to 5 cups whole wheat flour
> ½ cup golden raisins
> ½ cup dark raisins
> 1 cup ground walnuts
> 2 egg whites
> ¼ cup butter, softened
> ¼ cup Strawberry Jam (page 273)

Butter a large bowl. Flour a large baking sheet.

In another large bowl, blend together water and honey. Stir in yeast, and set aside until mixture bubbles up, about 10 minutes.

In a small saucepan, scald milk. Remove from heat, and stir in butter until melted. Allow to cool slightly. Add to yeast mixture along with beaten egg.

Sift flour into a medium-size bowl. Beat 3 cups flour into liquid ingredients, 1 cup at a time. Add as much of the remaining flour as dough will accept, working it in with your hands. Dough should be very stiff. Knead in a food processor in 2 batches for 1 minute, or until a ball forms; kneading can also be done by hand for 10 minutes, or with dough hooks for 5 to 7 minutes. If kneading was not done in a food processor, form dough into a ball. Place into prepared bowl, turning to coat all surfaces of dough with butter. Cover with plastic wrap, and let rise in a warm place until doubled in bulk, about 1 hour.

In a food processor, chop raisins. Remove to a bowl, and add walnuts, working in with hands until raisin pieces are separated and coated with nuts. Beat egg whites slightly, and add to raisin-nut mixture.

On a floured surface, punch dough down and form into a rectangle.

In a small bowl, cream together softened butter and jam. Spread on top of dough. Pile raisin-nut mixture in a line in center of dough, lengthwise, leaving a 1-inch border at each end. Fold one side of dough over filling. Then fold other side of dough over top to form a roll. Close ends by folding under and working together.

Place on prepared baking sheet, cover with plastic wrap, and let rise in a warm place until doubled in bulk, 30 to 45 minutes.

Preheat oven to 400°F. Remove plastic wrap, and bake on middle shelf of oven for 20 to 25 minutes, or until bread sounds hollow when tapped lightly on bottom with fingertips.

Cool on a wire rack.

Makes 1 loaf

Cookie Placecards

Children and adults both love these colorful party treats.

1 cup butter, softened
1 cup honey
2 tablespoons molasses
2 eggs
1 teaspoon vanilla extract
½ teaspoon almond extract
2½ cups whole wheat pastry flour
1 cup unbleached white flour
2 teaspoons baking powder
1 cup Decorator Frosting
   (page 267)
   natural food coloring of your
   choice

In a large bowl, beat together butter, honey, and molasses. Beat in eggs, vanilla, and almond extract.

Sift together whole wheat pastry flour, unbleached white flour, and baking powder into a medium-size bowl, and stir with a fork to blend. Add flour mixture to butter mixture, stirring to mix well. Roll dough into a ball, wrap in plastic wrap, and refrigerate until firm, preferably overnight.

Preheat oven to 400°F.

Divide dough in half. Roll out each half on a floured piece of wax paper to a rectangle ⅛ to ¼ inch thick. Cut into 5 × 2-inch rectangles, using a ruler as a guide, or cut into heart shapes, 5 inches across widest part and 5 inches from top to tip. Lift carefully with a spatula and place on a baking sheet with a nonstick surface. Bake on middle shelf of oven for about 6 minutes, or until lightly browned.

Cool thoroughly on wire racks.

Write names on cooled cookies with Decorator Frosting, using writing tip of decorating set and pastry bag. Color frosting, and use it to decorate placecards. Place on party table so that guests can find their places.

Makes about 2 dozen rectangles or 1 dozen hearts

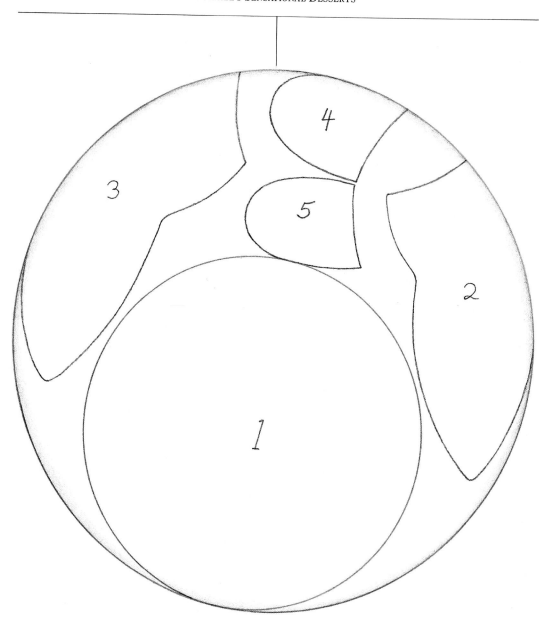

Easter Bunny Cake

2 cups Basic White Frosting,
    softened (page 268)
1 tablespoon unsweetened frozen
    grape juice concentrate or a few
    drops natural red food coloring
2 9-inch layers Lady Baltimore Cake
    (page 9)
¼ cup raisins
6 almond slivers

In a medium-size bowl, beat together white frosting and grape juice concentrate or food coloring.

Cut 1 cake layer as shown in illustration. Use second, uncut cake for body. Assemble cake as shown in illustration, using a little frosting to fasten pieces together.

Frost entire bunny. Use 2 raisins for eyes and 1 for the nose. On each side of the nose, place 3 almond slivers for whiskers. Make an outline of a bow tie and vest with remaining raisins.

10 to 12 servings

Framboise Fromage

2 packages (10-ounces each)
    unsweetened frozen raspberries,
    thawed and drained with juice
    reserved
1½ envelopes unflavored gelatin
16 ounces cream cheese, softened
1 cup heavy cream

Lightly oil a 6-cup mold.

Pour half of reserved raspberry juice into a small bowl. Sprinkle gelatin on top, and set aside for a few minutes to soften.

In a small saucepan, heat remaining juice just to a boil. Add softened gelatin, and stir until dissolved. Set aside to cool.

In a large bowl, beat cream cheese until fluffy. Beat in cooled gelatin mixture, and chill until thickened.

In a medium-size bowl, beat heavy cream until soft peaks form. Fold cream and raspberries into cheese mixture. Turn into prepared mold, and chill until set.

Turn out onto serving plate.

10 to 12 servings

Fourth of July It's-a-Grand-Old-Flag Cake   Page 185

Fourth of July
It's-a-Grand-Old-Flag Cake

    1 13 × 9-inch Italian Sponge Cake
      (page 10)
    1 cup heavy cream
    1 tablespoon honey
    ½ teaspoon vanilla extract
      about ½ cup large fresh blueberries
    2 cups sliced fresh strawberries

Place cake on an attractive serving dish or platter.

Beat cream in a medium-size bowl until soft peaks form. Beat in honey and vanilla extract. Spread whipped cream in an even layer over top of cake. Place 2 lines of blueberries at right angles in top left-hand corner so that they form a 4-inch square. Fill square with additional lines of blue-

berries. Leave a bit of white cream showing between berries.

Use overlapping sliced strawberries to form horizontal red stripes at top and bottom of the rest of the cake. Fill in with additional stripes, leaving cream showing between stripes. Refrigerate cake until serving time.

12 servings

VARIATION

Filled Fourth of July Cake: If desired, cake can be split to form 2 or even 3 layers. Use additional flavored whipped cream (double or triple recipe) and strawberries or blueberries, or a combination of both berries, between layers.

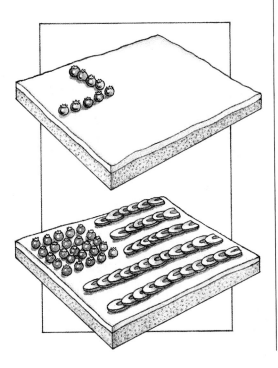

Frozen Christmas Confetti

    2 cups heavy cream
    2 tablespoons honey
    3 teaspoons brandy extract
      (optional)
    2 cups Custard Sauce (page 268),
      chilled
    1½ cups mixed dried fruit bits

Lightly oil a 6-cup ring mold.

In a large bowl, beat cream until soft peaks form. Beat in honey and brandy extract just until blended.

In a medium-size bowl, mix together Custard Sauce and fruit bits. Fold into whipped cream. Turn into prepared mold, cover, and freeze.

When ready to serve, dip mold into hot water for about 30 seconds. Turn over onto a serving plate. Slice with a sharp knife dipped in hot water.

8 to 10 servings

Eight Treasures Rice Pudding

To celebrate the Chinese New Year or any holiday, this fruit-studded pudding is decorative and easy to make.

¼ cup golden raisins
⅓ cup honey
½ teaspoon almond extract
4 cups hot cooked brown rice (moist rather than dry; use the maximum amount of water the directions suggest)
¾ cup pitted dates
2 slices dried pineapple, cut into pieces
2 dried pear halves, cut into pieces
1 slice dried papaya, cut into pieces
6 dried apricot halves, cut into slivers
4 dried figs, cut into round slices
¼ cup slivered almonds
1 cup pineapple juice
2 tablespoons honey
1 tablespoon cornstarch

Stir raisins, ⅓ cup honey, and almond extract into rice while it is still warm.

Cover dates with water in a small saucepan. Bring water to a boil and simmer for 5 minutes. Drain, reserving liquid. Mash dates, adding 1 or 2 tablespoons reserved liquid to make a spreadable paste.

Butter a 7- or 8-inch (1-quart) bowl. Starting at bottom of bowl, arrange fruit pieces in an attractive pattern, working up sides of bowl. Finish with a sprinkle of almonds above fruit. Gently cover fruit with a layer of rice, using about half of it. Next, make a thin layer of date paste, covering rice. Fill the center with remaining rice.

Place bowl in a steamer, cover, and steam for 20 minutes. (You can construct a steamer by using a colander and a large covered pan.)

While pudding is steaming, combine pineapple juice, 2 tablespoons honey, and cornstarch in a small saucepan. Stir until blended. Place over medium-high heat, and cook until sauce bubbles and thickens.

Loosen edges of pudding with a spatula or thin knife. Place serving plate over bowl. Invert to unmold. Pour pineapple sauce on top. Serve warm or at room temperature.

6 to 8 servings

Frozen Maple Sabayon with Raspberry Sauce

1 cup maple syrup
4 egg yolks
¼ cup lemon juice
1 teaspoon rum extract
1½ cups heavy cream, whipped
1 cup Raspberry Sauce (page 271)

In a deep saucepan, boil maple syrup to 230°F on a candy thermometer.

In a medium-size bowl, beat egg yolks until light. Pour hot (but not boiling) maple syrup in a very fine stream into egg yolks while beating constantly. Continue to beat until mixture is very thick. Beat in lemon juice and rum extract. Beat 2 minutes longer (until mixture has cooled a bit). Transfer egg yolk mixture to a large bowl, and fold in whipped cream. Freeze until firm.

Serve in stemmed glasses with a topping of Raspberry Sauce.

Sabayon can be chilled rather than frozen, if desired. It has a soft texture and can be served as a delicate pudding, or as a sauce for fresh fruit.

6 to 8 servings

Galettes de Noel

These deep-fried thin, crispy cookies are served warm right after they are made. Should anyone volunteer to help you make them, accept the offer, as the preparation is much easier if one person rolls the dough while another person fries the cookies.

    2 cups whole wheat pastry flour
    2 cups unbleached white flour
    1 teaspoon baking powder
    2 eggs
    ¾ cup milk
    ¼ cup butter, melted and cooled
        slightly
    2 tablespoons honey
    2 teaspoons grated orange rind
    1 teaspoon grated lemon rind
    ½ cup honey
    1 teaspoon ground cinnamon
        vegetable oil, for deep frying

Sift together whole wheat pastry flour, unbleached white flour, and baking powder into a large bowl.

In a medium-size bowl, beat eggs. Add milk, butter, 2 tablespoons honey, and grated rinds. Blend well using an egg beater. Pour liquid ingredients into dry ingredients, and stir to form dough. Knead in bowl until dough is smooth. If too sticky to handle, add a bit more flour. Form dough into balls the size of walnuts. Place on a platter, cover with plastic wrap, and refrigerate until ready to fry.

Prepare a dipping sauce for the cookies by mixing ½ cup honey with cinnamon in a small bowl.

When ready to serve, heat 4 inches of oil to 375°F in a large heavy pan. On a lightly floured surface, roll balls of dough into flat circles, ⅛ inch thick. Fry 2 at a time, turning once, until lightly browned. Drain on paper toweling. Serve warm with dipping sauce.

Makes about 25

Frozen Eggnog Logs

    2 recipes for Pastry Cream, omitting
        almond extract (page 272)
    1 teaspoon rum extract (optional)
    ¼ teaspoon freshly grated nutmeg
    1 cup heavy cream, whipped
    1 cup finely chopped pecans

Cool Pastry Cream slightly. Whisk in rum extract, if desired, and nutmeg. Fold whipped cream into Pastry Cream. Spoon mixture into 2 empty 20-ounce fruit or vegetable cans, or use 2 1-pound coffee cans, dividing the mixture between them. (It will not completely fill the coffee cans.) Cover with foil, and freeze at least overnight.

When ready to serve, unmold by removing bottoms of cans and pushing log through. Roll logs in pecans.

Let stand at room temperature for about 5 minutes before cutting into slices.

10 servings

Hanukkah Honey Nut Cake

½ cup golden raisins
½ cup dried apricots
1 cup coarsely chopped walnuts
2 tablespoons whole wheat flour
¼ cup hot water
½ teaspoon decaffinated instant coffee
¼ teaspoon baking soda
3 eggs, separated
1⅔ cups whole wheat flour
1 teaspoon baking powder
½ teaspoon ground cinnamon
¼ teaspoon ground nutmeg
¼ teaspoon ground allspice
¼ teaspoon ground ginger
1 cup honey
¼ cup vegetable oil

Preheat oven to 325°F.

Place raisins and apricots into a small bowl, cover with very hot water, and let stand for 10 minutes.

Drain fruit. Snip apricots into small pieces. Combine raisins and apricots with walnuts in another small bowl, and toss with 2 tablespoons flour.

Butter a 9 × 5 × 3-inch loaf pan, and then line it with wax paper. Butter the wax paper.

In a cup, mix together ¼ cup hot water, instant coffee, and baking soda.

In a medium-size bowl, beat egg whites until stiff peaks form.

In another medium-size bowl, sift together 1⅔ cups flour, baking powder, and spices.

In the large bowl of an electric mixer, beat honey and egg yolks together until well blended. Beat in oil until mixture is light and fluffy. Add flour mixture alternately with coffee mixture, beginning and ending with flour mixture.

When well blended, stir in about one-quarter of the beaten egg whites to lighten batter, and then gently fold in remainder of egg whites. Fold in fruit-nut mixture. Spoon batter into pre-pared pan, and bake on middle shelf of oven for 60 to 70 minutes, or until a cake tester inserted into the center comes out clean and dry.

Let cake cool in pan for 5 minutes; then turn out onto a wire rack to cool completely. Peel off wax paper.

When completely cool, wrap in foil, and store in bread box. Cake slices better if kept overnight before serving.

8 to 10 servings

Ginger Pumpkin Soufflé

This winter holiday dessert is really halfway between a soufflé and a puffy custard, but I like to call it a soufflé.

⅓ cup finely crushed crumbs from Orange-Ginger Cookies, divided (page 42)
3 eggs, separated
1 tablespoon milk
1 cup thick pureed pumpkin
¼ cup honey
2 tablespoons butter, cut into pieces
½ teaspoon ground ginger
⅛ teaspoon cream of tartar
½ cup heavy cream, whipped

Preheat oven to 350°F. Butter a 1-quart soufflé dish, and sprinkle insides with 1 tablespoon cookie crumbs.

Jolly Clown Cake   Page 196   Cookie Placecards   Page 181

In a medium-size bowl, beat together egg yolks and milk.

In a saucepan, combine pumpkin, honey, butter, and ginger. Bring to a simmer over medium-low heat, stirring constantly, and cook until butter melts.

Beat a small amount of pumpkin mixture into egg yolks. Gradually add more as you continue beating, until all of the pumpkin mixture is combined with egg yolks. Return to saucepan, and simmer for 2 minutes, stirring constantly. Remove from heat.

Beat egg whites in another medium-size bowl until foamy. Sprinkle with cream of tartar, and continue beating until stiff peaks form. Fold egg whites into pumpkin-egg mixture. Fold remaining cookie crumbs into batter. Spoon into prepared dish. Bake soufflé for 35 to 40 minutes, or until it has risen and browned.

Serve immediately with whipped cream topping.

6 servings

Italian Easter Braid

You will enjoy serving this Easter Morning breakfast treat, eggs baked in an almond- and anise-flavored sweet bread.

½ cup milk
1 tablespoon dry yeast
1 teaspoon honey
1½ to 2 cups whole wheat flour
1½ cups unbleached white flour
3 eggs, at room temperature, beaten
½ cup honey, slightly warmed
¼ cup butter, melted and cooled
1 tablespoon grated orange rind
1 teaspoon anise seeds, well crushed
⅛ teaspoon almond extract
½ cup golden raisins
½ cup slivered almonds
6 raw eggs in shells, tinted if desired (directions follow recipe)
½ cup Almond Glaze (page 266)

Scald milk in a small saucepan. Cool just until it feels very warm to your wrist.

In a small bowl, combine milk, yeast, and 1 teaspoon honey. Let stand until mixture bubbles up, about 5 minutes.

Mix together whole wheat flour and unbleached white flour in a medium-size bowl.

In a large bowl, beat together eggs, ½ cup warmed honey, butter, orange rind, anise seeds, and almond extract. Add yeast mixture and blend well. Add flour mixture, ½ cup at a time, to make a soft but workable dough. If using dough hooks, knead by machine for 5 to 7 minutes. By hand, knead on a lightly floured surface for 10 to 12 minutes. Place dough in a well-buttered bowl, and turn to butter all sides. Cover with plastic wrap, and let rise in a warm place until doubled in bulk, about 2 hours.

Flatten dough on a lightly floured surface, and let rest for 10 minutes to relax gluten. Roll out to about a 10 × 20-inch rectangle. Sprinkle with raisins and almonds, and roll up like a jellyroll. Flatten dough again, and roll out to a 10 × 15-inch square. Cut into 3 long ropes, and roll ropes to firm and lengthen them. Pinch ropes together at one end, and lay on a buttered jelly-roll pan. Begin to braid them, gently braiding in raw eggs in shells as you go. Coax braid into a circle around an oiled custard cup, and pinch closed. Cover lightly with plastic wrap, and let rise in a warm place until doubled in bulk, about 1½ hours.

Preheat oven to 350°F.

Bake bread on middle shelf of oven for 25 minutes. Gently remove custard cup (if necessary, use tip of a serrated knife), and continue baking for 10 minutes, or until bread sounds hollow when tapped and is a beautiful brown on top. Loosen bread from pan and place on a wire rack over a sheet of wax paper.

Spread Almond Glaze over bread while loaf is still warm. Cool on a wire rack. If keeping bread overnight, store in a bread box in a cool room.

Because this braid is traditionally light in color, some white flour has been used; if you prefer, you may use all whole wheat flour, in which case you will need about ¼ cup less.

Makes 1 loaf

Chantilly Peach Flan

Sweetened, flavored whipped cream is sometimes called Chantilly cream.

pastry for 1½ Tart Pastries 2
　(page 59)
⅓ cup Apple Jelly, divided (page 274)
½ cup heavy cream
1 tablespoon honey
¼ teaspoon almond extract
¼ teaspoon vanilla extract
　Creamy Cake Filling (page 273)
2 cups sliced peeled ripe peaches
　(nectarines may be substituted)

Preheat oven to 450°F.

Roll out chilled tart dough between 2 sheets of wax paper to about a ⅛- to ¼-inch thickness. Carefully remove 1 sheet of wax paper, and invert pastry over a 9-inch flan pan with a removable rim. Remove second sheet of wax paper, and fit pastry into pan without stretching it. Trim pastry at pan rim, pressing all around with tines of a fork. Prick pastry on bottom and sides at ½-inch intervals. Place pan on top shelf of oven, and reduce heat to 400°F. Bake for 15 to 20 minutes, or until lightly browned all over.

Cool in pan on wire rack.

In a small saucepan, melt jelly over low heat. When cool, brush bottom and sides of crust with 1 to 2 tablespoons melted jelly. Let stand for at least 30 minutes.

Whip cream in a small bowl until soft peaks form. Beat in honey and almond and vanilla extracts. Cover, and refrigerate until needed.

When ready to serve, spread Creamy Cake Filling over jelly. Top with peach slices. Brush fruit with the remaining melted jelly. Remove pan rim. Serve with Chantilly cream.

10 servings

Jack-o'-Lantern Cookies

Here is a sweet that will delight the trick-or-treat set—and their parents!

1 cup whole wheat pastry flour
1 cup unbleached white flour
1 teaspoon baking soda
1 teaspoon ground cinnamon
½ teaspoon ground cloves
½ teaspoon ground ginger
¼ teaspoon ground nutmeg
1 cup butter, softened
1 cup honey
1 egg
1 cup thick pureed pumpkin
1 cup uncooked quick oats
about ¼ cup milk carob chips
about ¼ cup raisins

In a medium-size bowl, sift together whole wheat pastry flour, unbleached white flour, baking soda, and spices.

Cream butter in a large bowl until light. Beat in honey, then egg and pumpkin. Stir in dry ingredients. Mix in oats. Chill dough until firm enough to handle.

Preheat oven to 350°F. Butter 2 baking sheets.

Scoop up ¼ cup dough. Roll between your palms to form a ball.

Tinted Easter Eggs for Italian Easter Braid

This technique can be applied to hard-cooked eggs as well as raw eggs in shells, depending on how you plan to use them. For the Italian Easter Braid, raw eggs are used so that they will not be overcooked while the bread is baking.

PINK

Combine 1 cup beet juice and 2 tablespoons white vinegar in a Pyrex cup. Immerse egg for 20 to 30 minutes. Rinse egg and allow it to dry in an egg holder or carton.

PURPLE

Cover 1 cup blueberries, fresh or frozen, with water in a small saucepan. Bring to a boil and simmer for 5 minutes. Drain, crushing berries; pour liquid into a Pyrex cup. Immerse egg for 20 to 30 minutes. Rinse egg and allow it to dry in an egg holder or carton.

YELLOW

In a Pyrex cup, dissolve 2 teaspoons turmeric in 1 cup boiling water. Immerse egg for 20 to 30 minutes. Rinse egg and allow it to dry in an egg holder or carton.

Place on a baking sheet, and press gently to make a ¼-inch-thick circle. Pinch 1 end to form a pumpkin stem. Repeat until you've used half of the dough to fill baking sheets, about 5 cookies to a sheet.

Use carob chips to make eyes and nose on each pumpkin face; use raisins to shape mouth. (Children love to do this!) Stagger baking sheets on 2 shelves near middle of oven, and bake for 25 minutes, or until lightly browned at edges.

Cool baking sheets. Form and bake the rest of the dough the same way.

Makes 20

Gingerbread People

The number of cookies that can be made with this recipe depends on the size of the cookie cutters used. Some are only a couple of inches high, others make cookies six inches tall. But small or tall, the recipe produces 4 batches of people.

3 cups whole wheat pastry flour
1 teaspoon baking soda
1½ teaspoons ground ginger
½ teaspoon ground allspice
½ cup butter
½ cup honey
¼ cup light molasses
1 egg
1 teaspoon white vinegar

Sift together flour, baking soda, ginger, and allspice into a medium-size bowl. Stir with a fork to blend.

In a large bowl, beat butter. Add honey and molasses, and beat in. Beat in egg. Lightly mix in dry ingredients and vinegar. Wrap dough with plastic wrap, and refrigerate until firm, about 1 hour.

Preheat oven to 350°F. Butter a baking sheet.

Divide dough into quarters. Roll out each portion on a lightly floured surface. Cut with cookie cutters, and place carefully on prepared baking sheet. If cookies are large enough, press raisins into dough for eyes and buttons. Bake on middle shelf of oven, allowing 6 to 8 minutes for small people, and 10 to 12 minutes for large ones.

Molasses Popcorn Balls

1 cup honey
⅓ cup light molasses
⅓ cup water
1 tablespoon butter
3 quarts popcorn

In a heavy medium-size saucepan, combine honey, molasses, and water. Cook slowly, stirring with a long-handled spoon until temperature on candy thermometer registers 250°F. Stir in butter until melted.

Place popcorn into a large bowl. Pour syrup over it, and stir well with a buttered spoon to coat all pieces. While mixture is still warm, form into balls about 3 inches in diameter with buttered hands.

Makes about 2 dozen

VARIATION
Maple Popcorn Balls: Substitute maple syrup for molasses.

Holiday Cookie Cottage

There are many recipes for cookie houses. Most of them are spectacular, but I've found that they take hours and hours to make and require very small amounts of ingredients that can't be purchased in very small amounts— thus leaving you with an array of things for which you have no use and have paid quite a large sum. These cookie houses are a major investment in both time and money. Years ago I designed a cookie cottage of my own, described below, and it's the easiest and least expensive one that I've come across.

IN ADDITION TO THE COOKIE
INGREDIENTS, YOU'LL NEED:

    a flat baking sheet (no sides)
    parchment paper or foil
    a pen or pencil
    tracing paper
    a piece of lightweight cardboard
     (about 10 × 12 inches)
    scissors
    a sharp knife
    a piece of corrugated cardboard
     (about 9 inches square)
    a pastry bag with a writing tip and
     a star tip
    Decorator Frosting (page 267)
    Vanilla Icing (page 268)
    raisins
    slivered almonds (optional)

TO MAKE THE COOKIES,
YOU'LL NEED:

    1½ cups unsifted whole wheat flour
    1¼ cups unsifted unbleached white
      flour
    1½ teaspoons ground cinnamon
    1 teaspoon ground ginger
    1 teaspoon ground nutmeg
    ½ cup butter, softened

    ¼ cup honey
    ½ cup molasses
    1 egg

Sift together whole wheat flour, unbleached white flour, cinnamon, ginger, and nutmeg into a medium-size bowl.

In a large bowl, beat butter until fluffy. Beat in honey, molasses, and egg.

With floured hands, work flour mixture into moist ingredients until well blended. Cover, and refrigerate for about 30 minutes.

Line a baking sheet with parchment or foil, and roll dough out on it. Return to refrigerator for 1 hour.

Preheat oven to 350°F.

Trace outlines of roof, front and back, and side of house and tree on tracing paper (see illustration). Cut 2 of each of the tracings out of lightweight cardboard. Place cardboard pieces on rolled-out dough. With tip of a sharp knife cut around each piece, removing dough in between pieces. (You can roll this dough out for cookies.) Cut indentations in, but not through, pieces of dough, following designs in illustration. Bake on middle shelf of oven until edges are slightly browned, 10 to 12 minutes.

Remove from oven and cool completely on wire racks.

Tape front, back, and sides of cardboard house together. Tape cardboard roof pieces together at peak.

Make 1 recipe for Decorator Frosting. Place half of frosting into pastry bag fitted with writing tip, and outline all indentations on cookie pieces. (If frosting is too thick, thin slightly with

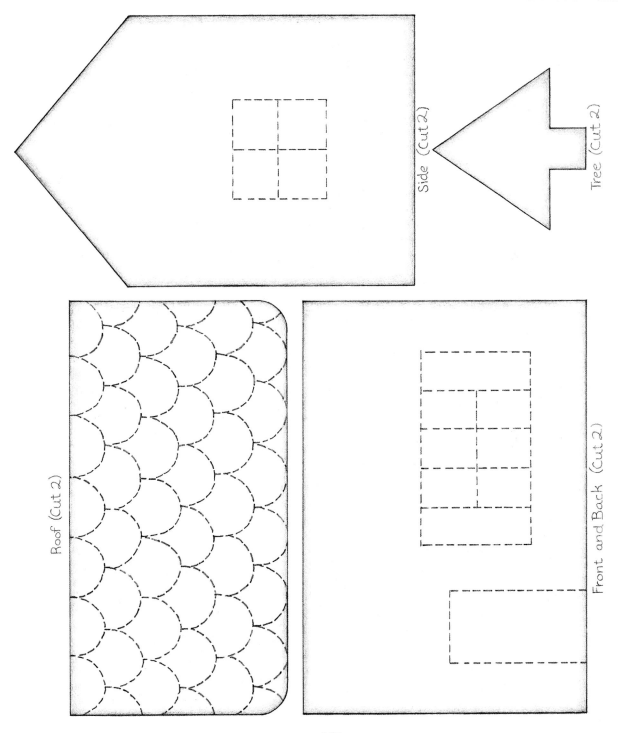

Side (Cut 2)

Tree (Cut 2)

Roof (Cut 2)

Front and Back (Cut 2)

195

honey. If not thick enough, beat in more instant nonfat dry milk.)

Divide remaining frosting in half. Stir in 5 or 6 drops of natural red food coloring into one half and 5 or 6 drops of natural green food coloring into the other half. With a knife, spread cookie trees with green frosting. Place pink frosting into clean pastry bag fitted with star tip. Fill in front door and shutters. Change to writing tip, and put dots on trees to resemble ornaments. (If desired, place green frosting into a clean pastry bag fitted with writing tip, and make wreaths on doors and windows.) Let pieces stand until frosting is thoroughly dry and set.

Make 1 recipe for Vanilla Icing. Brush front, back, and sides of cardboard house and backs of corresponding cookies with icing. Put cookie pieces in place against cardboard, placing a glass against each piece to hold it in place until icing dries. Brush surface of cardboard roof and backs of 2 roof-shaped cookie pieces with icing. Put roof together and set aside to dry.

Beat ½ to ¾ cup more of instant nonfat dry milk into remaining Vanilla Icing. (It should be quite firm but still pliable enough to push through decorator tip easily.) Place ½ cup into clean pastry bag fitted with star tip. Outline all joints of cookie house with icing. Put roof in place, and outline top and eaves (where roof joins house) with icing. If desired, form icicles under roof with writing tip, and outline roof with bits of raisins and slivered almonds.

Set cottage on corrugated cardboard. Beat about ½ cup more of instant nonfat dry milk into remaining icing. Spread around house and out to edges of corrugated cardboard. Press raisins into frosting to make a walk to front door. Make 2 "snowdrifts" of frosting—1 in front of the cottage by the window and 1 in back. Push trunks of trees into these mounds.

To make snowman, roll a ¾-inch ball and a ½-inch ball of icing between palms. Press balls together with smaller one on top. Press a raisin into top of head to make a hat, and press tiny pieces of raisin into front of head for eyes and nose. Lightly press snowman into frosting in front yard, adding more frosting if necessary to secure him in place.

Roll out 2 long pieces of icing between palms to make snowdrifts. Push into place on both sides of walk.

Let cottage set for 24 hours.

Jolly Clown Cake

This is my favorite birthday cake for little folks!

> 1 recipe for Italian Sponge Cake (page 10)
> 1½ recipes for Basic White Frosting (page 268)
> 4 Strawberry Almond Cookies (page 44), other round cookies may be substituted
> date sugar
> Coconut Sugar (page xxii)
> about ¼ cup milk carob chips
> a few drops natural red food coloring

Use 1 9-inch round layer cake pan and 1 9-inch square layer cake pan to bake Italian Sponge Cake according to recipe directions, except decrease baking time to 35 to 45 minutes. Cool layers on wire racks.

Cut a triangle from the square layer as shown in illustration. This will be the clown's hat. The round layer will be his head; trim top to make a straight edge. From scraps, cut a round pom-pom for top of hat and a neck for clown's head. Cut 2 small half-rounds to be clown's ears. (See illustration.)

Cover a board or tray with brightly colored foil to hold clown cake. Assemble parts and paste together with a little of the frosting. (See illustration.) Let cake dry for an hour or so before frosting. Brush off crumbs.

Frost entire clown's face and hat. Place 1 cookie on pom-pom, use 2 cookies for eyes, and carefully cut 1 cookie in half to place on ears. Sprinkle clown's hat with date sugar and Coconut Sugar. Make a mouth and nose with carob chips.

Color remaining frosting with food coloring. Place into a pastry bag, and use a decorative tube to pipe red frosting around cookie on pom-pom, to make a rim for hat, and to make a collar on neck. Use remaining carob chips to decorate collar and hat rim. Keep in a cool place until ready to serve.

12 servings

197

Passover Date Torte

¼ cup whole wheat pastry flour, divided
2 cups finely chopped dates
2 cups very finely chopped pecans
    or walnuts
8 eggs, separated
½ cup honey
1 tablespoon grated orange rind
¼ teaspoon cream of tartar

Preheat oven to 325°F. Butter a 9-inch springform pan. Sprinkle with 2 teaspoons flour.

In a medium-size bowl, mix dates and nuts with remaining flour.

Beat egg yolks in a large bowl. Beat in honey, then date-nut mixture and orange rind.

In another large bowl, beat egg whites until foamy. Sprinkle with cream of tartar, and continue beating until stiff peaks form. Fold into egg yolk mixture. Spoon batter into prepared pan, and bake on middle shelf of oven for 40 minutes, or until a cake tester or food pick inserted into the center comes out clean and dry.

Cool in pan on a wire rack. When cool, remove sides of pan.

12 servings

Noel Tortoni

½ cup raisins
2 quarts French Vanilla Ice Cream
    (page 131)
2 teaspoons vanilla extract
1½ teaspoons rum extract (optional)
½ cup chopped toasted almonds
1 cup milk carob chips

Place raisins into a small bowl, cover with boiling water, and set aside to plump for 15 to 20 minutes. Drain thoroughly.

Line 3 6-cup muffin tins with paper liners.

In a large bowl, cut ice cream into chunks. Stir until smooth and creamy. Mix in vanilla extract and rum extract, if desired. Fold in remaining ingredients. Turn into muffin tins, and place in freezer until very firm.

Cut 18 rounds of wax paper the size of the tortoni tops. To prevent tortoni from sticking together in freezer, cover each one with a wax paper round, pressing rounds gently onto surface. Remove tortoni from muffin tins, and store in plastic bag in freezer.

Makes 18

Mincemeat Cranberry Tarts

pastry for 1 Tart Pastry 2
    (page 59)
1½ cups Mincemeat "Lite" (page 70)
⅔ cup Cranberry Jelly, mashed
    (page 273)
18 cubes Cranberry Jelly

Preheat oven to 450°F.

Divide pastry into 2 portions. Roll out 1 portion between 2 sheets of wax paper into a 9 × 9-inch square. Remove top piece of wax paper. Cut dough into 3-inch squares. Fit each square into a 2½-inch fluted tart pan. Press edges to remove any overhang. Prick dough with a fork on bottom and sides. Repeat until all dough has been used, rerolling scraps. If you don't have 18 tart pans, you can make tarts in batches, reusing pans.

Place tarts on a large baking sheet on top shelf of oven. Reduce heat to 400°F. Bake for 15 minutes, or until lightly browned.

Cool tarts on wire racks until they can be handled comfortably. Invert on palm of hand and gently tap on bottom to remove from pans. Finish cooling on wire racks.

In a medium-size bowl, mix together mincemeat and mashed Cranberry Jelly. Bring to room temperature. When ready to serve, fill tarts. Top each one with a cube of Cranberry Jelly.

Makes 18

Kiffles

These crunchy rolled cookies with a sweet filling are guaranteed to please.

1 cup whole wheat pastry flour
1 cup unbleached white flour
1 cup cold butter
1 cup cold cottage cheese
½ cup Peach or Apricot Jam (page 276)
½ cup Prune Filling (page 272)
½ cup finely chopped almonds or pecans

Sift together whole wheat pastry flour and unbleached white flour into a medium-size bowl. Cut butter into chunks and drop into flour. With a pastry blender or 2 knives, cut butter into flour until mixture has a mealy texture. Add cottage cheese and cut it into mixture. Knead dough in bowl to form a compact ball. Wrap ball in plastic wrap, and chill for several hours.

Preheat oven to 350°F. Butter 2 baking sheets.

Pinch off about one-third of dough, and roll out ⅛ inch thick on a lightly floured surface to make a 10-inch circle. Spread with ¼ cup jam or Prune Filling. Sprinkle with 2 tablespoons nuts. Cut into wedges, roll them up starting at wide end, and place on prepared baking sheet. Repeat with remaining two-thirds of dough, one-third at a time, saving dough scraps to make a fourth circle. Bake for 20 minutes, or until golden brown.

Cool on wire racks.

Makes about 2 dozen

Strawberry Valentine   Page 204

Tutti-Frutti Roll

½ cup golden raisins
½ cup dark raisins
½ cup pitted prunes
½ cup dried apricots
½ cup finely chopped walnuts
⅓ cup Coconut Sugar (page xxii)

In a food processor, chop raisins, prunes, and apricots. Place fruit into a medium-size bowl, and mix with walnuts.

Using lightly buttered wax paper, form mixture into a roll, and then roll in Coconut Sugar. Cut crosswise into ½-inch pieces.

Makes 18 to 20 pieces

Ye Merrie Olde Plum Pudding

I like to decorate this Christmas favorite with sprigs of fresh holly and serve it with Orange Custard Sauce (page 270).

1 cup sifted whole wheat pastry flour, divided
1 cup finely chopped suet
3 cups mixed dried fruits (your choice: pitted dates, pitted prunes, currants, raisins, papayas, apples, apricots, pears)
1 cup unbleached white flour
1 teaspoon baking soda
1 teaspoon ground cinnamon
½ teaspoon ground cloves
¼ teaspoon ground nutmeg
4 eggs
½ cup honey
1 cup milk
1 tablespoon grated orange rind
2 cups dry whole grain bread crumbs

Mix ½ cup whole wheat pastry flour with suet and dried fruits in a large bowl.

In a medium-size bowl, sift together remaining whole wheat flour, unbleached white flour, baking soda, and spices.

In a very large bowl, beat eggs until light. Beat in honey, then milk and orange rind. Blend in flour mixture and bread crumbs. Fold in fruit-suet mixture.

Generously butter a 2-pound coffee can or equivalent mold. Pour in batter. Cover with buttered wax paper; then cover loosely with foil to allow for swelling. Tie a piece of kitchen twine around foil or use a large rubber band to form a tight seal. Stand can on a rack in a large pot. Fill pot with water to within 2 inches of top of can. Cover pot, bring water to a boil (slowly), and simmer pudding for 4 hours.

Remove can or mold from pot. Remove foil cover, and run a thin metal spatula around sides of can to ease pudding out. Cool. Wrap in aluminum foil, and refrigerate or freeze until needed. For best flavor, allow pudding to rest at least one day before serving.

To reheat, steam pudding in foil on a rack in a large covered pot for 1 to

2 hours. Use only a little water—it should not touch pudding. Watch that water does not boil away.

Serves 10 to 12

Pumpkin Cake Roll

CAKE
    4 eggs
    ½ cup honey
    ¾ cup pumpkin puree
    1½ teaspoons lemon juice
    1 cup sifted whole wheat pastry flour
    2 teaspoons baking powder
    1 teaspoon baking soda
    2½ teaspoons ground cinnamon
    1 teaspoon ground ginger
    ½ cup Coconut Sugar (page xxii)
FILLING
    8 ounces cream cheese, softened
    ¼ cup butter, softened
    ⅓ cup honey
    1 teaspoon vanilla extract

To make the cake: Preheat oven to 350°F. Butter and flour a 17 × 11 × 2-inch pan.

In a large bowl, beat eggs until foamy and lemon colored, about 3 minutes. Beat in honey, pumpkin, and lemon juice.

Sift together flour, baking powder, baking soda, cinnamon, and ginger into egg mixture. Beat for about 1 minute. Turn into prepared pan, and bake on middle shelf of oven for 10 to 15 minutes, or until cake springs back when pressed in the middle.

Sprinkle a tea towel with Coconut Sugar. Turn cake out onto towel, and roll towel and cake together from narrow end. (See illustration, page 8). Set aside to cool thoroughly.

To make the filling: In a medium-size bowl, beat together cream cheese, butter, honey, and vanilla. Unroll cake, and spread frosting over it. Roll up using edges of towel as a guide but not including it in roll. Chill until ready to serve.

10 to 12 servings

Prunes Stuffed with Almond Paste

The humble prune takes on a new sophistication when you prepare these confections. I like to include them in a cookie selection for variety.

    24 soft pitted dried prunes
        about ¼ cup Almond Paste (page 277)
    24 pecan halves
        about ½ cup Coconut Sugar (page xxii)

Make a slit on one side of each prune. Press ½ teaspoon Almond Paste into centers. Press a pecan half into Almond Paste in each prune. Reform prunes around stuffing so that it just peeks out a bit. Roll confections in Coconut Sugar until well coated. Place in miniature-size fluted paper liners.

Makes 2 dozen

Eight Treasures Rice Pudding   Page 186

Three-Story Holiday Cake

2¼ cups whole wheat pastry flour
2¼ cups unbleached white flour
  1 tablespoon baking powder
  1 teaspoon baking soda
  8 egg whites, at room temperature
  1 cup butter, softened
1½ cups honey
  1 teaspoon almond extract
1¼ cups milk
    Festive Frosting (page 266)

Preheat oven to 350°F. Butter and flour 3 8-inch round layer cake pans.

Sift together whole wheat pastry flour, unbleached white flour, baking powder, and baking soda three times.

In a large bowl, beat egg whites until soft peaks form.

In another large bowl, beat together butter, honey, and almond extract. Add flour, a little at a time, alternating with milk, and mix well. Gently fold in egg whites. Turn into prepared pans, and bake for 20 to 25 minutes, or until a cake tester or food pick inserted into the center comes out clean.

Cool in pans for 10 minutes. Turn out onto wire racks, and cool thoroughly.

Frost between layers, top, and sides with Festive Frosting.

8 to 10 servings

Torrone

Because Torrone entirely made with honey is softer than the traditional honey-sugar combination, I have devised sweet coatings to house the tender honey nougat.

NOUGAT
  3 egg whites
  1½ cups honey
  1 teaspoon vanilla extract
  ½ teaspoon almond extract
  3 cups nut meats (almonds, filberts, and/or pistachios are traditional)
COATING
  1 cup unsweetened flaked coconut
                or
  1 cup finely chopped almonds
                or
  1½ cups milk carob chips
  1 teaspoon butter

Generously butter a 10 × 10 × 2-inch pan.

In a medium-size bowl, beat egg whites until stiff peaks form.

Warm honey in a large, nonstick skillet, and then fold into egg whites. Spoon mixture into skillet. Bring to a very low simmer, over lowest heat, stirring constantly. When nougat shows a few bubbles, cook for 10 minutes longer, stirring constantly and lifting pan at any sign of sticking.

Remove from heat and stir in extracts and nuts. Spoon mixture into prepared pan. Chill in refrigerator.

When cold, coat candy in any of the 3 ways described below:

Coconut coating: Form a ball of nougat using 2 buttered teaspoons. Roll in coconut, covering nougat completely. Place ball in a miniature fluted paper liner. Repeat with the rest of nougat. Chill until firm.

Almond coating: Using the same method, coat nougat with almonds.

Carob coating: Invert nougat from pan onto a double thickness of wax paper.

Melt carob chips in top of a double boiler set over simmering water, adding butter. Remove pan from heat. With a table knife, spread about half of the melted carob over nougat. Chill until firm.

Turn nougat, carob-side down, onto a fresh double thickness of wax paper. Peel off first sheet of wax paper. Reheat remaining carob, and spread second side of nougat with it. Chill.

Cut into serving-size pieces. Dip knife into hot water as necessary.

Makes about 2 pounds

VARIATION

Orange Torrone: Substitute 1 tablespoon grated orange rind for vanilla and almond extracts. Substitute 1 cup macadamia nuts and 1 cup golden raisins for nut meats. Coat with coconut or melted carob. (I particularly like the carob coating with this recipe.)

Strawberry Valentine

This is an unusually moist cheesecake that appeals both to cheesecake lovers and to those who find ordinary cheesecake too dry for their liking.

2 cups crumbs from Basic Honey
    Cookies (page 46)
½ cup butter, melted
8 ounces cream cheese, softened
8 ounces creamed cottage cheese
4 eggs
⅓ cup honey
1½ teaspoons vanilla extract, divided
1 cup halved fresh strawberries
1 cup heavy cream
1 tablespoon honey
1 cup whole fresh strawberries

Preheat oven to 350°F. Butter bottom and sides of a 9-inch springform pan.

In a medium-size bowl, thoroughly mix together cookie crumbs and butter. Press onto bottom of springform pan to form a crust.

In a large bowl, beat cream cheese and cottage cheese together until fluffy.

Beat eggs in a small bowl, and then add to cheeses, mixing in until well blended. Beat in ⅓ cup honey and 1 teaspoon vanilla.

In a blender or food processor, puree halved strawberries. Beat into cheese mixture. Turn into prepared pan, and bake on middle shelf of oven for 1 hour and 10 minutes.

Turn oven off, but allow cake to remain in oven for another hour.

Remove cake from oven and cool thoroughly.

In another medium-size bowl, whip cream, 1 tablespoon honey, and ½ teaspoon vanilla together, until soft peaks form. Place cream into a pastry bag, and pipe onto cake in the shape of a heart. Decorate with whole strawberries.

8 to 10 servings

CHAPTER
10

Delectable Time-Savers

T hroughout this book you'll find many desserts that are quick and easy to prepare, but I've created this chapter especially for those occasions when you don't have time to browse through the book selecting a recipe that strikes your fancy. This chapter is for days when time really is at a premium.

Nothing is simpler yet more elegant than an assortment of fresh fruits in season served alone or with a just-ripe Brie or Camembert or a wedge of cheddar cheese—it's the quintessence of easy desserts. And fresh berries topped with yogurt or cream take only seconds to prepare and are oh, so good.

Having desserts frozen and at the ready is, of course, very helpful.

Unfrosted cakes, fruit pies, and cookie dough all freeze well. The pies can be popped into the oven without defrosting.

For instant dessert decorations, I often freeze seedless grapes, placing them in a single layer on a baking sheet in the freezer and then storing the frozen grapes in a freezer bag. They quickly turn the plainest of desserts into company fare. Frozen cake crumbs are also a fast dessert topping.

One of the first rules for saving time in the kitchen is to keep equipment and staples organized so that they're within easy reach. And you need a workspace that's kept uncluttered so that you don't waste precious time clearing it. Then, before you start making a dessert, assemble all the ingredients and equipment you'll need.

Planning is a large part of time saving. If you decide ahead of time what dessert you'll be making, you can

Petits Pots au Carob   Page 222

have some of the ingredients ready for use. For instance, eggs can be separated and kept in jars in the refrigerator. (The yolks should be stored whole in a jar of cold water.) Much of the chopping and slicing can be done in advance, too. Cream can be whipped and stored, covered, in the refrigerator. I always keep an airtight container full of chopped nuts and one with ground nuts in my refrigerator, ready whenever they're needed. One sure way to save time is to plan an entire oven meal, including the dessert—all to be cooked in one oven, at one time, at one temperature.

If you've neglected to plan in advance, and you need a fast dessert, you can speed up the preparation by bringing ingredients to room temperature rapidly. Put butter on a plate and place it near a steaming pot, a pilot light, or other source of heat to soften it; measure milk into a container, and set it in warm water; submerge eggs in tepid water.

Keep an ample batch of homemade cake mix on hand (page 216). This eliminates several steps in cake making and is a big help on hectic days. Cookie dough (page 214) and piecrusts (page 218) can also be made in bulk.

Make double or triple recipes when you have time, and freeze the extras for later use. (See page xxv for information on freezing desserts.) All you need is a larger mixing bowl, and you'll have two desserts for the work of one. If you can't fit two batches of cookies, two cakes, or two pies on the same oven shelf, stagger them so that they'll get even heat. Halfway through the baking process, reverse their positions in the oven.

Many cakes and puddings can be cooked in the same dish in which they're mixed. This makes it possible to go from mixing to oven to table without muss or fuss.

The food processor is invaluable when it comes to hurry-up baking. But in a standard-size processor, only about 2½ cups of solids or 1½ cups of liquids can be processed efficiently at one time. This means that for large recipes or for baking in quantity, processing must be done in batches. If you're going to use the food processor often as a time-saving tool, you may want to invest in a professional model with a large-size work bowl that will handle larger amounts.

The blender is another valuable tool when you have ingredients to chop, grate, or puree, but it doesn't work as efficiently as a food processor; and for most jobs, you must stop the motor and scrape down the sides frequently.

The food processor is a multi-talented tool, and I wouldn't be without one. The steel cutting blade is the most versatile and the one most often used. There's nothing the plastic mixing blade can do that the steel blade doesn't do as well. Fitted with a steel blade, many processors will knead bread in a matter of seconds. They'll chop nuts and fruits if you use an on/off motion and will grind them if you let the processor run for about 30 seconds.

The blender won't knead bread, but it will chop, grate, puree, and liquify, and it's a marvel for making quick, lump-free sauces.

Whether you use a food processor or a blender to chop and grate, or do these tasks by hand, you'll save time by chopping enough for more than one recipe. The extra ingredients can be frozen or refrigerated until you need them.

With the steel blade, a food processor can beat several eggs or egg yolks in a jiffy, getting the yolks to the "ribbon" stage in about 1 minute (a job that takes about 10 minutes with an electric beater), but the processor does a poor job on egg whites since it works too fast to incorporate the air necessary to make them puffed up and fluffy.

Dried fruits, which are so difficult and time consuming to cut up by hand, are a breeze to do in a food processor. Fit it with the steel cutting blade, add up to a cup of dried fruit and a little flour to prevent sticking, and then process with an on/off motion until the fruit is the size you want. If there's any loose flour, shake it off unless it's part of the recipe.

The blender also acquits itself well on dried fruits, but it takes a little longer and won't chop as much at one time. You'll do best to start with ⅓ cup and stop the machine often, turning the fruit over so that the pieces on the bottom won't get pulverized while those on top stay whole.

For creaming butter, I find there's nothing as efficient as an electric beater or mixer. It works best when the butter is softened, but if you don't want to take the time for this, just cut the butter into 1-inch cubes before beating it. It will stick to the beaters initially, but as it creams it will pull away from

them. Cream cheese behaves the same way as butter, so I generally use an electric beater on it, too.

The electric beater is unsurpassed for whipping cream. The food processor can be used for this task, but its efficiency is debatable. Some cooks say it does the job well, others say it doesn't work at all. In my experience, it does a fair job when you're on a particularly tight schedule and just don't have the few extra minutes required to whip the cream with an electric beater or by hand. But the food processor won't produce the volume of fluffy whipped cream you'll get using other methods.

Since the food processor works so fast, I recommend using an on/off motion during processing so that you can check its progress and not over-process. If the food isn't chopped quite enough when you check it, you can give the machine another whirl or two, but if what you wanted chopped has been processed too much, and you've pureed ingredients you wanted only to chop, there's nothing to do but start over.

When time is short, you may take several minutes off the cooking time of many recipes by cutting pieces smaller than the recipe calls for. An apple pie with chopped apples, for instance, bakes more rapidly than one with sliced apples.

You may find that making the finishing touches for a dessert are more time consuming than making the basic dessert itself. Some frostings are fussier to prepare than the cakes they adorn. When time is of the essence, you can't go wrong by replacing complicated frostings and other toppings or fillings with whipped cream. And, of course, some cakes are even more delicious without frosting.

Cleanup is an unavoidable part of food preparation that's often forgotten in figuring time requirements. I always do my preparation on a dishwasher-safe white polyethylene chopping board, which can be wiped off quickly and popped into the dishwasher for a more thorough cleaning. One of the advantages of this type of cutting board is

that it doesn't harbor bacteria as do the wooden ones.

Cookie dough and piecrusts can leave a mess. Rolling out the dough for either of them between pieces of wax paper is another way to hasten cleanup. You can roll up the paper and dispose of it, leaving no counters to scrub.

Many of these suggestions will only save you seconds or minutes. But they add up, and that's how time saving works.

Almond Cream

1 egg yolk
8 ounces cream cheese, softened
1 cup sour cream
1 cup heavy cream
3 tablespoons honey
½ teaspoon almond extract

Blend all ingredients in a food processor or blender. Keep chilled, and serve over any fresh berries.
Preparation time: 3 minutes

Yields about 3 cups

Baked Banana Puddings

3 eggs
1½ cups milk
½ cup honey
¼ teaspoon ground ginger
¼ teaspoon ground cinnamon
½ teaspoon ground cloves
2 ripe bananas, chunked

Preheat oven to 325°F. Place 6 custard cups in a roasting pan that will accommodate them comfortably.

Place ingredients in a blender container in the order given, and process until well blended. Pour mixture into custard cups. Place pan in oven; add hot water to pan up to ½ inch from top of custard cups. Bake for 35 minutes, or until a table knife inserted into the center comes out clean.

Serve warm with a topping of unsweetened whipped cream, if desired, or chilled.

Preparation time (not including baking): 10 minutes

6 servings

Bananas Supreme

2 tablespoons butter
2 bananas
¼ cup chopped pecans
2 tablespoons honey
   ground cinnamon, for sprinkling

Preheat oven to 350°F, and while it is heating, melt butter in a gratin dish in the oven, removing before it turns color.

Slice bananas lengthwise and in half, and turn them over in melted butter to coat all sides, leaving bananas in gratin dish. Sprinkle with pecans, and drizzle honey over all. Add a sprinkle of cinnamon, and bake on middle shelf of oven for 20 minutes.

Serve warm.

Preparation time (not including baking): 8 minutes

2 servings

VARIATION

Hot Banana Splits: Top Bananas Supreme with French Vanilla Ice Cream (page 131), Basic Carob Syrup (page xviii), and a ripe cherry or strawberry for decoration.

Basic Cookie Logs

Make these logs when you have leisure time; then when you are harried, you can quickly slice them and bake an easy dessert.

2¼ cups whole wheat pastry flour
½ teaspoon baking soda
½ cup butter, softened
⅓ cup honey
1 egg
1½ teaspoons vanilla extract

Sift together flour and baking soda into a medium-size bowl, stirring with a fork to blend.

In a large bowl, beat butter until fluffy. Beat in honey, then egg, and vanilla. Mix in flour. Divide dough in half, and roll into 2 logs. Wrap in wax paper, and refrigerate until firm. (These will keep for 2 weeks in the refrigerator.)

Preheat oven to 350°F. Butter a baking sheet.

Slice logs into ⅛-inch-thick slices. Place on prepared baking sheet, and bake on middle shelf of oven for 8 to 10 minutes, or until lightly browned.

Makes 3 to 5 dozen

VARIATIONS

Carob Nut Rounds: Add 3 tablespoons ground walnuts and 2 tablespoons Basic Carob Syrup (page xviii) to dough before making logs.
Orange Treats: Substitute orange extract for vanilla extract. Add 1½ teaspoons grated orange rind to dough before making logs.

Coconutties: Stir ¾ cup unsweetened flaked coconut into dough. Substitute lemon extract for vanilla extract.

Carob Fondue with Strawberries

1 cup heavy cream, divided
1 tablespoon cornstarch
¼ cup Basic Carob Syrup (page xviii)
¼ cup honey
2 teaspoons vanilla extract
4 cups fresh strawberries (other fresh fruit chunks may be substituted)

In a cup, mix together ¼ cup heavy cream and cornstarch until cornstarch is dissolved. Stir together in a small saucepan cornstarch mixture, ¾ cup heavy cream, carob syrup, and honey. Cook over medium heat, stirring constantly, until fondue thickens, about 5 minutes. Add vanilla extract.

Serve in fondue pot surrounded by fresh strawberries for dipping.

Recipe may be doubled.

Preparation time: 10 minutes

4 servings

Colorful Ambrosia

2 oranges, peeled, seeded and chopped
2 bananas, sliced
1 cup fresh blueberries

Ginger Peaches   Page 217   Minute Macaroons   Page 219

1 cup seedless green grapes
1½ cups unsweetened flaked coconut
½ cup heavy cream
1 tablespoon honey
1 teaspoon vanilla extract
1 cup yogurt, sweetened with 1
  tablespoon honey or maple syrup
  and flavored with ¼ teaspoon
  vanilla extract
½ cup chopped pecans

Mix together oranges, bananas, blueberries, grapes, and coconut in a large bowl.

Whip cream in a small bowl, adding honey and vanilla. Fold yogurt into cream. Mix with fruit, and serve in dessert glasses. Top with pecans.

Preparation time: 10 minutes

6 to 8 servings

Easy Cake Mix

6 cups whole wheat pastry flour
6 cups unbleached white flour
15 teaspoons baking powder
1½ cups instant nonfat dry milk

Sift ingredients together in about 6 batches, alternating ingredients. Sift 2 more times to blend. Cover tightly and store in a cool, dry place.

Preparation time: 10 minutes

Makes about 4 cakes

TO USE:
Quick Carob Cake

Serve plain or with Coconut Cream Frosting (page 267).

3¼ cups sifted Easy Cake Mix
4 eggs, separated
1 cup honey
⅔ cup water
2 teaspoons vanilla extract
3 tablespoons Basic Carob Syrup
  (page xviii)
⅛ teaspoon cream of tartar

Preheat oven to 350°F. Butter a 2-piece tube pan.

In a large bowl, beat together cake mix, egg yolks, honey, water, and vanilla, and beat for 2 minutes. Beat in carob syrup.

In a medium-size bowl, beat together egg whites and cream of tartar. Fold into carob mixture. Turn into prepared pan, and bake on middle shelf of oven for 40 to 45 minutes, or until a cake tester or food pick inserted into cake comes out clean.

Cool in pan 10 minutes. Run knife around tube and edge of pan, and turn cake out onto a wire rack to cool.

Preparation time (not including baking): 15 minutes

8 to 10 servings

Golden Layers

Fill and frost with Carob Whip (page 266).

⅓ cup butter
1 cup honey
4 eggs, separated
¾ cup water
2 teaspoons vanilla extract
3½ cups Easy Cake Mix
⅛ teaspoon cream of tartar

Preheat oven to 350°F. Butter and flour 2 8-inch layer cake pans.

In a large bowl, beat butter until fluffy. Beat in honey, then egg yolks, water, and vanilla. Gradually add cake mix, beating for 4 minutes.

In a medium-size bowl, beat together egg whites and cream of tartar until whites are stiff. Fold into batter. Turn into prepared pans, and bake on middle shelf of oven for 30 to 35 minutes, or until a cake tester or food pick inserted into the centers comes out clean.

Cool in pans for 10 minutes. Turn out onto wire racks to cool completely.

Preparation time (not including baking): 10 minutes

6 to 8 servings

Crunchy Chip Cake

Good plain or frosted and filled with whipped cream.

Follow the recipe for Golden Layers, folding ¾ cup milk carob chips into batter.

Preparation time (not including baking): 10 minutes

6 to 8 servings

Easy Orange Cake with Broiled Frosting

CAKE
¼ cup milk
2 tablespoons butter
2 eggs, at room temperature
½ cup honey
¾ cup whole wheat pastry flour
¾ cup unbleached white flour
½ teaspoon baking powder
½ teaspoon baking soda (be sure there are no lumps)
¼ cup orange juice
1 teaspoon grated orange rind

FROSTING
2 tablespoons butter
2 tablespoons honey
2 tablespoons orange juice
¾ cup unsweetened flaked coconut

Preheat oven to 350°F. Butter an 8 × 8-inch baking pan.

To make the cake: In a small saucepan, heat together milk and butter just enough to melt butter. Set aside.

Beat eggs in a large bowl until light and thick. Beat in honey and then milk mixture. Stir in whole wheat pastry flour, unbleached white flour, baking powder, and baking soda, blending well. Stir in orange juice and grated orange rind. Pour batter into prepared pan, and bake on middle shelf of oven for 25 minutes, or until center of cake springs back when lightly pressed and a cake tester or a food pick inserted into the center comes out clean and dry.

To make the frosting: In a small skillet, melt butter with honey and orange juice. Mix in coconut. Spread over hot cake and, place under heated broiler about 1 minute, or until coconut browns lightly. Watch carefully while broiling.

Serve warm or at room temperature.

Preparation time (not including baking): 15 minutes

8 servings

Ginger Peaches

2 tablespoons butter
1 tablespoon honey
1 teaspoon ground ginger
½ teaspoon ground cinnamon
3 cups thinly sliced peeled peaches
½ cup yogurt

In a large skillet, melt butter, stirring in honey, ginger, and cinnamon. Add peaches, and cook, stirring often, until peaches are soft and sauce has thickened. Turn into 4 dessert dishes, and top with yogurt.

Preparation time: 10 minutes

4 servings

Currant-Stuffed Baked Apples

½ cup dried currants
⅓ cup honey
¼ cup uncooked quick oats
½ teaspoon ground cinnamon
2 teaspoons lemon juice
6 large apples
3 tablespoons butter

Preheat oven to 350°F. Lightly butter the bottom of an 8 × 8 × 2-inch pan.

Place currants in a small bowl, cover with boiling water, and set aside to plump for 15 to 20 minutes.

Mix together honey, oats, cinnamon, and lemon juice.

Core apples, leaving a 1-inch plug in bottom. Split skin in 2 places at top edges.

Drain currants, and mix with oats. Fill apples, and place them in prepared pan. Dot each with ½ tablespoon butter, add water to bottom of pan to about a 1-inch depth, and bake on middle shelf of oven for about 60 minutes, or until tender.

Preparation time (not including baking): 8 minutes

6 servings

Ever-Ready Pie Dough

Make these in advance, and roll out when you need a pie in a hurry.

4½ cups whole wheat pastry flour
1 cup butter, divided
½ to ¾ cup ice water

Place half of flour and ½ cup butter, cut into chunks, into a food processor. Blend until fine crumbs form. Add ice water, a few drops at a time, through feed tube, blending until dough is moist enough to form a ball. Remove and process remaining ingredients in the same way.

Divide each batch in half, and roll each into a ball. Wrap in plastic wrap and then foil. Refrigerate for up to 1 week, or freeze for up to 2 months.

Makes 4

Hummingbird Cake

Sometimes known as Captain Bird Cake, this fruit-and-nut-filled favorite makes a lot of cake in a little time with no frosting necessary.

1½ cups honey
3 eggs
1 cup vegetable oil
1½ teaspoons vanilla extract
1½ cups whole wheat pastry flour
1½ cups unbleached white flour
1 teaspoon baking soda
1 teaspoon ground cinnamon
1 can (8 ounces) unsweetened crushed pineapple, undrained
2 ripe bananas, diced
1 cup grated fresh or unsweetened flaked coconut
1 cup chopped pecans

Preheat oven to 350°F. Butter a 13 × 9-inch baking pan.

In a medium-size bowl, beat honey, eggs, oil, and vanilla until well blended.

In a large bowl, sift dry ingredients together. Pour honey-egg mixture into dry ingredients, and stir until just blended. Fold in remaining ingredients. Spoon batter into pan, and bake for 45 minutes, or until center springs back when lightly pressed and a cake tester or food pick inserted into the center comes out clean and dry.

Preparation time (not including baking): 15 minutes

18 servings

Minute Macaroons

1 egg
3 tablespoons honey
2 tablespoons half-and-half
1 teaspoon vanilla extract
2½ cups unsweetened flaked coconut

Preheat oven to 350°F. Butter a baking sheet.

Beat egg, honey, half-and-half, and vanilla in a medium-size bowl. Mix well with coconut. Form into 20 to 24 balls by pressing together firmly with hands. Bake on middle shelf of oven for 12 to 15 minutes, or until lightly browned.

Remove from baking sheet immediately.

Preparation time (not including baking): 10 minutes

Makes 20 to 24

Raspberry Cream Loaf

1 Old-Fashioned Pound Cake (page 11)
2 cups fresh raspberries
¼ cup honey
1 cup heavy cream
2 teaspoons honey
¼ teaspoon vanilla extract
carob powder, for sprinkling

Slice pound cake lengthwise into 3 layers. Mix together raspberries and ¼ cup honey in a medium-size bowl, mashing raspberries slightly. Place bottom layer of cake on a serving dish. Spoon half of raspberries over cake. Do the same with second layer. Place upper layer of cake on top.

In a small bowl, whip cream until soft peaks form. Beat in 2 teaspoons honey and vanilla. Frost cake with whipped cream. (If time permits, place some of the cream into a pastry bag, and pipe a trim around edges of cake.) Sprinkle carob powder from a salt shaker lightly down the center. Refrigerate until ready to use.

To cover without disturbing whipped cream frosting, insert a cake tester or straw into center of cake to hold plastic wrap off the surface, like a tent. Before serving, remove tester or straw, and smooth cream.

Preparation time (not including baking): 15 minutes (20 minutes if you use a pastry bag to decorate)

8 to 10 servings

Makes-Its-Own-Crust Date-Custard Pie

2 cups milk
4 eggs
⅓ cup honey
½ cup whole wheat pastry flour
¼ cup butter, cut into pieces
2 teaspoons molasses
1½ teaspoons vanilla extract
½ teaspoon baking powder
¼ teaspoon ground cloves
1 cup chopped dates

Preheat oven to 350°F. Butter a 10-inch pie plate.

Combine all ingredients except dates in a blender container. Cover and blend at low speed for 3 minutes. Pour filling into pie plate. Stir in dates. Bake on middle shelf of oven for 40 to 50 minutes, or until a knife inserted 1 inch from the center comes out clean. Pie will rise, then fall, like a custard.

Preparation time (not including baking): 10 minutes

Makes 1

VARIATION

Makes-Its-Own-Crust Fruit Pie: Any diced, cooked fruit, such as peaches, pears, or nectarines, may be substituted for dates. Substitute ground cinnamon for cloves.

Papaya Pudding

2 ripe papayas
2 tablespoons honey
2 tablespoons lemon juice
1 cup heavy cream
¼ cup finely chopped pecans

Peel and chop papayas. Puree fruit in a food processor or blender. Blend in honey and lemon juice.

In a medium-size bowl, whip cream until soft peaks form. Fold in papaya mixture. Spoon pudding into 6 serving dishes, and chill. Top each with a dusting of chopped pecans.

Preparation time: 20 minutes

6 servings

Peach Melba

Dame Nellie Melba's operatic performances are all but forgotten, still her name lives on due to this elegant dessert named after her by a French chef who also happened to be an opera bug.

1 quart French Vanilla Ice Cream (page 131)
8 unsweetened canned peach halves, chilled
2 cups Raspberry Sauce (page 271)

Place 1 generous scoop of ice cream into each of 8 dessert dishes. Arrange 1 peach half, cut-side down, over each scoop of ice cream. Top with Raspberry Sauce, and serve immediately.

Preparation time: 5 minutes

8 servings

Pear Almond Custards

2 cups unsweetened canned pears
2 cups milk
4 eggs
⅓ cup honey
1 teaspoon almond extract
nutmeg, for sprinkling

Preheat oven to 325°F. Place 8 custard cups in a roasting pan. Heat water in a kettle.

Divide pears among custard cups.

In a blender container, combine milk, eggs, honey, and almond extract, and process until blended. Pour over pears, and then sprinkle with nutmeg. Place pan on middle shelf of oven, and pour hot water into roasting pan almost to the tops of custard cups. Bake custards for 30 to 50 minutes, or until a knife point inserted into the centers comes out clean.

Remove from water bath and cool. Serve at room temperature or chilled. If desired, Raspberry Sauce (page 271) makes a nice accompaniment.

Preparation time (not including baking): 10 minutes

8 servings

Quick Frozen Strawberry Soufflé

An easy-to-make refreshing frozen soufflé.

4 cups fresh strawberries
⅓ cup honey, or to taste
1 envelope unflavored gelatin
2 tablespoons cold water
1½ cups heavy cream

Construct a collar for a 1-quart soufflé dish (page 120).

Set aside a few pretty berries for decoration. Puree the rest in a blender, adding honey.

Sprinkle gelatin over cold water in a cup, and set aside to soften for 5 minutes.

In a small saucepan, combine gelatin with ½ cup puree, stirring over low heat until gelatin is completely dissolved.

In a large bowl, combine gelatin mixture with remaining puree.

Whip cream until soft peaks form. Fold cream into puree. Spoon mixture into prepared soufflé dish, and freeze until firm. When frozen, cover with plastic wrap until ready to serve.

Remove from freezer, decorate with reserved berries, and let stand at room temperature a few minutes before serving.

Preparation time (not including construction of soufflé collar or freezing): about 20 minutes

4 to 6 servings

Currant-Stuffed Baked Apples   Page 218

Strawberry Whip

¼ cup cold water
1 envelope unflavored gelatin
2 cups fresh strawberries
¼ cup honey
1 teaspoon lemon extract
2 ice cubes
1 cup heavy cream
6 whole fresh strawberries
  (optional)

Pour water into a small saucepan, and sprinkle gelatin on top. Set aside for 5 minutes to soften.

In a blender, puree strawberries with honey. Add lemon extract.

Heat gelatin, stirring until dissolved, about 2 minutes. Remove from heat, and add ice cubes, stirring until melted.

In a large bowl, beat cream until soft peaks form. Beat in strawberry mixture and gelatin. Pour into 6 dessert glasses, and refrigerate until set.

Decorate with strawberries, if desired.

Preparation time: 8 minutes

6 servings

Strawberry Fool

2 cups fresh strawberries
  honey, to taste
1 cup heavy cream
1 tablespoon honey
½ teaspoon vanilla extract

In a blender or food processor puree strawberries. Stop blender or processor, and stir in honey.

In a medium-size bowl, beat heavy cream until it begins to thicken. Add 1 tablespoon honey and vanilla, and continue beating until soft peaks form.

Fold strawberry puree into whipped cream just until you see streaks of strawberry in a ripple design. Divide among 4 dessert glasses.

Preparation time: 5 minutes

4 servings

Petits Pots au Carob

This is the perfect company dessert when you're short on time but still want to serve something elegant.

1 cup milk
1 envelope unflavored gelatin
1¼ cups milk carob chips
½ cup honey
3 eggs
½ teaspoon almond extract
½ cup heavy cream

Pour milk into a small saucepan, sprinkle gelatin on top and mix. Set aside for a few minutes to soften.

Blend carob chips, honey, eggs, and almond extract in a food processor.

Heat milk mixture, stirring constantly, until gelatin dissolves and milk is scalding. Add to carob chip-egg mixture, and process until smooth, keeping feed tube covered to avoid splashing. Pour into demitasse cups, and chill in refrigerator for at least 1 hour.

Whip cream in a small bowl. Top each cup with a dollop of cream just before serving.

Preparation time (not including chilling): 20 minutes

6 to 8 servings

Quick Blueberry Crisp

3 cups fresh blueberries
1 tablespoon honey
1½ tablespoons cornstarch
¼ cup water
½ cup uncooked quick oats
¼ cup toasted wheat germ
¼ cup raisins
2 tablespoons butter, melted
¼ cup date sugar

Preheat oven to 375°F.

In a medium-size saucepan, mix together blueberries and honey.

In a cup, mix cornstarch and water until blended, and then add to berries. Cook over medium heat, stirring constantly, until mixture bubbles and thickens, about 8 minutes. Remove from heat, and turn into a 9 × 5 × 3-inch pan.

Mix together remaining ingredients in a medium-size bowl. Spread over blueberries, and bake on top shelf of oven for 10 minutes.

Serve warm with heavy cream or vanilla ice cream.

Preparation time (not including baking): 10 minutes

6 servings

Raspberry Orange Pudding

1½ cups milk (for a richer pudding, half-and-half or light cream may be substituted)
1 package (10 ounces) unsweetened frozen raspberries, thawed and drained with juice reserved
2 tablespoons cornstarch
1 medium-size orange, peeled, seeded, and chopped

In a medium-size saucepan, combine milk, reserved raspberry juice, and cornstarch. Cook over medium heat, stirring constantly, until mixture thickens.

Remove from heat. Stir in raspberries and orange pieces, divide among 4 dessert dishes, and chill for at least 30 minutes.

Preparation time: 10 minutes

4 servings

CHAPTER
11

Glorious
Gifts of Love

There's no nicer gift than a present of homemade sweets prettily packaged. It expresses both thoughtfulness and true generosity. This is something that even the person who has everything will appreciate.

A hostess gift of homemade goodies is always welcome. However, if you bring cookies, candy, or preserves when you're invited to someone's home, do make it clear that your gift is to be enjoyed at the convenience of the hostess, now or at another time. And be sure that your gift is something that will last a day or two, until the chance comes to savor it.

I like to select a reusable container for packaging that then becomes part of the gift. Of course, this is not at all necessary—any nice-looking container that you don't expect to have returned will do—but I think it adds to the distinctiveness of the gift.

When I give a loaf of my Irish Cinnamon Raisin Bread with a jar of jam, I enjoy presenting them in a basket with a ribbon tied around it and a big bow. If it happens to be holiday time, I often include a bottle of cider, the festive-looking, sparkling kind. For cookies, I use attractive tin canisters, and Honey Butter goes into a ceramic crock. I like the old-fashioned glass-topped jars for preserves, with special labels that give the name and date made. Candies or Petits Fours look attractive in fluted paper cups (the miniature ones are small enough for candy) nestled in a flat tin container.

If you don't want to shop for a basket or tin to hold baked goods, a decorated paper plate and a simple wrap of colored cellophane will give your present a festive appearance. And

Presentation Cherry Roll   Page 229

rather than buying a crock or fancy jar, you can save the pretty ones that come your way for the time when you will want to fill them with candy or fruit butters.

Occasionally, and only if I believe it will be of interest, I include the recipe with my gift. I must admit that I like the idea of listing the wholesome ingredients I use to make these delicious treats.

Cookies, of course, are the most versatile of food gifts. I like to give an assortment at holiday time. The easy way to do this is to make one batch a day, and freeze them as you go along. Then, when you're ready, defrost and assemble one or more assortments. You'll find more about freezing cookies, cookie assortments, and mailing cookies in the chapter "Naturally Smart Cookies."

If a gift of food needs refrigeration, be certain to tell the recipient, and be clear about how long it will keep. I often make refrigerator jams and preserves that are not processed for shelf life. When I give these as gifts, the label clearly says, "Keep Refrigerated."

Since a food gift must always be taken from one place to another, it's wise to choose good travelers. My idea of good travelers are those sweets which will not easily crumble or perish quickly in warm weather. That's why I avoid giving delicate pastries or cream-filled desserts as gifts.

Many of the desserts in this book make lovely gifts (most of the cookies and candies, for instance), but in this chapter, I have assembled some of the ones that are special favorites. Some require a bit of time to prepare, but others are easily made and just as pleasurable to receive.

I think especially nice occasions for giving homemade sweets are when welcoming a new neighbor or as a hostess gift. The right sweet treat from your kitchen as a birthday present is sure to please. Wrap up some cookies as a thank-you gift to someone who has been especially kind, or present them as a cheer-up gift for the convalescent whose diet permits such indulgence. Of course, as holiday gifts for an office crew or anyone with whom you would like to share the joys of the season, nothing conveys personal, heartwarming wishes more convincingly than goodies personally made by you.

Presentation Cherry Roll

This roll looks lovely wrapped in red cellophane (over plastic wrap) and tied with a wide white ribbon. Since the dessert requires refrigeration, it is only appropriate when a gift is to be presented in person.

CAKE

    5 eggs, separated
    ½ teaspoon cream of tartar
    ¼ cup honey
    1 teaspoon vanilla extract
    ½ cup sifted whole wheat pastry
      flour
    ½ cup sifted unbleached white flour

FILLING

    8 ounces cream cheese, softened
    ¼ cup butter, softened
    2 tablespoons heavy cream
    ¼ cup honey
    1½ teaspoons vanilla extract
    1 cup fresh sweet cherries, halved
      and pitted

To make the cake: Preheat oven to 350°F. Line a 15 × 10 × 1-inch jelly-roll pan, with parchment paper cut to fit.

In a medium-size bowl, beat to-gether egg whites and cream of tartar until stiff peaks form.

In a large bowl, beat egg yolks until lemon colored. Add honey and vanilla, and beat for 5 minutes.

In a small bowl, sift together whole wheat pastry flour and unbleached white flour. Stir with a fork to blend, and then fold into egg yolks. Fold in egg whites, and spread batter on prepared pan. Bake on middle shelf of oven for 12 to 15 minutes, or until cake springs back when pressed with fingertips.

Sprinkle flour on a tea towel. Turn baked cake out onto towel, and remove parchment paper. Trim off all edges, and roll cake up with towel. (Towel should be rolled in cake. See illustration on page 8.) Set aside to cool thoroughly.

To make the filling: In a medium-size bowl, beat together cream cheese and butter until fluffy. Beat in cream. Add honey and vanilla, and beat for 1 minute.

Drain cherries thoroughly, and fold into cream cheese mixture.

Unroll cooled cake. Spread filling on entire top, and roll up again. Refrigerate seam-side down on a plate.

10 to 12 servings

Easy Shortbread Fans

1½ cups whole wheat flour
1¼ cups unbleached white flour
½ cup butter
⅓ cup honey

Preheat oven to 350°F. Lightly flour a baking sheet.

Sift together whole wheat flour and unbleached white flour into a large bowl. Cut up butter and add. Cut butter into flour with a pastry blender or 2 knives until mixture is coarse and grainy. Add honey, and work in with floured hands (the dough will be slightly crumbly).

On a floured surface, pat dough into a rectangle about ¼ inch thick. Cut into 4 5-inch rounds. You will have to reroll dough to do this. Cut rounds into 4 equal pieces. Score each piece with a sharp knife as shown in the illustration. Place on prepared baking sheet, and bake on middle shelf of oven for about 20 minutes, or until lightly browned.

Cool on wire racks.

Makes 16

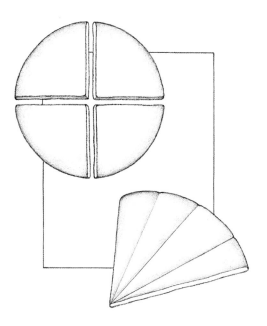

Miniature Fruit Cakes

These tasty fruit cakes can be made in advance and frozen until gift time.

1 cup golden raisins
1 cup chopped dried prunes
1 cup mixed dried fruit
1 cup chopped walnuts
½ cup sifted whole wheat pastry flour
4 eggs
½ cup honey
1½ teaspoons vanilla extract
½ cup sifted unbleached white flour

Preheat oven to 325°F.

In a large bowl, mix together raisins, prunes, mixed fruit, and walnuts. Toss with whole wheat pastry flour.

In a medium-size bowl, beat eggs and honey. Add vanilla extract. Beat in unbleached white flour. Pour into bowl with fruit, and mix well. Turn batter into a 12-cup nonstick muffin tin. (Cups will be almost full.) Bake on middle shelf of oven for about 35 minutes, or until golden.

Turn out onto wire racks to cool.

Makes 1 dozen

Beautiful Braided Bread

1 cup lukewarm milk
2 tablespoons dry yeast
1 tablespoon honey
1¼ cups milk
½ cup honey
½ cup butter
7 cups whole wheat flour
1 egg

Butter a large bowl and a large baking sheet.

Pour warm milk into a small bowl. Mix in yeast and 1 tablespoon honey. Let stand until mixture bubbles up, 5 to 10 minutes.

In a medium-size saucepan, heat 1¼ cups milk to scalding. Remove from heat, and stir in ½ cup honey and butter, stirring until butter has melted. Turn into a large bowl, cool slightly, and then add yeast-milk mixture.

Mix in flour, 1 cup at a time, until dough is very stiff, using as much flour as liquid will accept. Knead in a food processor in 2 batches until dough forms into a ball, about 1 minute; or knead by hand on floured surface for 10 minutes, or with dough hooks for 5 to 7 minutes. Place ball of dough into prepared bowl, turning over to butter all surfaces. Cover with plastic wrap, and let rise in a warm place until doubled in bulk, about 50 minutes.

Punch down, and shape with hands into a rectangle, about 11 × 8 inches. Cut lengthwise into 5 equal pieces. Roll each strand to round off corners. Braid dough by placing strand 2 over strand 3 (2 is now 3, and 3 is now 2). Place strand 5 over strand 2. Place strand 1 over strand 3. Repeat braid-ing to end of dough. Work ends together, and turn ends under loaf. Place on prepared baking sheet, cover with plastic wrap, and let rise in a warm place until doubled in bulk, about 40 minutes.

Preheat oven to 400°F.

Remove plastic wrap. Beat egg in a cup, and brush on top and sides of braid. Bake on middle shelf of oven until braid sounds hollow when tapped lightly on bottom with fingertips, about 20 minutes.

Makes 1 loaf

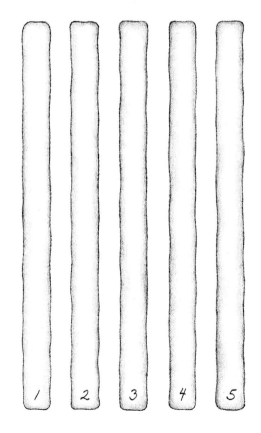

Spiced Pears   Page 241

Irish Cinnamon Raisin Bread

If you are familiar with Irish brown bread, you will notice that this is a near relative. It is meant to be served at room temperature, not warm, for finer slicing.

    1 cup raisins
    3 cups whole wheat flour
    2 cups unbleached white flour
  2½ teaspoons baking soda
    ¼ cup butter (temperature will
        depend on method of mixing)
  1½ cups sour milk (page xxiv) or
        buttermilk, at room
        temperature
    ½ cup honey, slightly warmed
    1 tablespoon molasses
  2 to 4 teaspoons ground cinnamon

Place raisins into a small bowl, cover with boiling water, and set aside to plump for 15 to 20 minutes.

Preheat oven to 425°F. Butter 2 8-inch layer cake pans.

In a large bowl, sift together whole wheat flour, unbleached white flour and baking soda. With your fingers, rub in softened butter until flour is mealy but not lumpy. Or combine flour mixture with soda in a food processor, and cut in cold butter until mixture resembles meal.

Mix together milk, honey, and molasses in a medium-size bowl. Pour into dry ingredients. (Do not use food processor for this step.) Stir until just combined. Drain raisins, and fold into dough. Dough may be sticky but manageable. If too sticky, add a bit more flour.

Turn dough out onto a generously floured surface. Sprinkle flour on top, and with floured hands, pat it into a 1-inch-thick rectangle. Sprinkle with cinnamon. Fold dough into thirds as you would a sheet of letter paper. Cut dough in half. Pat each half into a circle using additional flour as needed. Place each circle into a prepared pan. With a floured knife, cut a ¾-inch-deep cross into each loaf. Bake on middle shelf of oven for 20 minutes.

Reduce heat to 350°F, and bake for 10 more minutes, or until a cake tester or food pick inserted into the center comes out dry. Do not overbake.

Remove breads from pans, and cool completely on wire racks. If desired, wrap well in foil, and freeze until needed.

Makes 2 loaves

Peanut-Raisin-Carob Clusters

½ cup butter
3 tablespoons honey
2 cups milk carob chips
1 cup roasted peanuts
½ cup raisins

Line a baking sheet with wax paper.

In top of a double boiler set over simmering water, melt butter. Add honey and carob chips, and stir constantly until carob has melted. (Mixture will be thick.) Remove from heat, and stir in peanuts and raisins.

Drop by tablespoonfuls onto prepared baking sheet. Refrigerate on baking sheet until hard.

Store in tin in refrigerator.

Makes about 2 dozen

Trail Mix

Package this mix in a pretty canister for the perfect hostess gift. What follows is one of my favorite combinations, but feel free to substitute any dry ingredient you particularly like for any of those listed below.

2 cups unsalted dry roasted peanuts
2 cups unsalted dry roasted soybeans
2 cups raisins
1 cup dried papaya chunks
1 cup dried banana slices
1 cup sunflower seeds
1 cup lightly toasted pumpkin seeds
1 cup walnut halves
1 cup cashews

Place all ingredients into a large bowl or pan, and mix lightly but thoroughly. For use away from home, package each half cup of mix in a small plastic bag, and close it securely. For home snacking, store in canisters or jars.

Yields 12 cups

VARIATION

Chipper Trail Mix: Substitute 2 cups milk carob chips for walnut halves and cashews.

Peanutty Coconut Candy

½ cup mild honey
¾ cup peanut butter
1 teaspoon vanilla extract
¾ cup uncooked quick oats
1 cup instant nonfat dry milk
¾ cup unsweetened shredded coconut, divided
¼ to ½ cup orange juice

In a medium-size bowl, mix together honey, peanut butter, and vanilla until well blended. Mix in oats, dry milk, ¼ cup coconut, and enough orange juice to just moisten all ingredients. (The oiliness of the peanut butter will dictate how much orange juice is needed.)

Grease palms with butter, and roll bits of batter between hands to form 1-inch balls. Roll balls in remaining ½ cup coconut. Store in covered container in refrigerator.

Makes about 3 dozen

Petits Fours

There's no getting away from it—frosting these little cakes is a fussy job. But they make such a delicious, impressive gift they're well worth the effort.

⅓ cup butter
6 eggs, separated
½ cup honey
1 teaspoon vanilla extract
½ cup sifted whole wheat pastry flour
½ cup sifted unbleached white flour
2 teaspoons baking powder
1 teaspoon baking soda
4 tablespoons Basic Carob Syrup (page xviii)
1 cup Apricot Preserves (page 276)
1 cup Strawberry Jam (page 273)
4 cups Vanilla Icing (page 268)
2 cups Decorator Frosting (page 267)
natural green, red, and yellow food coloring

Preheat oven to 350°F. Butter and flour 2 8 × 8 × 2-inch pans.

In a small saucepan, melt butter. Set aside to cool slightly.

In a large bowl, beat together egg yolks, honey, and vanilla for 5 minutes.

In a medium-size bowl, sift together whole wheat pastry flour, unbleached white flour, baking powder, and baking soda. Mix into egg yolks. Beat in cooled butter.

In another large bowl, beat egg whites until stiff peaks form. Fold into batter. Pour half of batter into 1 prepared pan. Fold carob syrup into second half of batter, and then turn into the other prepared pan. Bake on middle shelf of oven for about 30 minutes, or until tops spring back when pressed lightly with fingertips.

Cool for 10 minutes in pans, and then turn out onto wire racks to cool thoroughly. With a sharp knife, cut off edges of cakes. Cut cakes into 1½-inch squares. Cut each square in half crosswise (so that there's a top and a bottom). Spread Apricot Preserves on bottoms of carob squares. Replace tops. Spread Strawberry Jam on bottoms of yellow squares. Replace tops.

Divide Vanilla Icing into 4 batches. Add a few drops of green coloring to 1 batch; a few drops of red coloring to another batch; a few drops of yellow coloring to the third batch; leave the last batch white. Frost tops and sides of squares with colored frostings, making 12 of each color and 2 multicolored. Set aside until frosting becomes firm.

To prevent hardening, make Decorator Frosting just before you're ready to use it. Divide frosting into 3 batches. Put a few drops of green coloring in 1 batch; a few drops of red coloring in another batch; and a few drops of yellow coloring in the last batch, making the colors darker than those in the Vanilla Icing. Decorate Petits Fours, forming bows and flowers with a pastry tube fitted with appropriate openings.

Makes 50

Easy Peanut Butter Fudge

½ cup honey
¼ cup butter
1 cup milk carob chips
1 cup peanut butter
1 teaspoon vanilla extract

Line an 8 × 8 × 2-inch pan with wax paper.

In top of a double boiler set over hot, not boiling, water, heat together honey, butter, and carob chips, stirring constantly, until butter and carob are melted. Stir in peanut butter and vanilla.

Turn into prepared pan, and chill until set, about 1 hour.

Cut into 1-inch squares.

Makes 64

Ribier Grape Jam

As a gift to accompany my Irish Cinnamon Raisin Bread (page 232), I like to use small (½ cup or less) jars of this jam, tucking one jar in with each loaf. Before making jam, read the general instructions in the beginning of the chapter, "Triumphant Toppings, Fillings, and Sweet Spreads."

7 cups stemmed Ribier grapes
1 large tart apple
  about 1¼ cups honey

Crush grapes in an 8-quart stainless steel pot. With Ribier grapes, which are quite firm, I do this by pinching each grape with my fingers to insure even crushing. Core and slice apple thinly into pot. Bring mixture to a simmer (there should be enough liquid, but, if not, add ½ cup water), cover, and cook for 20 minutes.

Strain mixture through three layers of dampened cheesecloth or a jelly bag; for a thicker consistency (the one I prefer), simply put mixture through a food mill twice. Measure juice, pouring it back into pot. Add one-third to one-half as much honey as you have juice. Bring to a rolling boil, and then simmer over medium-high heat until it reaches jam consistency, about 30 minutes. Toward the end of the cooking time, you have to be very careful to prevent the jam from sticking, stirring it often, and watching it carefully. Test by placing 1 tablespoon jam on a cold plate and refrigerating for a few minutes. It should not run when you tip plate; and when scooped up with a spoon, it should mound up.

Skim off foam. Pour into hot sterilized jars. If not refrigerating jam, follow directions for processing on page 262. If refrigerating, cover and let stand at room temperature overnight before chilling in refrigerator.

Makes about 2 half pints

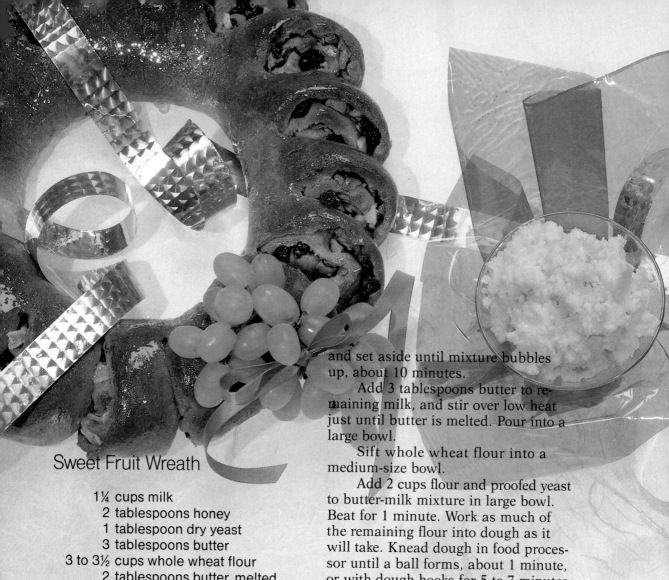

Sweet Fruit Wreath

   1¼ cups milk
   2 tablespoons honey
   1 tablespoon dry yeast
   3 tablespoons butter
3 to 3½ cups whole wheat flour
   2 tablespoons butter, melted
   2½ cups mixed dried fruit bits

Butter a medium-size bowl.

In a small saucepan, heat together milk and honey until very warm, about 110°F. Pour half of warmed milk mixture into a small bowl. Mix in yeast, and set aside until mixture bubbles up, about 10 minutes.

Add 3 tablespoons butter to remaining milk, and stir over low heat just until butter is melted. Pour into a large bowl.

Sift whole wheat flour into a medium-size bowl.

Add 2 cups flour and proofed yeast to butter-milk mixture in large bowl. Beat for 1 minute. Work as much of the remaining flour into dough as it will take. Knead dough in food processor until a ball forms, about 1 minute, or with dough hooks for 5 to 7 minutes, or by hand for 8 to 10 minutes.

If kneaded with dough hooks or by hand, roll dough into a ball. Place into prepared bowl, turning to coat all surfaces. Cover with towel or plastic wrap, and let rise in a warm place until doubled in bulk, about 45 minutes.

Butter a large baking sheet.

Punch dough down on a lightly floured surface, and roll into an 18 × 9-inch rectangle. Brush with melted butter. Spread fruit bits on dough all the way to the ends at top and bottom, but leave a 1-inch margin on each side. Roll up lengthwise, jelly-roll style. Form into a circle, joining ends together by moistening with a little water. Place on prepared baking sheet.

With sharp scissors, cut wreath three-quarters of the way across, making cuts 1 inch apart. Twist each piece and lay it on its side so that fruit shows. Cover and let rise in a warm place until doubled in bulk, about 30 minutes.

Preheat oven to 350°F.

Bake on middle shelf of oven for 25 to 30 minutes, or until golden brown.

Serves 16 to 20

Honey Butter

½ cup butter, softened
½ cup honey

In the small bowl of an electric mixer or in a food processor, blend butter and honey until mixture is fluffy and thoroughly mixed. Chill. Keep refrigerated until ready to use.

Yields about 1 cup

VARIATION

Cinnamon Honey Butter: Blend in ½ teaspoon ground cinnamon. This is especially tasty with raisin bread toast!

Miniature Banana-Fruit Breads

2 cups sifted whole wheat pastry
   flour
2 cups sifted unbleached white flour
2 teaspoons baking soda
1 cup butter, softened
1 cup honey
3 eggs
4 large bananas, mashed (2 cups)
¾ cup chopped dried apricots
¾ cup chopped dates
¾ cup chopped walnuts (optional)

Preheat oven to 350°F. Butter 6 5 × 3 × 2-inch miniature loaf pans, and line bottoms with thin, plain paper. Butter the paper.

Sift together whole wheat pastry flour, unbleached white flour, and baking soda in a medium-size bowl.

In a large bowl, cream butter until light and fluffy. Beat in honey, then eggs, and then bananas. Stir in dry ingredients. Fold in fruit and nuts, if desired. Bake for 35 minutes, or until a cake tester inserted into the center comes out clean. Breads should have risen and split at the top before testing.

Cool for 5 minutes in pans. Remove breads from pans, and peel off paper. Allow to finish cooling on wire racks. When completely cool, wrap breads in foil. Refrigerate until ready to use.

These breads can also be baked in 2 9 × 5 × 3-inch loaf pans, if you prefer. Increase baking time to 50 minutes.

Makes 6 loaves

Petits Fours   Page 234

Siena Sweetmeats

If you want something with real food value to replace candy bars, this will do very well. Just cut it into the appropriate shape, and wrap each bar in plastic wrap.

¾ cup honey
½ cup whole wheat pastry flour
1 tablespoon powdered carob
2 teaspoons ground cinnamon

1 cup chopped mixed dried fruit
  (raisins may be substituted)
1 cup coarsely chopped mixed nuts
  (almonds and filberts are
  traditional, but you may use
  any combination you like or
  just unsalted peanuts)
1 tablespoon grated orange rind

Preheat oven to 275°F. Generously butter a 9- or 10-inch square pan.
Pour honey into a large nonstick

skillet, and cook over lowest heat ("warm" is fine) until it simmers. Allow to simmer for 10 minutes, stirring occasionally. At this very low heat, it will not boil over or burn.

In a small bowl, mix together flour, carob, and cinnamon to blend.

In a medium-size bowl, combine fruit, nuts, and orange rind.

After removing honey from heat, stir in flour mixture. When well blended, stir in fruit-nut mixture. Spread candy in prepared pan. Bake for 30 minutes.

Cool for 10 minutes. Turn out onto a double thickness of wax paper, and refrigerate until firm. Cut into serving pieces or bars. Wrap each in plastic wrap. Store in an airtight container in a cool place.

Makes about 1 pound

Very Berry Cheesecake

This moist cheesecake can be made using just one berry topping. However, it won't look as spectacular as it does with the colorful use of all three berries.

CAKE
    2 cups crumbs from Basic Honey
        Cookies (page 46)
    5 tablespoons butter, melted
    24 ounces cream cheese, softened
    ⅓ cup honey
    3 eggs
    1 cup sour cream
    2 teaspoons vanilla extract

TOPPING
    ¾ cup fresh raspberries
    2 teaspoons honey
    2 tablespoons cornstarch, divided
    ¾ cup water, divided
    ¾ cup fresh blueberries
    2 teaspoons honey
    ¾ cup fresh blackberries
    2 teaspoons honey

To make the cake: Preheat oven to 350°F.

In a 9-inch springform pan, mix together cookie crumbs and butter until well blended. Press firmly on bottom of pan.

In a large bowl, beat cream cheese until fluffy. Beat in honey, eggs, and then sour cream and vanilla. Pour on top of prepared crust. Bake on middle shelf of oven for 1 hour and 10 minutes.

Cool in pan. Run knife around edge. Release springform, and carefully slide cheesecake onto a plate with spatula.

To make the topping: In a small saucepan, combine raspberries and 2 teaspoons honey.

Dissolve 2 teaspoons cornstarch in ¼ cup water, then stir into raspberry mixture, and heat to a boil, stirring constantly. Boil until thickened, about 2 minutes.

Cool completely. Cook blueberries and blackberries in the same manner.

Spread cooled blackberries in a circle around outer edge of cake. Spread raspberries in a circle inside blackberries. Spread blueberries in the middle.

10 to 12 servings

Grape Charlotte Russe

Pieces of sponge cake or pound cake may be substituted for the Ladyfingers. This would make a lovely contribution when you're asked to bring a dessert. Do keep it chilled until serving time.

½ cup cold water
2 envelopes unflavored gelatin
3½ cups milk, divided
¼ cup honey
2 tablespoons cornstarch
5 egg yolks, beaten
⅓ cup unsweetened frozen white grape juice concentrate
1 teaspoon vanilla extract
1½ cups heavy cream, divided
about 40 Ladyfingers (page 10)
about 25 seedless green grapes, halved
about 25 purple grapes, halved and seeded

Pour cold water into a small bowl, and sprinkle gelatin on top. Set aside for a few minutes to soften.

In a 2-quart saucepan, mix together 3 cups milk and honey.

Dissolve cornstarch in remaining ½ cup milk. Add to milk mixture in saucepan. Heat to scalding, stirring constantly. Add softened gelatin, and stir until dissolved. Pour a little of the scalded milk mixture into egg yolks, whisking as you do so. Return to sauce-

pan, and cook mixture over medium heat, for 15 to 20 minutes, or until slightly thick, stirring constantly.

Remove from heat. Stir in grape juice concentrate and vanilla. Refrigerate until thick but not set.

In a medium-size bowl, beat 1 cup cream until soft peaks form. Fold into thickened grape filling.

Line sides and bottom of a 9-inch springform pan with Ladyfingers, cutting off rounded ends of those used on bottom. Turn filling into prepared pan. Chill until set.

Decorate top of charlotte with grapes. Working from the outside, make a circle of green grapes. Leave a space, and then make a circle of purple grapes. Repeat all the way to the center.

Beat remaining cream in a small bowl, and pipe it around top of filling and between rows of grapes. Remove charlotte from springform pan.

10 to 12 servings

VARIATION
Carob Charlotte: Substitute 3 tablespoons Basic Carob Syrup (page xviii) for grape concentrate. Decorate with strawberries.

Fruit Leather

This method of preserving fruit when it's plentiful provides a chewy confection that relies mostly on the fruit itself for sweetness. Children love it as a little "extra" gift at holiday time. Fruit leather will keep for about a year. Experiment. It can be made with most fruits—alone or in combination.

> 8 pounds apricots or peaches, pitted
>   but not peeled
> ½ cup honey
>   Coconut Sugar (page xxii)

Place fruit in a large heavy pot. Cover, and cook over low heat in enough water to cover until soft. Drain well. Remove skins, and puree in a food processor or food mill in batches. Add honey, mixing in well.

Lightly oil 2 large baking sheets. Spread fruit pulp evenly on prepared baking sheets. Place baking sheets in 120°F oven, leaving door slightly ajar, until pulp is dried into sheets, about 12 hours.

Lift gently from baking sheets, and place on wire racks to cool. When leather has lost its stickiness, dust both sides lightly with Coconut Sugar. Roll each sheet in wax paper, and store in a cool, dry place.

Makes 2 sheets

Spiced Pears

I like to present these in the old-time glass-topped canning jars, but any pretty jar will do. They are served as a condiment or relish, as you would applesauce.

> 2 cups water
> 1 cup honey
> 1 cup cider vinegar
> 3 cinnamon sticks
> 2 teaspoons whole cloves
> 10 large or 12 medium ripe Bartlett
>   pears

Combine all ingredients except pears in a large stainless steel or enamel-coated pot. Bring to a boil, reduce heat, and simmer for 5 minutes, stirring occasionally.

Peel pears thinly. Slice in half lengthwise, leaving stem on one half. Remove core with a sharp paring knife. Gently place pears in pot of warm liquid, cover, and poach for 30 minutes. If pears rise above liquid, gently stir occasionally so that they will be evenly flavored.

When tender, allow to cool in liquid. Place pears with their liquid, cloves, and cinnamon sticks in well-washed jars, cover, and refrigerate. Allow to stand a few days before serving.

Yields 3 quarts

Applesauce-Prune Cake

Not only is this cake delicious when first baked, it is even better on the second day.

  1 cup whole wheat flour
  1 cup unbleached white flour
1½ teaspoons baking soda
  1 teaspoon ground cinnamon
  ½ teaspoon ground cloves
  ¼ teaspoon ground nutmeg
  1 cup pitted prunes
  ½ cup coarsely chopped walnuts
    (optional)
  ½ cup vegetable oil
  ½ cup honey, slightly warmed
  3 tablespoons molasses
  1 egg
  ½ teaspoon grated lemon rind
  1 cup thick unsweetened
    applesauce

Preheat oven to 325°F. Butter a 12 × 7 (or 8) × 2-inch baking pan.

Into a medium-size bowl, sift together whole wheat flour, unbleached white flour, baking soda, and spices.

Cut prunes into pieces. Place prunes and walnuts, if desired, into a small bowl, and mix with 1 tablespoon flour mixture.

In a large bowl, beat oil, honey, and molasses together until well blended. Beat in egg and lemon rind. Stir in applesauce. Mix in dry ingredients until just blended. Fold in prune mixture. Spoon batter into prepared pan, and bake for 45 minutes, or until a cake tester inserted into the center comes out clean and dry.

Cool in pan on wire rack.

10 to 12 servings

CHAPTER 12

Diet Desserts

Desserts have their place in a dieter's menu. They offer variety, as well as good nutrition (if carefully planned), and they help to keep one firmly set on the path of good resolution. In this chapter, you'll find some of my favorite low-cal treats—desserts that are attractive, light, and, most important, tasty.

Fruit is the natural alternative to rich desserts that dieters want to avoid. Fresh fruit—a favorite of mine—is always a good choice, but at times I like to create something a bit fancier for dieters. A pleasing and different presentation can be enough to turn a plain fruit into a dessert with a capital D. Careful peeling, slicing, and decorating always makes fruit special, and a hint of spice sprinkled over it enhances the fresh flavor and makes up for the lack of any additional sweetener.

I like fresh pears with a sprinkling of ground ginger. Cinnamon or nutmeg are especially compatible with apples, and cinnamon is also good on fresh blueberries (think how welcome a hint of cinnamon is in apple and blueberry pies). Try a quarter teaspoon of vanilla extract drizzled on crushed raspberries. A light dusting of ground cloves or allspice is an interesting addition to mango, and a dash of powdered carob gives bananas a pleasant, new flavor. Fresh lime juice enhances the sweetness of melon. Rum extract gives a different twist to fresh pineapple. Crushed fresh mint leaves or ginger slices are refreshing in a fruit compote.

Cooking fruits gives them a different taste and texture, and makes them seem more like desserts. Baked apple slices are a favorite of mine. Broiled

Apples Alaska   Page 249

247

grapefruit is a citrus elevated beyond the breakfast category, and bananas take on a new appeal and sophistication when they're baked.

Desserts can be delectable without heavy sweetening, so for dieters, an important consideration is to omit or drastically reduce these additional calories. This means avoiding most pies, cookies, and cakes and concentrating on light, airy puddings and fresh fruit concoctions that are equally pleasing.

Since an airy texture usually means fewer calories, by simply whipping gelatins and puddings, you can serve pleasingly heaped-up portions that are nonetheless lower in calories. You can also cut down on fats by substituting low-fat milk for regular milk, cottage cheese for cream cheese, low-fat yogurt for cream, and flavorful reductions of fruit juice for butter-rich sauces. It is surprising how many desserts lend themselves to this sleight of hand.

Devotees of ice cream often can be appeased by frozen ices that are simply made of fruit and crushed ice blended in a food processor. Of course, there are no calories at all in the ice portion. A frozen banana has the rich, smooth texture of ice cream without the fat. I like to keep a few bananas in the freezer for low-calorie snacks. The fruit's own skin is all the packaging it needs. After the banana is frozen, simply peel back the skin, and as soon as you can cut into the fruit with a spoon, it's ready to eat.

Tip: Never put a bowl of dessert on the table when dieters are eating. Serve it in individual dishes, and immediately put any leftovers out of sight.

For dieters' desserts, use individual dishes that are pretty to look at but don't hold a great deal. A stemmed sherbet glass, for instance, holds much less than a fruit dish and looks prettier, too. A few berries on the underlining plate (where ordinarily you might have served a crisp cookie) adds a low-calorie festive touch.

Unsweetened flaked coconut is an easy decoration to use in making simple desserts a bit more special. A dusting of powdered carob is attractive, too. Frozen grapes (at about four calories each) add a very elegant touch to a simple whipped gelatin dessert. With a little thought, a cook can preserve the mystique of dessert and still pare away a lot of those unwanted calories.

Crustless Raspberry Cheesecake

This tastes just as good as classic cheesecake, and it has far fewer calories.

> 2 cups part-skim ricotta
> 3 eggs
> 2 tablespoons cornstarch
> 2 tablespoons honey
> 1½ teaspoons lemon extract
> 1½ cups fresh raspberries
> ¼ cup Red Currant Jelly (page 273), optional

Preheat oven to 325°F. Butter a 9-inch pie plate.

In a large bowl, beat ricotta and eggs together until smooth. Beat in cornstarch, honey, and lemon extract. Turn into prepared pie plate, and bake on middle shelf of oven for 1 hour.

Cool on wire rack, and then chill. Top with raspberries.

In a small saucepan, heat jelly. Drizzle over top of berries, and refrigerate cake.

8 servings

Apples Alaska

A particularly pretty dessert without a bit of calorie-adding sweetener or fat in it.

> 3 baking apples (use a variety that is not too tart, such as Cortland or McIntosh)
> cinnamon, for sprinkling
> 2 egg whites
> ¼ teaspoon cream of tartar
> ½ teaspoon vanilla extract

Preheat oven to 350°F.

Core apples, but do not peel. Split apples in half and lay them, cut-side up, in a baking dish that will hold them upright. Sprinkle with cinnamon, and bake on middle shelf of oven for about 30 minutes, or until tender when pierced with a knife point.

While apples are baking, beat egg whites in a small bowl until foamy throughout. Sprinkle with cream of tartar, and continue beating until they form stiff peaks but are not dry. Beat in vanilla. Cover bowl with a plate.

When apples are tender, remove from oven and increase heat to 400°F. Divide meringue among apples, spooning an attractive mound on top of each. Return to oven, and bake until meringue is golden brown.

Allow to cool for about 15 minutes, so that they are just warm but not hot, and serve.

6 servings

Broiled Grapefruit Sections

> 2 cups skinned, seeded grapefruit sections, well drained
> 2 tablespoons honey
> ½ cup unsweetened flaked coconut

Place grapefruit sections in a single layer in 4 individual ovenproof gratin dishes. Drizzle honey over grapefruit, ½ tablespoon per portion. Place under broiler until sizzling. Sprinkle with coconut, and broil until topping is just golden. Do not overcook.

Serve at once.

4 servings

Baked Apple Rings

4 apples (use any good cooking
 apple, such as Cortland or Granny
 Smith)
2 tablespoons butter, melted
2 teaspoons honey
 cinnamon, for sprinkling

Preheat oven to 350°F. Butter a baking sheet.

Core apples, but do not peel. Slice into ½-inch rounds. Place on prepared baking sheet.

Mix butter and honey in a cup, and brush mixture on rings. Sprinkle with cinnamon, and bake for about 15 minutes, or until soft but not mushy.

4 servings

Fruit Compote Exotica

It would be difficult for a dieter to feel deprived when having a cup of this luxurious melange for dessert.

2 kiwi fruit
2 pomegranates
1 ripe papaya
1 ripe mango
3 Asian pears
1 orange
2 limes
3 slices peeled ginger root
 unsweetened flaked coconut, for
 sprinkling

As you prepare ingredients, combine them in a large bowl. Peel and slice kiwis into half rounds. Quarter pomegranates and scoop out fruit with a grapefruit spoon; don't include any pith. Peel, seed, and cut papaya into bite-size chunks. Peel, pit, and cut mango into bite-size chunks. Peel, core, and slice pears. Squeeze juice from orange and limes, and stir into fruit. Squeeze ginger to release flavor; stir into compote. Chill to blend flavors.

Remove ginger before serving. Sprinkle each portion with coconut.

8 1-cup servings

Lemon Fluff

2 eggs, separated
2 cups skim milk
1 envelope unflavored gelatin
¼ cup honey
2 teaspoons lemon extract
 frozen seedless green grapes
 (page 209), optional

In a small bowl, beat egg yolks.

In a medium-size saucepan, mix together egg yolks and milk. Stir in gelatin, and set aside for about 5 minutes to soften. Add honey, and cook over low heat, stirring constantly, for 5 minutes. Remove from heat, and mix in lemon extract. Pour into a large bowl, and chill until thick but not set.

In a medium-size bowl, beat egg whites until stiff peaks form. Fold into lemon mixture. Spoon into 6 dessert dishes, and chill until set. Decorate with frozen grapes, if desired.

6 servings

Delicious Dessert Shake

1 cup fresh strawberries
¼ cup unsweetened frozen orange
    juice concentrate
1 cup skim milk
½ cup yogurt
½ teaspoon vanilla extract
½ teaspoon ground cinnamon
1 tablespoon honey (optional)

Combine all ingredients in a blender or food processor, and process until smooth.

2 servings

Pineapple Snow

1 cup canned unsweetened crushed
    pineapple, well drained
1 cup finely crushed ice
¼ cup Mint Syrup (page 270)
    fresh mint leaves (optional)

Combine pineapple, ice, and Mint Syrup in a blender. Process until frothy and light in color, about 30 seconds. Pour into dessert dishes, and, if desired, decorate with mint leaves. Serve immediately.

4 servings

Lemon Fluff   Page 250   Orange-Pineapple Fluff   Page 252
Lime Melba   Page 252

Orange Charlotte

10 to 12 Ladyfingers (page 10), split
½ cup cold water
2 envelopes unflavored
    gelatin
1½ cups skim milk
½ cup honey
3 eggs
1½ cups orange juice
1 teaspoon orange extract

Lightly oil sides and bottom of a 2-quart, straight-sided mold. Line sides with Ladyfingers.

Pour cold water into a cup, and sprinkle gelatin on top. Set aside for a few minutes to soften.

In a large saucepan, heat together milk and honey.

In a medium-size bowl, beat eggs for 1 minute. Add 1 cup milk mixture to eggs, and stir to blend. Pour back into milk mixture in pan, and continue to heat, stirring constantly, until mixture starts to thicken. Stir in gelatin, heating until dissolved. Remove from heat, and mix in orange juice and extract. Pour into a bowl, and chill until thickened but not set, about 1 hour.

Beat until fluffy. Turn into prepared mold, and chill until set.

To serve, unmold onto plate.

6 servings

Lime Melba

½ cup nonfat dry milk
½ cup cold water
1 tablespoon lime juice
2 tablespoons honey

3 peaches, peeled, pitted, and
    halved
Raspberry Sauce "Lite" (page 271)

Mix dry milk, water, and lime juice in the small bowl of an electric mixer. Whip until light and fluffy. Blend in honey. Continue to beat until thoroughly mixed.

Place each peach half in a stemmed sherbet glass. Top with whipped dry milk. Pour 2 tablespoons Raspberry Sauce "Lite" over all.

6 servings

Orange-Pineapple Fluff

2 cups orange juice
1 envelope unflavored gelatin
½ cup canned unsweetened crushed
    pineapple, well drained
½ teaspoon orange rind
1 orange, peeled, seeded, and
    separated into sections
fresh mint sprigs (optional)

Pour orange juice into a small saucepan. Add gelatin, and stir mixture over low heat until gelatin is completely dissolved. Turn into a small bowl, and chill until set.

Spoon gelatin into a medium-size bowl, and beat with a hand-held electric mixer or egg beater until light and fluffy. Fold in pineapple and orange rind. Spoon into stemmed sherbet glasses and chill.

When ready to serve, decorate each serving with an orange section and a sprig of fresh mint, if desired.

4 to 6 servings

Pineapple Pudding

1 cup pineapple juice, divided
1 envelope unflavored gelatin
1½ cups canned unsweetened
   crushed pineapple, well drained
2 teaspoons honey (optional)
½ teaspoon lemon extract
1½ cups yogurt

Pour ½ cup pineapple juice into a small saucepan, and sprinkle gelatin on top. Let stand for about 5 minutes to soften.

Warm mixture over low heat, stirring constantly, until gelatin dissolves.

In a large bowl, mix together pineapple, ½ cup pineapple juice, honey, if desired, and extract. Thoroughly stir in gelatin mixture. Chill until thickened but not set.

Fold in yogurt, and spoon pudding into 6 dessert dishes. Chill until set.

Serve within 4 hours or dessert may separate.

6 servings

Pumpkin Pudding

4 cups pumpkin puree
⅓ cup honey
2 eggs
2½ teaspoons ground cinnamon
½ teaspoon ground nutmeg
½ teaspoon ground allspice
2 tablespoons cornstarch
1½ cups skim milk, divided

Preheat oven to 350°F.

In a large ovenproof bowl, beat together pumpkin and honey. Beat in eggs, and then stir in spices.

Dissolve cornstarch in ½ cup milk. Beat cornstarch mixture and 1 cup milk into pumpkin. Bake on middle shelf of oven for 1 hour and 10 minutes. Cool, and then chill before serving.

10 servings

Strawberry Parfait

1 recipe Dieters' Vanilla Pudding
   (page 103)
1 cup quartered fresh or frozen and
   thawed strawberries
1 cup Raspberry Sauce (page 271)
4 whole fresh strawberries (optional)

Place ¼ cup pudding into each of 4 parfait glasses. Top with 2 tablespoons berries, and then 2 tablespoons Raspberry Sauce. Repeat layers. Decorate with whole strawberries.

4 servings

Vanilla Pots de Crème

½ cup instant nonfat dry milk
2 cups boiling water
2 tablespoons honey
2 teaspoons vanilla extract
3 eggs, well beaten

Preheat oven to 350°F.

In a medium-size bowl, mix together milk, water, and honey. Stir in vanilla. Pour a little of the mixture into eggs. Return to bowl, and blend. Spoon mixture into 6 ovenproof cups.

Place a shallow pan on middle shelf of oven. Arrange filled cups in pan. Then pour water into pan so that it comes half way up sides of cups. Bake for about 30 minutes, or until just set.

Chill before serving.

6 servings

Spanish Cinnamon Cream

2 cups skim milk
1 envelope unflavored gelatin
2 tablespoons honey
1 teaspoon ground cinnamon
2 eggs, separated
1 red Delicious apple
2 tablespoons lemon juice
    ground cinnamon, for sprinkling

Scald milk in top of a double boiler set over simmering water. Slowly stir in gelatin until dissolved. Blend in honey and cinnamon.

Beat egg yolks in a cup. Gradually add about ½ cup hot milk mixture to egg yolks while beating. Empty contents of cup into top of double boiler, and whisk pudding over simmering water until thick and smooth. Remove from heat, and cool.

In a small bowl, beat egg whites until stiff peaks form. Fold into cooled pudding. Spoon pudding into 6 stemmed sherbet glasses. Chill until firm.

When ready to serve, core and slice apple, but do not peel. Top each serving with apple slices brushed with lemon juice. Sprinkle with cinnamon.

6 servings

CHAPTER
13

Triumphant Toppings, Fillings, and Sweet Spreads

A truly sensational dessert, the kind that elicits rave reviews, often is a combination of recipes put together in an interesting and attractive way to take advantage of contrasts in taste, texture, and temperature. In this chapter, I've provided some of my favorite sauces, frostings, and fruit spreads so that basic desserts can be dressed up with toppings and fillings that are especially appealing.

Since I don't use sugar (and, ordinarily, recipes for these frostings and fruit spreads depend heavily on sugar), you'll find my alternatives use different ingredients and methods than those to which you may be accustomed. My frostings, for example, rather than using a pound of confectioners' sugar, are made with really nutritious foods like egg whites, nonfat dry milk, or cream cheese and yet are just as tasty as traditional frostings, maybe more so. And my jams and preserves for filling tarts and cakes are simply fruit and honey cooked together until they jell.

To add the one last touch that makes a dessert special or, as they say, "to put the icing on the cake," you'll need a number of these sweet basics in your repertoire.

DECORATING CAKES

Not every cake needs a frosting. Cakes made with honey are much moister than most sugar-based cakes and can be enjoyed without this additional sweetening. Most of the cakes I make are served plain—or with a simple fruit or custard sauce—but for special occasions, such as birthdays, it's fun to get a bit artistic about cake decorating.

For this purpose, you may want to buy a good cake decorating set consisting of a cloth bag and decorating tips. Natural food coloring puts all the colors of the rainbow at your fingertips.

A frosting and an icing are practically the same thing, except that an icing contains egg white and is usually thinner.

Uncooked frosting is a better basis for fancy cake decoration than cooked frosting or whipped cream.

To fill and frost an 8- or 9-inch layer cake, you'll need about 2 cups of frosting. If you have a lazy susan, put the cake plate on it to make the job easier. If the cake is lopsided, trim it as necessary. Place the bottom layer upside down on the cake plate. Tuck strips of wax paper around the cake to catch drips of frosting. (Remove these before serving.) Spread the filling about 3/16 inch thick, unless otherwise specified in the recipe, and let it set for a few minutes before placing the top layer on it, right side up.

Brush the cake free of crumbs. Frost the sides first. Then pile the remaining frosting in the center of the top of the cake, and swirl it out quickly and evenly over the top to overlap the edges a bit on all sides. Dip your knife in hot water to smooth the frosting. Let the frosting harden before decorating.

Decoration can be as simple as a sprinkle of coconut, a circle of fresh berries, or a dash of powdered carob. Or you can press chopped nuts into the sides of the cake while the frosting is still soft and then let it harden. A light-colored frosting looks pretty with a contrasting glaze poured over the top and allowed to drip down the sides.

But if you want to go beyond these easy alternatives, prepare an icing or Decorator Frosting (page 267) in one or more colors that contrast with the basic frosting. Prepare the decorating bag and tip according to the directions that came with it. (I like to line the cloth bag with a plastic bag, pull the corner of it through the decorating tip, and snip it off with scissors. This makes it much easier to clean up or to change colors.)

Next, fill the bag with icing. Pipe the pattern you've selected with firm, steady pressure. You may want to practice a little on a sheet of wax paper first, then scoop up the icing and put it back into the bag. Any set of cake decorating equipment you buy will give you instructions on how to make stars, leaves, and flowers galore as well as decorative edgings.

You can write a wish on a birthday cake using the plain writing tip; it's advisable to practice first on a piece of wax paper to be sure the words will fit.

Even when you frost the easy way, with whipped cream, I think it's nice to save some cream to pipe around the edges. This little bit of extra effort makes a cake look as if it just came from the hands of a professional chef.

PRESERVING FRUIT SPREADS

Although some standard cookbooks give directions for using a mixture of honey and sugar, none recommends preserving fruit spreads with honey alone. My experience is that you can indeed, make perfectly lovely jellies, jams, and preserves using honey, with no sugar at all, and that's the way I do it. Honey gives a slight flavor to fruit (as opposed to sugar, which imparts sweetness without any discernible flavor), but the fruit taste definitely predominates. Many classic desserts depend on a fruit spread ingredient, and for those I use my own homemade products with excellent results.

I often (but not always) rely on the natural pectin of the fruit for jelling, instead of using processed pectin, powder or liquid. For those fruits which are low in natural pectin, I include a high-pectin ingredient, such as apple or boiled-down apple juice.

Homemade Apple Pectin

Add ⅔ cup of this mixture to 1 quart of low-pectin fruit (see table, Acid and Pectin Content of Common Fruits) when making jelly.

2 cups water
16 large tart juicy apples, washed

Pour water into a large stainless steel kettle, and bring to a boil. Do not core or peel apples, as the seeds, cores, and skin contain the lion's share of pectin. Just cut them in half, lay them cut-side down on a cutting board, and, using a long knife, cut halves into slices and put them right into the pot. When all the apples are in the pot and water is boiling fast, reduce heat, cover, and simmer for 30 minutes; apples will be very soft.

Fit a colander with 6 layers of rinsed cheesecloth. Drain apples in colander over a large bowl (without pressing on fruit if pectin is to be used in the making of clear jelly) for 10 to 12 hours.

Pour juice into a medium-size saucepan, and reduce to two-thirds the original volume by boiling rapidly, uncovered. Cool liquid. Pour ⅔ cup into individual freezer containers, and freeze until needed.

Makes about 3 batches

NOTE

If, like me, you dislike throwing away the apple pulp, don't do it! Put it through a food mill, and it becomes apple sauce. Or add ½ cup honey, 1 teaspoon ground cinnamon, ½ teaspoon ground cloves, and cook over very low heat for 30 minutes, or until very thick and smooth. Then you will have 2 cups of apple butter. Keep refrigerated.

Fruit spreads made with honey have to be cooked longer than those made with sugar, so a given quantity of fruit yields a bit less spread. Honey-based spreads must be carefully watched toward the end of the cooking time to prevent them from sticking to the bottom of the pan. Other than that, the preserving process is the same.

There are three ways of putting up fruit spreads. The first is to make a small batch and simply refrigerate it in clean jars. The spread will keep this way for a month or more. The second way is to freeze the spread; it will keep for six months or more. If you don't use very much jelly or jam, these two methods are recommended because they're so easy. It will encourage you to use your own homemade product instead of sugar-filled store-bought products.

The third method of putting up fruit spreads is to eliminate all bacteria and give the product a shelf life. This enables you to preserve a year's supply of fruit that's available for only one short season a year, such as Concord grapes or raspberries.

Fruit spreads come in many varieties. Jelly is made from strained fruit juice so that it's transparent and shimmering. Jams include the fruit pulp, chopped or crushed, cooked just until the spread will mound up in a spoon; I prefer jams to jellies, since there's no waste of good fruit when you make a jam. Fruit butters also include the fruit pulp, cooked much longer and strained to produce a thick, fine-textured spread. Conserves generally contain a combination of fruits, nuts, and raisins. Marmalades consist of soft slices of citrus fruit suspended in jelly. Preserves are whole fruits suspended in soft jelly.

The basic ingredients of fruit spreads are fruit, acid, pectin, and a sweetener. Fruits naturally contain acid and pectin, but in varying amounts. A fruit low in one or the other necessary ingredient may need to have a supplement added in order to jell, such as lemon juice to add acid or tart apple juice to add pectin, or in some cases,

powdered pectin. Since unripe fruit is higher in both acid and pectin than ripe fruit, sometimes it's enough just to include a portion of unripe with ripe fruit. Therefore, if a recipe calls for a certain amount of unripe fruit, it's important to include it. The chart on the opposite page rates fruits for acid and pectin.

GENERAL DIRECTIONS FOR MAKING FRUIT SPREADS

You'll need an 8- to 10-quart stainless steel kettle, a thermometer (the same kind you use for candy or deep-fat frying), and a jelly bag and stand, or the equivalent arrangement of a colander lined with six thicknesses of rinsed cheesecloth propped up above a large bowl. One package of cheesecloth, which is 3½ yards, is enough to do this. (I have a three-tiered wire basket for fruit hanging in my kitchen, which I find very useful for holding my cheesecloth-lined colander above a bowl on the counter top.) For fruit spreads that are not going to be refrigerated or frozen, you'll need a boiling water bath canner with a rack for holding jars and a jar lifter with a good grip.

And then, of course, you'll need jars. It's my advice to avoid melted paraffin entirely and use the can-or-freeze glass jars with the metal two-piece vacuum covers and rims. The metal covers (not the screw-on rims) need to be replaced with new ones each time the jars are reused. For fruit spreads, the smallest (half-pint) size is best, but they're also the hardest to find. Buy them well before the canning season!

Acid and Pectin Content of Common Fruits			
	HIGH	MEDIUM	LOW
ACID	tart apples apricots blackberries blueberries citrus fruits cranberries currants pineapple tart plums raspberries rhubarb	tart cherries grapes sweet plums strawberries	sweet apples sweet cherries figs melons nectarines peaches pears quinces
PECTIN	tart apples citrus fruits cranberries currants tart plums	sweet apples blackberries blueberries cherries (tart or sweet) grapes melons sweet plums quinces raspberries	apricots figs nectarines peaches pears pineapple rhubarb strawberries

If a fruit spread is going to be refrigerated and eaten within a few weeks, any jars with good screw-on lids can be used to contain it. You should, however, wash and heat the jars just as you would if preparing the fruit for shelf storage.

When you are ready to cook, the lids should be simmered in water heated to 180°F for 5 minutes, then left in the hot water until ready to use. The jars should be washed in hot soapy water, rinsed well, and left in hot water until ready to use. Or you can wash them in

263

a dishwasher, leaving it closed to keep the jars hot.

A hot jar should never be placed on a cold surface or in a drafty place. Boiling liquid should never be poured into a cold jar. Sudden wide temperature changes can cause the glass to crack or shatter.

Follow the individual recipe directions in the preparation of ingredients. Many fruit spread recipes require you to cook the spread to the "jelling point" and to perform a test to be sure you have reached it. There are three tests for the jelling point, and it's not excessive to try two of them when making jelly; I always do.

Test one: A fruit spread will jell when the cooked mixture reaches a temperature 8°F above the temperature of boiling water. First check the temperature of boiling water, since it varies in different locations. Then add eight degrees to figure when the jelling point should be reached. When you're ready to make the jelly, place the thermometer in the cold fruit mixture, and watch its temperature as the fruit cooks.

Test two: Dip a cold spoon into the cooking mixture. Tip the spoon and allow the mixture to run off. When the last two drops run together and fall off the spoon as a sheet or flake, the jelling point has been reached. (See illustration.)

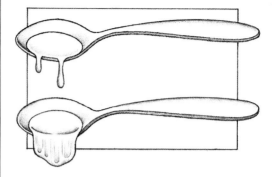

Test three: Put a stack of saucers in the freezer. When you believe the jelling point has been reached, pour a teaspoon of the mixture on a cold saucer, and return it to the freezer. In about three minutes, the juice should form a jelled mass that holds together. If clots separate, the fruit needs further cooking.

If the jam recipe you're using calls for the fruit mixture to be cooked until it mounds in the spoon, that simply means it should heap up rather than run when you half-fill a cold spoon. To find out exactly what the finished product will be like, try test three also.

When the fruit mixture is ready, carefully pour the boiling liquid into hot jars to within ⅛ inch of the top. If necessary, wipe the top and threads of the jar with a clean damp cloth. Cover the jars, and screw the bands on tightly. Invert each jar for a few seconds.

Sometimes there won't be enough spread to completely fill the last jar. Simply refrigerate it and use the contents within a few weeks.

If the recipe requires you to process the fruit spread by the boiling water method, place the jars in the canner rack, cover with water (1 inch above the top of the jar), and boil for the required time. Lift them out with the jar lifter. Do not place them on a cold surface.

Allow hot jars of fruit spread to stand and cool overnight before storing in a cool dark place. As the air in the top of each jar cools, it contracts, causing the metal cover to make "ping" sounds and contract inward, becoming slightly concave and bonded to the glass rim. This indicates a good vacuum seal has been achieved. If a jar does not do this, it's better to refrigerate it, as the seal may not be perfect.

Almond Glaze

3 tablespoons honey
5 tablespoons Almond Butter (page
    277)

In a small skillet (with a nonstick surface, if possible), heat honey, stirring constantly, until it bubbles. Stir in Almond Butter to make a smooth paste. Spread over warm bread or cake immediately.

Yields about ½ cup

Carob Fudge Glaze

¾ cup sifted powdered carob
½ cup boiling water
3 tablespoons honey
3 tablespoons butter, cut into pieces
1 teaspoon vanilla extract

Place carob into a small saucepan. Slowly pour in boiling water while whisking to blend. Continue to whisk over low heat. Add honey and blend. Add butter and blend. Remove from heat, and stir in vanilla.

Use to glaze cupcakes or cake. Chill to harden.

Yields about 1 cup

Carob Whip

1 cup heavy cream
2 tablespoons Basic Carob Syrup
    (page xviii)
2 tablespoons honey

In a small, chilled bowl, beat cream with an electric beater until slightly thickened. Add carob syrup and honey, and continue to beat until cream is thick and forms mounds.

Yields about 2 cups

Cashew Frosting

5 tablespoons honey
5 tablespoons Cashew Butter
    (page 277)
2 tablespoons nonfat dry milk
½ teaspoon vanilla extract

Combine honey, Cashew Butter, and nonfat dry milk in a small skillet, and stir over low heat until mixture is soft and spreadable. Remove from heat and stir in vanilla. Use while still warm to frost cookies.

Yields about ½ cup

Festive Frosting

1 cup raisins
1 cup maple syrup
12 egg yolks, slightly beaten
1 cup honey
¾ cup butter, cut into chunks
1½ cups pitted frozen sweet
    cherries, thawed, drained, and
    quartered
1½ cups unsweetened flaked coconut
1 cup chopped walnuts

Place raisins into a medium-size bowl, and pour maple syrup over them. Soak raisins in syrup for several hours or overnight.

In top of a double boiler, combine egg yolks and honey. Add butter, set over simmering water, and cook, stirring constantly, until mixture thickens, 20 to 25 minutes.

Remove from heat, and mix in cherries, coconut, walnuts, and raisin mixture. Chill before spreading.

Yields 6 to 8 cups

Orange Frosting

8 ounces cream cheese, softened
¼ cup unsweetened frozen orange juice concentrate
¼ cup honey
½ teaspoon orange extract

Place ingredients into a medium-size bowl, and beat together until smooth.

Yields about 1½ cups

Cranberry Frosting and Filling

2 cups fresh cranberries
½ cup water
1 cup honey
½ teaspoon grated orange rind
¼ teaspoon ground cinnamon
8 ounces cream cheese, softened

In a medium-size saucepan, combine cranberries and water. Bring mixture to a boil. Cook over low heat for 10 minutes, stirring often and watching that mixture does not stick towards the end of cooking time. Add honey, orange rind, and cinnamon, and continue cooking for 4 minutes longer, stirring often. Sieve cranberries through a fine-meshed strainer. Discard skins and seeds. Chill jelly.

When ready to spread, cream the cheese until fluffy, and blend in jelly. This can be done in a food processor or by hand. Use while mixture is still soft.

Yields 1½ to 2 cups

Decorator Frosting

This frosting must be used immediately as it hardens quickly. It's not meant to frost a cake, but to be used for decorative purposes only.

2 egg whites
½ teaspoon cream of tartar
¼ cup honey
2 teaspoons vanilla extract
2 cups instant nonfat dry milk*

In a medium-size bowl, beat egg whites and cream of tartar together until frothy. Beat in honey and vanilla. Slowly add dry milk, beating until stiff and glossy.

To achieve desired color, add a few drops of natural food coloring.

Yields about 1¼ cups

*It is essential that the nonfat dry milk have a very fine texture for this recipe.

Coconut Cream Frosting

1 cup heavy cream
1 cup Pastry Cream (page 272)
1 cup unsweetened flaked coconut

In a medium-size bowl, beat cream until soft peaks form. Fold in Pastry Cream and coconut.

Yields about 4 cups

Seven-Minute Frosting

4 egg whites, at room temperature
6 tablespoons honey
⅛ teaspoon cream of tartar
1 teaspoon vanilla extract

In top of a double boiler set over simmering water, beat egg whites, honey, and cream of tartar with an electric beater for 5 minutes.

Remove from heat. Add vanilla, and beat for another 2 minutes. Frosting will be stiff. Allow to cool before using.

Yields about 4 cups

VARIATIONS
Almond Seven-Minute Frosting: Substitute ½ teaspoon almond extract for vanilla extract.
Lemon Seven-Minute Frosting: Substitute 1 teaspoon lemon extract for vanilla extract.

Basic White Frosting

⅓ cup honey
8 ounces cream cheese, softened
1 teaspoon vanilla extract

In a large bowl, beat together all ingredients until well blended, about 3 minutes.

VARIATIONS
Almond Frosting: Substitute ½ teaspoon almond extract for vanilla extract.
Lemon Cheese Frosting: Substitute 1 teaspoon lemon extract for vanilla extract.

Yields about 1½ cups

Vanilla Icing

2 egg whites
¼ teaspoon cream of tartar
¼ cup honey
2 teaspoons vanilla extract
1 cup instant nonfat dry milk*

Beat egg whites and cream of tartar in a medium-size bowl until frothy. Beat in honey and vanilla. Gradually beat in dry milk. If icing is not firm enough, add more nonfat dry milk.

Yields about 2 cups

*It is essential that the nonfat dry milk have a very fine texture for this recipe.

VARIATION
Anise Icing: Substitute anise extract for vanilla extract.

Custard Sauce

2 cups milk, divided
4 teaspoons cornstarch
3 tablespoons honey
3 egg yolks
1½ teaspoons vanilla extract

In a cup, mix ¼ cup milk with cornstarch. Pour into a medium-size saucepan, adding remaining milk and honey. Bring to a boil over medium heat, stirring constantly.

In a small bowl, whisk egg yolks briefly. Add ¼ cup hot milk to egg yolks, and pour mixture into remaining hot milk. Bring to a boil, stirring until thickened. Remove from heat and stir in vanilla.

Yields about 2 cups

Apricot Sauce

2 cups fresh or unsweetened canned
    apricot puree (peaches or half
    peaches and half apricots may be
    substituted)
3 tablespoons honey*
1 tablespoon cornstarch
¼ cup water
½ teaspoon lemon extract

In a medium-size saucepan, combine puree and honey.

Dissolve cornstarch in water, and add to puree mixture. Cook over medium heat, stirring constantly, until thickened and bubbly.

Stir in lemon extract. Put through medium-fine strainer. Chill.

Yields about 1¾ cups

*Some apricots are much sweeter than
    others. This measure is simply a guide.
    Your own taste should be the final authority.

Fresh Mango Sauce

1 large ripe mango, peeled and
    cubed
½ cup orange juice
¼ cup honey

In a food processor, puree mango. Add orange juice and honey through feed tube with motor running, and continue to process until well blended. Pour into a pitcher and use immediately.

To make sauce in a blender, first add orange juice and honey, then mango. Blend until smooth.

Yields about 1½ cups

Carob Fudge Sauce

½ cup sifted powdered carob
1 cup minus 2 tablespoons boiling
    water
½ cup honey
¼ cup butter
1 teaspoon vanilla extract

Place carob into a heavy, deep medium-size saucepan. Stir in boiling water until mixture is smooth. Blend in honey. Bring to a boil, stirring constantly. Reduce heat and simmer sauce for 8 minutes, stirring occasionally.

Remove from heat, and whisk in butter until melted. Stir in vanilla.

Store in a covered jar in refrigerator. To reheat, open jar, and place into a pan of water. Heat water to warm sauce. Stir before serving.

Yields 1½ cups

Blueberry Honey Sauce

*This versatile sauce can be used on
pancakes, waffles, and ice cream.*

6 tablespoons butter
1 tablespoon cornstarch
¾ cup honey
3 cups fresh or frozen blueberries
½ teaspoon vanilla extract

In a large saucepan, melt butter. Blend in cornstarch, and stir in honey and blueberries. Bring to a boil over medium heat, stirring constantly. Boil for 5 minutes.

Stir in vanilla, and cool before serving.

Yields about 2 cups

Hard Sauce

½ cup butter, softened
½ cup honey
1 teaspoon brandy extract
2 teaspoons lemon extract

In a medium-size bowl, beat butter until fluffy. Beat in honey and extracts. Chill well before serving.

Yields about 1 cup

Mint Syrup

Fresh mint is a useful and easy herb to grow; in fact, it multiplies so fast that it's necessary to keep it restricted to a small area. In addition to the well-known spearmint and peppermint, other lesser known "flavors" such as pineapple mint and orange mint are especially delightful. Mint syrup, besides being a tangy, fragrant ingredient in desserts, makes a pleasant sweetener for cooling summer drinks.

1 cup fresh mint leaves, well packed (3 tablespoons dried mint may be substituted)
1 cup boiling water
1 cup honey

Place mint leaves into a small saucepan, and pour boiling water over them. Simmer over very low heat for 5 minutes. Remove from heat, cover, and let steep for 1 hour.

Drain off liquid and reserve it. Discard leaves.

Combine mint liquid and honey in a large saucepan. Bring to a boil over high heat. Allow to boil for 5 minutes undisturbed (to soft ball stage, if you wish to use a thermometer), watching that mixture does not boil over.

Yields about 1⅓ cups

Orange Custard Sauce

3 tablespoons honey
4 egg yolks
1 cup half-and-half
⅛ teaspoon orange extract

In top of a double boiler, whisk together honey and egg yolks until mixed. Slowly stir in half-and-half with a metal spoon. Set over simmering water, and cook, stirring constantly, until mixture thickens enough to coat the back of the spoon.

Remove from heat, and stir in orange extract. Cool well before serving.

Yields about 1¼ cups

Cherry Sauce

4 cups fresh sour cherries
1½ cups orange juice
¼ cup honey
1 tablespoon lemon juice
3 tablespoons cornstarch
¼ cup water

Pit and halve sour cherries. In a large saucepan, simmer cherries, orange juice, honey, and lemon juice for 10 minutes, stirring often. Blend cornstarch and water. Stir into cherries, and continue to cook, stirring constantly, until mixture thickens.

Yields about 3 cups

Rhubarb Sauce

For a sauce with a pretty color, choose pink-hued rhubarb stalks at the market.

½ pound rhubarb
½ cup honey
¼ cup water
1 tablespoon cornstarch
¼ cup cold water

Cut rhubarb stalks into 1-inch lengths. Place into a medium-size saucepan with honey and ¼ cup water. Bring to a boil, reduce heat, and simmer, stirring often, for about 10 minutes, or until rhubarb is quite tender.

Stir cornstarch into ¼ cup cold water until there are no lumps. Pour into sauce, and cook, stirring constantly, until it clears and thickens. Serve warm over pancakes or plain cake.

Yields about 1½ cups

Raspberry Sauce

This versatile sauce is delicious on French Vanilla Ice Cream (page 131), adds a note of elegance to pound cake, turns plain vanilla pudding into a company dish, can be used on pancakes, and is essential to Peach Melba.

1 cup frozen raspberries, thawed and drained with juice reserved
2 teaspoons cornstarch
¼ cup Red Currant Jelly (page 273)

Place drained raspberries into a small saucepan.

Dissolve cornstarch in ¼ cup reserved juice. Add to raspberries along with jelly, and bring to a boil, stirring constantly, until thickened. Remove from heat and strain.

Yields about 1 cup

VARIATION
Raspberry Sauce "Lite": Omit red currant jelly.

Yields about ½ cup

Pineapple Filling

2 cups unsweetened canned crushed pineapple, undrained
2 tablespoons cornstarch
2 tablespoons honey, or to taste

Place pineapple into a medium-size saucepan. Stir in cornstarch until dissolved. Bring to a boil over medium-high heat, stirring constantly. When mixture bubbles and thickens, remove from heat and stir in honey. (If you like a slightly tart flavor, you can leave out honey altogether.) Cool before using.

Yields about 2 cups

Ricotta Cheese Filling

2 cups ricotta cheese
1 egg, beaten
3 tablespoons honey
½ teaspoon grated lemon rind

In a medium-size bowl, beat all ingredients together to blend thoroughly. Use as a filling for Danish pastry or any pastry in which the filling will be cooked.

Yields 2¼ cups

271

Orange Filling

¼ cup cornstarch
2 cups orange juice, divided
2 tablespoons honey
½ teaspoon lemon extract

In a small bowl, dissolve cornstarch in ½ cup orange juice.

In a medium-size saucepan, heat remaining orange juice, honey, and cornstarch mixture to boiling, stirring constantly. Boil for 2 minutes, while stirring.

Remove from heat, mix in lemon extract, and allow to cool.

Yields about 2 cups

VARIATION
Orange Topping: Reduce cornstarch to 1½ tablespoons.

Lemon Filling

1½ cups water
⅓ cup cornstarch
¾ cup honey
3 egg yolks, beaten
¾ cup lemon juice
1 teaspoon butter

Pour water into a small bowl, and dissolve cornstarch in it. Place mixture into a medium-size saucepan with honey, and cook until thickened, stirring constantly.

Pour a little of the hot mixture into egg yolks, whisking constantly. Return to saucepan, and continue cooking for 2 minutes, stirring constantly.

Add lemon juice and butter, and stir until butter is dissolved.
Cool thoroughly before serving.

Yields about 2½ cups

Prune Filling

1 cup prunes
1¼ cups water
¼ cup honey
   stick of cinnamon
1 slice lemon, ½ inch thick, with
   rind
¼ teaspoon ground cloves

Combine all ingredients in a medium-size saucepan. Bring to a boil, reduce heat, and simmer, covered, for 45 minutes.

Strain mixture, reserving juice. Remove pits from prunes. Discard pits, cinnamon stick, and lemon slice. Puree prunes. If mixture seems too thick, add a bit of the reserved prune juice.

Yields 1¾ cups

Pastry Cream

1 cup milk
1 tablespoon cornstarch
2 egg yolks
¼ cup honey, warmed slightly
¼ teaspoon vanilla extract
¼ teaspoon almond extract

Pour milk into a medium-size bowl. Stir cornstarch into milk until completely dissolved.

Whisk together milk-cornstarch mixture, egg yolks, and honey. Pour into a medium-size saucepan and cook over medium heat, stirring constantly, until mixture bubbles and thickens. Remove from heat, and stir in extracts. Cool.

Yields about 1½ cups

VARIATIONS

Creamy Cake Filling: Increase cornstarch to 5 tablespoons. Double all other ingredients.

Yields about 3 cups

Lemon Cream: Increase cornstarch to 2 tablespoons. Omit vanilla and almond extracts. Add 1 teaspoon finely grated lemon rind.

Vanilla Cream: Increase cornstarch to 2½ tablespoons. Omit almond extract.

Berry Jam or Jelly

Use this pattern recipe to make strawberry, raspberry, blackberry, blueberry, red currant, or any other berry jam. Before starting to cook, read the general instructions at the beginning of this section.

JAM
4 cups fresh berries
½ cup water
1½ cups honey

Place berries and water into an 8-quart pot, and bring to a boil, stirring often. Stir in honey. Boil until jam mounds up in a spoon. Spoon hot jam into hot sterilized jars to within ⅛ inch of the top, seal, and process in a hot water bath for 15 minutes.

Makes about 4 half-pints

JELLY
Extract juice as follows:

For soft berries, such as strawberries or raspberries, place 6 to 8 cups into a large bowl, add ½ cup water, and crush berries. Cover, and refrigerate for several hours.

For firm berries, such as cranberries,* red currants, or blueberries, add 1 cup water, bring to a boil, and cook, covered, for 10 minutes, or until berries are quite soft.

Strain through a jelly bag or a colander lined with 6 layers of rinsed cheesecloth. Let stand for several hours to make a transparent jelly. If you are satisfied with an opaque jelly, you can shorten the straining time by squeezing the bag. I recommend that you do this with cranberries to obtain an adequate yield of juice.

When straining process has been completed, measure juice. Add one-third to one-half as much honey as you have juice. Pour mixture into an 8-quart pot, bring to a boil, and cook until it passes 1 or 2 of the tests for jelly on page 264. Pour hot jelly into hot sterilized jars leaving ⅛ inch of headspace, seal, and process in a boiling water bath for 15 minutes. Let stand overnight before storing in a cool, dark place.

Makes about 4 half-pints

*This is the recipe to use for making Jellied Cranberry Sauce.

Fresh Mint Jelly

Before making jelly, read the general instructions at the beginning of this section.

4 to 5 pounds tart juicy apples (about one-quarter underripe)
4 cups water, divided
1 cup fresh mint leaves, well packed
about 2½ cups honey

Remove stem and blossom end of apples but don't peel or core them. Slice into a large stainless steel pot. Add 3 cups water. Bring to a boil, reduce heat, and simmer for 25 minutes, or until very soft. Strain through 3 layers of dampened cheesecloth in a colander. Reserve juice.

In a small saucepan, bring 1 cup water to a boil. Stir in mint leaves. Remove from heat, cover, and let steep for 1 hour. Strain mixture, squeezing leaves. Discard leaves and reserve juice.

Measure apple juice and pour into a large stainless steel pot. Add half as much honey as you have juice. Bring to a boil, stirring to blend in honey. Boil rapidly until juice passes any of the jelly tests on page 264, about 30 minutes.

Measure jelly and add 2 tablespoons mint juice for every cup. Bring to a boil, and test again for jelly point, cooking about 5 minutes longer. Skim off foam, pour into hot sterilized jars, leaving ⅛ inch of headspace, and seal. Process for 10 minutes in a boiling water bath.

Yields 3 to 4 half-pints

VARIATION
Apple Jelly: Simply omit mint. If you wish, you may add 1 tablespoon lemon juice for each cup apple juice before boiling to jelly point. Or add cinnamon to taste at end of cooking time while mixture is still simmering. Bonus Applesauce: Since I hate to waste the pulp of the apples after extracting the juice, I put the pulp through a food mill (to remove seeds, core, and skin) and add honey and cinnamon to taste, heating just enough to blend in honey thoroughly.

Yields 5 to 6 cups applesauce

Citrus Marmalades

These piquant fruit spreads can be made with any kind of citrus fruit or a combination of citrus fruits.

2 cups thinly sliced citrus fruit rind
4 cups chopped citrus fruit pulp
6 cups water
about 3 cups honey

Before starting, read the general instructions at the beginning of this section.

Place rind and fruit into a large pot. Add water, bring to a boil, cover, and simmer for 5 minutes. Let stand overnight in a cool place.

Bring mixture to a boil again, and cook, with cover ajar, until rind is tender, about 1 hour.

Measure fruit and liquid, adding ½ cup honey for every cup of fruit and juice. Cook rapidly, stirring often, to jelling point, about 45 minutes. Take care that mixture does not overcook and does not stick toward the end of the cooking time. Pour boiling hot into hot sterilized jars, leaving ¼ inch of headspace. Seal, and process in boiling water bath for 10 minutes.

5 to 6 half-pints

VARIATIONS

Cherry Marmalade: Add 4 cups pitted fresh sweet cherries to 2 cups orange rind and 4 cups orange pulp. Proceed as above.
Pineapple Marmalade: Add 4 cups chopped fresh pineapple to 2 cups orange rind and 4 cups orange pulp. Proceed as above.

Grape Jelly

Before making jelly, read the general instructions at the beginning of this section.

12 cups Concord grapes
about 2¼ cups honey

Use about one-quarter slightly underripe grapes with three-quarters ripe grapes. Stem and measure grapes. Crush by handfuls into an 8-quart stainless steel pot. There should be ½ inch or more of juice at bottom of pot; if not, add a little water. Bring to a simmer and cook for 10 minutes, covered.

Strain through a jelly bag or a triple layer of dampened cheesecloth. Pour juice into a pitcher, and refrigerate overnight. The next day, strain to remove crystals that have formed.

Measure juice, pour into pot, and add one-third to one-half as much honey as you have juice. Bring to a boil, stirring to blend in honey. Boil rapidly until mixture passes any of the jelly tests on page 264, about 15 to 20 minutes.

Skim off foam, pour into hot sterilized jars leaving ⅛ inch of headspace,

and seal. Process for 10 minutes in a boiling water bath.

Yields about 4 half-pints

VARIATION

Unsweetened Grape Juice: If you wish, you can process grape juice rather than making jelly. After juice has been strained to remove crystals, bring to a simmer, pour into hot sterilized jars, seal, and process for 10 minutes in a boiling water bath. Or simply refrigerate and use fresh.

Yields about 2 pints

Quick Strawberry Jam

4 cups fresh strawberries
1 cup honey
2 tablespoons lemon juice
1 envelope unflavored gelatin

Quarter strawberries. (If berries are small halve them.)

In a medium-size saucepan, cover berries with honey.

Pour lemon juice into a cup, sprinkle gelatin on top, and stir. Then add to strawberries and honey. Cook over low heat, stirring constantly, until honey takes on a pink color. Increase heat to medium and bring to a boil, stirring constantly. Allow to boil without stirring for 30 minutes.

Remove from heat and cool. (Jam will thicken as it cools.) Pour into a sterilized jar, and refrigerate. Keeps 2 weeks.

Makes about 1 pint

Peach or Apricot Preserves

This recipe will also make Peach or Apricot Jam, for which alternate directions are given. Before making preserves, read the general instructions at the beginning of this section.

8 cups sliced peeled peaches (two-
    thirds ripe, one-third underripe)
            or
8 cups peeled pitted apricots (two-
    thirds ripe, one-third underripe)
    and ⅓ cup lemon juice
1 cup water
2 cups honey

Place peaches or apricots and lemon juice into a large stainless steel pot. Add water, bring to a boil, and simmer until very soft, about 15 minutes.

At this point, if you want to make jam, crush fruit with a potato masher. If you want to make preserves, leave pieces of fruit whole.

Add honey to hot fruit, and stir to blend well. Boil, uncovered, over medium-high heat, stirring often, until mixture passes test for jam on page 264, about 40 minutes. Toward the end of the cooking time, stir frequently; mixture will stick if not watched carefully.

Pack into hot sterilized jars leaving ⅛ inch of headspace, and seal. Process in a boiling water bath for 15 minutes.

Yields 3 to 4 pints

VARIATIONS
Spiced Peach Preserves (or Jam): In a square of cheesecloth, securely tie up 1 teaspoon whole cloves, ½ teaspoon whole allspice, and 1 stick of cinnamon. Place into pot with fruit. Remove after honey has been added and mixture has boiled for 20 minutes, when it is beginning to get quite thick.

Instant Apricot Jam: Because so many dessert recipes call for apricot jam and the season for fresh apricots is very short, here's a quick substitute you can make in a few minutes at any time of year.

Place 1 cup dried apricots and ¼ cup honey into a food processor. Chop fruit very fine. Add ½ to ¾ cup boiling water through feed tube, and continue to process until you have a smooth jam consistency. Remove mixture to a small saucepan. Taste to correct sweetness; if desired, stir in more honey. Cook over medium heat, stirring constantly, until mixture simmers. Simmer 3 minutes, stirring often. Remove from heat, pack into a clean, hot jar, and seal. When jar cools, refrigerate until needed.

Walnut Butter

Try this butter on fresh apple slices.

2 cups walnut meats
2 to 3 tablespoons honey

Blanch walnuts by covering with water in a small saucepan, and bringing water to a boil. Drain and rinse walnuts.

In a food processor, grind nuts until soft and spreadable, blending in honey to produce a smoother texture. Store in refrigrator. Keeps for about 2 weeks.

Yields about 1 cup

Almond Butter

For a special treat, spread Almond Butter between two plain cookies to make a cookie sandwich.

2 cups whole or slivered
    blanched almonds
3 tablespoons honey
1 tablespoon vegetable oil, or
    more as needed
⅛ to ¼ teaspoon almond extract

In a food processor, grind almonds until soft and pasty. Occasionally stop machine to break up ground nuts that pack down below blade. Add honey, 1 tablespoon oil, and almond extract. If necessary, add more oil to achieve a spreadable texture. Store in refrigerator. Keeps for about 2 weeks.

Yields about 1 cup

VARIATION
Almond Paste: Follow the same method as for Almond Butter, omitting vegetable oil. Increase honey to ⅓ cup or more, adding enough to make a kneadable paste. Increase almond extract to ½ teaspoon. Wrap with plastic wrap. Keeps for months under refrigeration. Bring to room temperature, and knead briefly before using.

Cashew or Peanut Butter

2 cups cashew or peanut meats

In a food processor, grind nuts until butter is shiny with oil and spreadable. Occasionally stop machine to break up ground nuts that pack down below blade. Taste to determine that texture is smooth. Store in refrigerator. Keeps for 2 weeks or more.

Yields about 1 cup

Fruit Butters

I especially like fruit butters because they use the pulp of the fruit, are not heavily sweetened, and are very easy to make (there's no fuss about reaching the jelling point).

BASIC RECIPE
8 cups cooked fruit pulp
2 cups honey, or to taste (it's all right to use less or more according to the sweetness of the fruit)
flavoring (see below)

APPLE BUTTER
For 8 cups pulp, include:
4 teaspoons ground cinnamon
2 teaspoons ground cloves

APRICOT BUTTER
For 8 cups pulp, include:
¼ cup lemon juice
½ teaspoon ground nutmeg

PEACH BUTTER
For 8 cups pulp, include:
1 teaspoon ground cinnamon
½ teaspoon ground nutmeg

PEAR BUTTER
For 8 cups pulp, include:
1 teaspoon grated orange rind
juice of 1 orange
½ teaspoon ground nutmeg

Before making butter, read the general instructions for preserving fruit spreads at the beginning of this section.

If you're not using fruit pulp left over from making jelly, prepare fruit by cooking it, in just enough water to prevent sticking, until quite soft, about 30 minutes.

Press fruit through a food mill. Measure pulp, and add honey and additional flavorings according to amount you have, using basic recipe as a guide. Place flavored pulp into a large heavy pot, and simmer until spread is thick, stirring frequently. This will take from 15 to 30 minutes, depending on juiciness of fruit.

Spoon hot butter into hot sterilized jars. Seal, and process in a boiling water bath for 10 minutes.

Yields 4 to 5 pints

Index

Page numbers in boldface indicate tables; page numbers in italic indicate photos.